What is a Group?

A New Look at Theory in Practice

edited by

Chris Oakley

REBUS PRESS

Rebus Press
76 Haverstock Hill
LONDON
NW3 2BE

Printed and bound in Great Britain
by Biddles Ltd, Guildford and King's Lynn

ISBN 1-900877 07 4

Library of Congress Cataloging-in-Publication Data

What is a group?: a new look at theory in practice edited by
Chris Oakley. -- 1st ed.
    p.   cm.
Includes bibliographical references and index.

1. Group psychoanalysis.   I. Oakley, Chris.

RC510.W48   1999   99-44128
616.89'152--dc21   CIP

CONTENTS

FOREWORD

The time is shortly before Christmas 1994 and three dreamers are ensconced in the comfortable leather armchairs of the staff bar at University College, London. The dreamers are Kirsty Hall, Oliver Rathbone and Sharon Morris. We like the idea of starting a publishing company. Single authored books, we calculate, will take three months to produce. Edited collections are a little more complicated, we note, and so might take up to six months... Our abject ignorance is a kind midwife to our project... Yet now, in 1999, our original idea has finally flowered. *The Encyclopaedia of Psychoanalysis* has been born. And, despite all the delays and setbacks, our vision is still intact...

Rebus Press is a non-partisan publishing company. We aim to bring a range of psychoanalytic ideas to a wide readership, namely: the experienced psychoanalyst or psychotherapist; the student, in the guise of either clinician or academic; and, last but certainly not least, the interested person in the street. We pose the question: are the original ideas which psychoanalysis brought to the world now dead, or are they alive and kicking in the work of subsequent writers, waiting to be brought forward afresh and anew for each generation of readers? In turn, we hope that through *The Encyclopaedia of Psychoanalysis*, Rebus Press will stimulate the next generation to take up the baton and produce further creative thinking.

The *Encyclopaedia* series does not set out to tell people what to think. It encourages readers to be fascinated, lured into reading 'just one more chapter', to puzzle over conflicting points of view and, on occasion, to grapple with difficult and complex ideas. Why? Well, if psychotherapists and psychoanalysts encounter the Byzantine complexity of human suffering in their daily work, then our view is that the practitioner will find assistance in this supremely difficult task by being gently helped to think for him or herself. Being told what to think and what to do does not produce good psychoanalysis or good psychotherapy, and it seems there is far too much 'instruction' of this kind already in circulation.

I wish to thank all our contributors to the *Encyclopaedia* series—past, present and future. As they have discovered—or, indeed, will discover in due course—Rebus Press is unique. We do not settle for statements such as: 'following Melanie Klein it is clear that...' or 'as Jacques Lacan has demonstrated...' We insist on *explanation*, wherever possible. As a result many of the people who have written for this series have had long, passionate, interesting, and—very occasionally—acrimonious discussions about their papers with the individual editors of our books, with the chief editor of Rebus Press, Duncan Barford, and with me. Consequently, where ideas do seem unclear, this is often because it is the intention of the author to leave the reader in doubt. Doubt *can* be a productive position from which to carry out an analysis of one's own thought, or an assessment of one's opinion about a book and—indeed—is regarded by some as the only viable position from which to conduct psychoanalysis or psychotherapy...

The *Encyclopaedia* series has a consistent format. In most of the books you will find papers which are informed by Freudian, Jungian, Kleinian, Lacanian and Object Relations perspectives. You may also find papers where the perspective of the author is hard to pin down... Good! Keep the 'doubt' working! In each volume we attempt to offer a wide range of opinion, and the majority of papers have been specially commissioned and written for the series. In a few cases, we have published work which has already appeared elsewhere but perhaps in a format which has not been easily accessible. In some instances a paper has appeared in another language, and has been specially translated for this series.

The aim of the *Encyclopaedia* is to present a coherent body of ideas, yet within a structure sufficiently loose to allow the reader to interpret the papers for him or herself. We are hoping and aiming for a wide-ranging reaction to the contents of these volumes. Feedback, constructive criticism, ideas for future projects in the series, possible papers for future inclusion—all of these and more are most welcome.

Kirsty Hall MA
Commissioning Editor
e-mail k.hall@rebuspress.co.uk

NOTES ON CONTRIBUTORS

PHILIP BOXER, B.Sc.(Eng.), M.Sc.(Bus.Admin.) has been a strategy consultant since the late 1970's, working within businesses across many different sectors of industry, both public and private, facilitating the process of strategy formation and development. He is a member of the Institute of Management Consultants, an Associate Member of the Centre for Freudian Analysis and Research, and the Chairman of the 'Just Ask' Charity.

ROBIN COOPER Ph.D is a psychotherapist and group-analyst working in full-time private practice. He is a member of the Institute of Group Analysis and the Philadelphia Association, and has for thirty years been actively involved in the therapeutic community households of the Philadelphia Association.

STEVEN GANS Ph.D was trained as a philosopher at Penn State University. He taught Philosophy at Vermont, and has written on existential and phenomenological themes, including one of the earliest papers in English on the work of Emmanuel Levinas. In the 70s and 80s he trained and worked with the Philadelphia Association on their philosophical approach to psychoanalysis. He now practises privately in London. His book *Just Listening: Therapeutic Conversations*, co-authored with Leon Redler, published by Free Association Press, is scheduled to appear next year.

MICHAEL HALTON is a psychoanalytic psychotherapist, member of the Tavistock Society of Psychotherapists (adult section), and a member of the British Confederation of Psychotherapists. He works part-time for the health service as a Consultant Clinical Psychologist at the Whittington Hospital in London, and also in private practice. In addition, he teaches and supervises at the Tavistock Clinic and other psychotherapy organisattions.

ERIC HARPER is a member of the Site for Contemporary Psychoanalysis, and is at present working at The Trauma Centre for Survivors of Violence and Torture in Cape Town.

EARL HOPPER, Ph.D, is a psychoanalyst and a group analyst. He is an honorary tutor at the Portman and Tavistock Trust, and a past president of the International Association for Group Psychotherapy. He is the author and co-author of many papers on psychoanalysis and groups.

OTTO KERNBERG M.D., is a training and suspervising analyst at the Columbia University Center for Psychoanalytic Training and Research, professor of psychiatry at Cornell University Medical College, and director of the Institute for Personality Disorders at the New York Hospital-Cornell Medical Center, Westchester Division. He is the author and co-author of ten books.

CHRIS OAKLEY is a psychoanalyst working with the Site for Contemporary Psychoanalysis and has considerable experience of working in Philadelphia Association community households. He is the author of various articles on psychoanalysis. His more recent publications include contributions to 'Returns of the French Freud: Freud, Lacan and Beyond' (ed. Todd Dufresne, London: Routledge, 1997) and to 'Where id was: challenging normalisation in Psychoanalysis' (ed. Tony Molino and Christine Ware, City Lights Books,1999).

ALAN ROWAN is the manager of the Department of Clinical Psychology and Psychological Therapies at the Chase Farm Hospital in London. He trained as a clinical psychologist, specialising in Family/Systemic therapy and has since undergone a training in psychoanalysis within the Lacanian orientation with both the School of Psychoanalysis, St. Vincent's Hospital in Dublin, and with the Centre for Freudian Analysis and Research in London.

NORMAN VELLA, M.A in psychoanalysis, has been working in therapeutic communities for 28 years and has been a group analyst since 1980. He is a member of the Institute of Group Analysis.

A NOTE ON TEXTS

All references to Freud's writings are based on *The Standard Edition of the Complete Psychological Works of Sigmund Freud* (24 volumes), translated by James Strachey, published by Hogarth Press and the Institute of Psycho-Analysis (1961).

INTRODUCTION

Chris Oakley

Any anthology or collection of papers is—potentially—something of a compromise. But it clings to a vague and insistent hope that it may transform itself into something more than the sum of its disparate parts.

Indeed, the question arises as to whether there is *any* inherent common purpose suffusing these chapters, beyond a response to the initial proposal to produce a book on 'group psychoanalysis'. In the case of this compilation, we decided to tilt in the direction of a pick 'n' mix of psychoanalytic notables—some names that might add weight to such a collection—co-joined with some emerging chancers, all struggling for a wee spot in the sun, all with their separate agendas and idiosyncrasies. The result is this curious manifesto of odd cullings, in which any purported links between the contributors would be more an effect of the contingent than of any meticulous planning.

Possibly the very notion of a *text book*—for this is, rather, a book of *texts*—lures the reader into a fantasy of enclosure, into an expectation of an account which covers the whole field, an invitation to 'come on in and read all about it; we've got it *all* down!'. Indubitably this would be misleading, for there was never any intention to squeeze these random samplings into a package for export, nor to fit them into any particular syllabus.

So much contemporary psychoanalytic writing arrives dead on the page. It merely papers over the fissures that open onto the profoundly alarming abyss of anxious uncertainty, which we encounter as we endeavour to address the hurt of our being and our attempts to understand this. It is with a certain defiance—a brash humility, even—that this slender volume gestures towards *something other*. Is it possible to surf the Zeitgeist of these troubled psychoanalytic times, and offer up the possibility of access to the marginal, whilst simultaneously leavening this with something bordering on the orthodox? Indeed, it would certainly be implausible to attempt to define what is included in this book by means of a memorable label—for instance: *The Independent Tradition, French Freud*, etc.—or via the colonisation of a particular geographical location—*The Palo Alto Group, The Tavistock School*... For this volume is much more in the vein of an album 'by various artists'.

Whilst purposefully shying away from any attempt to chart a general or prevailing group analytic milieu—far less a recording of a history—what we have here is more a celebration of a few elective outsiders. What is valued is often the more remote, the difficult—the 'fractured', even—all of which might, hopefully, inaugurate a faint adrenaline rush. Consequently, there has been no attempt to identify 'the best' or the 'most important' among the contributors or the theorists whose work is addressed, or even to conduct an overarching survey of 'group psychoanalysis'.

Psychoanalytic writers can so often be a quarrelsome crowd. One often anticipates demands of 'who else is involved?' and a withholding of work unless the project is underwritten by some suitable co-journeymen. But, for the most part (the odd envies and resentments from the also-rans notwithstanding), this project was uncontaminated by such capers.

I began with a low-key sniffing around: being passed over, passing over, passed on by certain people to others... I found my way by stalking possibilities, lurching into random moments... Philip Boxer—for instance—was picked up over lunch in the bar of London's Hotel Russell. I just liked the man's style, and stumbled with him and others via cogent suggestions, eventually arriving at the final compilation. Ultimately, those who are here wanted it the most, for with only a little guidance people were encouraged to follow their own desire, to articulate particular themes around certain pivotal figures or historical moments—with Kirsty Hall's deft hand always at my elbow, steering a path through the thickets of inertia. Hopefully what has emerged is something both intelligent and provocative; perhaps Steve Gans and Norman Vella are exemplary contributors in this respect. Michael Halton and Robin Cooper produce some fresh thoughts about two of the original innovators in the field, Bion and Foulkes. Earl Hopper engages in a valorisation of the socio-cultural dimension at play within unconscious process. Otto Kernberg provides us with an individual blend of thoughts around Freud's classic text, *Group Psychology and the Analysis of the Ego*, Melanie Klein and Elias Cannetti, before arriving at his own views in connection with the contribution of narcissism to an understanding of group process. Eric Harper and Alan Rowan mount a lucid account of a Lacanian approach to groups, whilst wondering at the same time whether this venture is not lodged in the realms of impotence and impossibility. But if this book produces in its readers even the faintest trace of an invocation to think about group analysis differently, or to disrupt prevailing stagnancies, then it will all have been worthwhile.

* * *

It was Schopenhauer who saw us as entangled in the heart of our being with something incorrigibly *alien*. He termed it 'The Will', and suggested that out of it 'we' are formed. 'The Will' is, in itself, utterly meaningless and without objective, and insistently indifferent to us, yet it simultaneously sustains in us an illusory veil of purpose. Freud was not unimpressed by this conceptualisation, and installed in his theory the concept of desire which, whatever *we* might say, will always say what *it* wants (hence the psychoanalyst's love of parapraxes), and implicitly cares for nothing but itself. Lacan called it *'Das Ding'*, the Thing, or—as the Slovenian philosopher Slavoj Zizek underscores it in his re-readings of Lacan: The Real. One might equally refer to it as life and life only, as that which makes us what we are and which is, at the same time, impenetrable, unrepresentable and obscenely enjoyable. If such ideas are taken seriously, then what significance do they have for a theory of—or an analysis of—what goes on in groups?

At times, in these chapters, one may note a mild tilt in the direction of a preference for 'theory' or textual exegesis, but hopefully not at the expense of the specificities of clinical practice. Inevitably there will be considerable congestion around a number of the customary sites of initiative within the group psychoanalytical field: Foulkes, Klein and Bion, amongst others. But perhaps it is also possible to discern a distillation of something more latent, a potential *reversal* of the more habitual maxims or aims of psychoanalytic treatment... Rather than a project enmeshed in a concern with conformity, maturity, the 'authenticated self'—and the like—we might find instead a site within which psychoanalysis itself is entangled, as a co-conspirator in 'the critique of the subject'.

Partially one of the effects of the Real is that it dismantles any sense that one might rendezvous with the real nature of ourselves. This aspiration is now relegated to the illusory, downgraded locus of a fantasy, a means by which one attempts to fend off the compulsive anxieties that cling to desire. Potentially, however, we come by this route to recognise that man's habitual state is to be constantly and continuously entangled in a phantasmal mendacity. Fantasy can no longer be taken as a straightforward counterpoint to what we take reality to be; rather, it is the stopper in the hole, the plug in the lack in our being, which is actually the condition upon which the multiplicity of fictions that we call 'reality' depends. Following Hegel, for Lacan this *'spaltung'*, this primordial wound inaugurated by the irredeemable rupture from the immediacy of the natural, is the site from which our desire unstaunchably flows. The Real is an indivisible remainder; it is that which cannot be subsumed under any system of representation or model. The consequence of this is that we can never be identical to ourselves. In that case, neither is it be possible for any group process to be rendered totally transparent.

Draped over this only dimly perceived absence is a contagion of possible readings and responses, all vigorously propped up by an insistent demand that herein resides the 'truth'. Indeed we can never be entirely outside of this. But for both Freud and Lacan—amongst others—at the heart of meaning there will always be a persistent residue of *non-sense*. This is always something other than the signifiable or representable, in which case the Real does not 'exist' as such, but can only be acknowledged via its effects.

Following Zizek, every signifying system, every form of interpretation, will contain that which ultimately stumbles up against a particular threshold, the effect of which is to point out that the system cannot be totalised. The system does not quite hold together, and although we are driven in our myriad and varying ways to continue to try to bring about a complete signification, this honest endeavour inevitably fails. We can recognise this point of view as the classically post-structuralist form of the story: what constitutes any sign is its difference from other signs, therefore it is impossible for any sign or 'story'—aka *theory*—to be complete unto itself, precisely because its very identity can only be formed through this aforementioned difference.

However, this is also—potentially—a Hegelian or dialectical narrative, to the extent that truth is viewed not so much as in opposition to error, but rather is the *result* of it. Our mistakes and oversights, inevitable as we know them to be, have been always already taken into account by truth *en route*, as part of the very process by which it is approached. Indeed, truth itself is somewhat 'misleading', for rather than the objective with which we might rendezvous, truth is that which frames both the possibility, and the process of trial and error, which are all so entangled together in this impossible project. As any psychoanalyst or group analyst will know, it is these crucial misrecognitions that are essential to the enterprise. Woven into the requirement that one undergoes the experience of personal or group analysis in the context of training to be an analyst, is this encounter with the potential rupture of the fantasy—indeed, of any lingering illusion—that we will one day meet some ultimate truth, some transcendental knowledge of which someone (usually in the place of the analyst) will gain possession.

Given these considerations, we should acknowledge the fact that, for the healthy development of any language, incorporation and acceptance of foreign elements is not only likely, but entirely essential. All enduring intercourse with others—for it is from this that everything emerges—will result in the borrowing of words from *their* language. Indeed, this is indispensable when it comes to the cross-fertilisation of ideas.

Freud anxiously admonished practitioners of 'wild analysis', by pointing out that it might do more harm to psychoanalysis itself than to individual patients. However, is there not a very real possibility that its very vitality is dependent upon the potentiality of new forms of thinking? Ultimately, the debate hinges upon what precisely is meant by this term 'wild'.

There will be countless moments or points of contact which culture sets up between people, leaving indelible traces in their language. New objectives, notions, conceptualisations—ideological, philosophical, psychoanalytical and personal—all leading to new configurations of ideas and word formations... But this is what is so conspicuously lacking in much of the prevailing psychoanalytic literature in this country and beyond. In the fifty years since the publication of Foulkes' *Group Analysis* the psychoanalytic establishment has become increasingly eaten up with tension, frustrated at being neither especially talented nor able to partake of very much pleasure. One effect of this has been a congealment into forms of hatred—not appropriate hate, directed at those who abuse or oppress, but rather an irrational and (in many instances) an ignorant hatred, saturated with fear in the face of difference. Given this state of affairs, we should increase the sense of importance we attach to appreciating the significance of alternative forms of cultural production. This should be done without deciding in advance what kinds of relationships can be developed between emerging discourses and practices, and the more classical forms of psychoanalytic legitimisation. By valuing the diversity of contributions to the theoretical culture of psychoanalysis, which take place against the backdrop of an increasingly fragmented milieu, we may come to recognise a curious and unexpected complexity with regard to our sense of unity. This might emerge despite an absence of any consensus between the members of the group.

It was Freud, in *Group Psychology and the Analysis of the Ego*, who emphasised that a bond unites us in group settings, producing an inevitable libidinal resonance within this or that association, society, or school of psychoanalysis. This depends upon a blind fidelity to an all-powerful leader. The social bond is established through the very existence of this beloved chief. It can only be maintained as long as the '*Führer*' (for this is how Freud translated Le Bon's '*meneur*') is himself sustained, through an identificatory love which underwrites the possibility of group cohesion. The assumption is that the disappearance of the tie to the leader will occasion a destruction of these bonds—a form of 'every man for himself'.

Granted, a disruption of a dominant and habitually idealised fantasy in a community setting provokes a proliferation of fissures across the surface of the social microcosm, accompanied by members of the group turning on one another. In other words, the dislocation of the mutual ties between group members is coterminous with the dismantling of the libidinal tie to the leader—who represents the prevailing fantasy that society is 'one', 'united', 'unanimous', all flying in formation and ultimately undifferentiated

This is perhaps best exemplified in the use of the term 'mass' which, following Arendt, is a fundamental term used in contemporary totalitarianism. It is the work of the French philosophers Lacoue-Labarthe and Nancy which has underlined how there is an relationship between this insistence on the 'mass' as 'an organic unity', and similar insistences upon the unity of the subject. To put it another way, the mass, the group, the association—and the like—can erect itself as a 'subject' only via the introduction of the subject *par excellence*: the authoritarian *Führer*. It is the narcissistic ego-ideal and ideal ego upon which both the 'undivided subject' and the undivided 'masses' depend, in order to shore up this notion of the compact whole.

However, if we are to take Lacan's thesis seriously—which is so suffused with the ideas that flowed from Kojève's influential lectures in France in the 1930s—are we not obliged to deconstruct relentlessly any idea of a grounding super-ego, in order to resist the temptation it offers to shore up our faltering and always suspect identity? And does this not apply at the level of the individual, the group or organisation, *and* the discursive register? For in the analytic encounter, there should be no-one and nothing to mirror or to bolster the subject's increasingly ruptured, ultimately false and misleading ego. Unless, that is, one is working in the field of psychosis. This is not to prioritise Lacan, but merely to require his thought and writings to go to work. This is always already set in the context of the interweave of one specific psychoanalytic oeuvre working on, joining up with, other bodies of psychoanalytic thought.

Inevitably, however, we must confront the fear of 'obscurity', which is one of the motivating forces in the compulsive, totalitarian drive towards conformity and homogeneity. Contemporary psychoanalytic politics is saturated by a dread of an immutable law of that fundamental dynamic of our being—*seduction*. Here, 'full signs' do not operate, but remain obscure and enigmatic. The consequence of this dread is a capitulation in the face of the demand to place everything under the sign of luminous legibility. However, taking up a position on the run from this project of incorrigible transparency does not lead inevitably to a collapse into the dualistic, in that it does not automatically inaugurate the counter-position of revelling in some 'brute meaninglessness of things'.

Any group or community is inevitably vexed by the problem of our ultimate inability to gain access to the 'other'. The 'other' is always alien, irreducible, and incomplete, and therefore unknowable as a whole. Consequently any introduction to the work, the project of group analysis, lies not in the *whole* of the project but rather in the *hole* which informs and sustains it—the gap or yawning abyss wherein is unveiled the truth of 'the subject supposed to know'.

Perhaps what is communal—the common ground that is to be shared with others—is precisely this recognition that we are never self-transparent, never completed, nor even wholly bound to our own cultural context, for we are always to some extent out of sync with it. The hollow fictions of mastery, truth, closure, subjectivity—the 'twilight of the idols', indeed—and the transference onto fantasised sites of legitimating authority such as Freud and Lacan can be potentially un-handcuffed from the Father-Signified, which is merely the locus of a narcissistically configured ideal. In their place we might pass from an inappropriate certainty of consciousness, towards the unmasterable gap or hole in our ceaselessly spiralling desire. Thus a communality may be built upon realisation that there will always be that which eludes our grasp, and that it is in the overlap of these multiple absences that a possibility of a meeting can arise.

FREUD ON GROUPS

Norman Vella

Introduction

Why should we pay attention to what Freud said about groups? In his opinion each member of a group suffers a profound alteration, in which: 'liability to affect becomes extraordinarily intensified, while... intellectual ability is markedly reduced' (Freud 1921: 88).

It would seem that there is still a stylistic imperative to quote Freud near the beginning of any paper on psychoanalytic theory. It acts in much the same way as the notion of precedence does in Law. I would like to suggest—only half-seriously, perhaps—that there is a phylogenetic basis for this, as outlined by Freud himself in *Civilization and Its Discontents* (Freud 1930: 132). Here, Freud states that ambivalence and guilt over the murder of the primal father are inherited by all subsequent generations. I would associate the primal father's murder with the injuries our contemporary theories inflict upon ideas which Freud held precious. Inevitably, current theory disagrees with the primal father's adherence to instinct theory and the Oedipus complex. The divergence into separate psychoanalytic schools recapitulates the scattering of the original band of brothers, after which each promotes his own distinctive tribal theoretical profile. Guilt for the murder of the father's theory leads to infusions of love, gratitude and ambivalence. Guilty theorists therefore seek to atone for their heresy with a rich crop of deferential references to the master.

Freud described society, mob, army and church, but never wrote about therapy groups. In fact there is some evidence that he disliked the early experiments of the 20s and 30s in group therapy. Consequently, it is by drawing upon his texts on *culture* that I shall attempt to draw out Freud's account of what motivates humans as social beings, and what constitutes the nature of social ties between people. I shall then attempt to reconcile this with a contemporary account of group theory.

Problems of group theory

Malcolm Pines (Pines 1978) writing on Freud's attitude to groups, relates an incident which occurred in the 1920s. Trigant Burrow,

President of the American Psychoanalytic Association, and former analysand of Jung, attempted to make a transference interpretation to a patient, Clarence Shield. Rejecting Burrow's offering, Shield expressed his belief that the psychopathology being interpreted was also, in part, a function of the analytic setting and the unequal balance of power in the room. In response, Burrow—in the same 'great American spirit of Independence'—changed seats and role, and discovered that it is indeed not just who you are and who you were which influences the transference. He realised that roles dictate entirely different meanings for the two individuals who adopt them.

Burrow sent these findings to Freud, and advocated greater egalitarianism within the psychoanalytic setting. This was his small contribution to the sum of analytic knowledge. The Master, however, was unimpressed. The connection between this event and Burrow's subsequent expulsion from the International Psychoanalytic Association is a matter of speculation, or of further research…

Freud quotes Le Bon: 'by the mere fact that he forms part of an organised group, a man descends several rungs in the ladder of civilization' (Freud 1921: 77).

The conductor's role in group therapy is—mainly—to analyse the group, leaving members to free associate and become (collectively) one another's therapists. The difficulty which Freud—but also modern psychoanalysis—may find with this model centres upon the supposed uncertainty in assessing the accuracy of members' counter-transference responses to each other, and the increased distance of the group conductor from material produced by individual members.

This barrier against accepting that patients can help one another may have its origins in a closed-shop professionalism, which claims a monopoly on knowledge under the dictum that the analyst must always have been analysed in order to analyse. In addition, the thrust of individual therapy is envisaged as 'vertical' and 'deeper', while that of the group is 'horizontal'.

The main problem with attempting to link group therapy and current psychoanalytic theory to Freud is his life-long commitment to drive theory. Even his sociological texts seek a central position for the instincts. Concerns about instinct theory were voiced before 1939, but the trend since Freud's death has been away from drives and in favour of object relations theory, ego- or self-psychology. Jung and Fromm had already begun to erode the emphasis Freud had placed on sexuality, and this was followed by a sceptical response to the theory of the death instinct. Sociology, meanwhile, avoids awarding prime importance to inner conflict and instincts, instead regarding instinctual expression as culturally determined. A theory of groups which seeks greater convergence with Freud's ideas must—therefore—find a more central position for the Oedipus complex and the superego, and must also share Marcuse's enthusiasm for a dual instinct theory.

Which offers the greatest explanatory value: a single psychoanalytic school, or an eclectic 'pick and mix' of elements from widely different models? The literature on groups favours the latter, and offers ideas organically grown by contributors of varying theoretical persuasions. This is understandable, given the difficulty of establishing an optimal fit between any one particular psychoanalytic school and group theory. Yet an alignment of group theory with a single school might introduce academic rigour, and encourage more internal consistency. The most pragmatic argument against a single theoretical underpinning, however, is that all the main psychoanalytic schools are already represented in this field, so an attempt at unification would pose risks of sectarian schisms.

The way in which the group 'is more than the sum of its parts' is an enduring theoretical problem. The central role of the notion of 'group' in many other disciplines—for example, systems theory, family therapy, social psychology and sociology—confuses any attempt to find a well-defined niche for group theory.

Brief review of the literature

The three central texts by Freud which deal with the problems of groups are *Totem and Taboo* (1913b), *Group Psychology and the Analysis of the Ego* (1921), and *Civilization and Its Discontents* (1930).

These represent a progressive inquiry over 18 years into the question of social humanity. It would be as wrong to regard these works as studies in mythology, ethnology, social psychology and sociology as it would be to regard the Oedipus complex as a theory of child psychology. The texts are essentially *psychoanalytic interpretations* of these allied subjects, and are motivated by the desire to advance *individual* psychology by setting it in wider contexts, rather than an interest in the social for its own sake.

By isolating these works, one can see how each text builds on previous themes. Evidence is taken from prehistory, neurotics, crowds and children, which are all taken as sites of regression. *Totem and Taboo* has been regarded by contemporary ethnologists as a speculative and somewhat flawed work. Through the myth of the Primal Father, and his murder by the band of Brothers, it outlines the earliest human social relations, by connecting the murder of the Father with the Oedipus complex.

Myth is also the thematic foundation of *Group Psychology and the Analysis of the Ego*. This is a much greater work, which examines the nature of the 'vertical' and 'horizontal' libidinal ties that bind people into groups, with or without a leader. Here, Freud distinguishes between identification and object-choice, and elaborates the function of the ego-ideal, the precursor of the superego; but most of all the central role of the 'leader' is heavily underscored.

Where *Group Psychology and the Analysis of the Ego* had highlighted libidinal impulses, *Civilization and Its Discontents* concentrated upon the destructive impulse, a derivative of the death instinct, which itself was first introduced in *Beyond the Pleasure Principle* (1920) and formed Freud's third theory of instinct. The structural theory incorporated the superego as a distinct psychical agency. The addition of the death instinct provides an intra-psychic model of aggression which allows Freud to analyse the function of guilt and civilization.

Case material from Group Y #1

Group Y was a twice-weekly group held in a day-time therapeutic community for the mentally ill. This account will later seek to demonstrate that the fusion of libidinal and destructive ties tips over all too easily in favour of the latter. In this case the aggressors were the women, which reminded me never to trust my own presumptions about any group. In fact, this group exhibited a death instinct which reminded me of the behaviour of a flock of sheep. At best, it seemed, they would simply fail to thrive, but at worst they would self destruct...

Totem and Taboo

Freud uses research into primitive tribes and neurotics in order to provide a backdrop against which the horror of incest assumes its full significance. Case material from 'Little Hans' and Ferenczi's patient 'Little Arpad' connects anthropological findings on primitive mentality with the 'magical thinking' of children and neurotics. Freud is then able to link repression and obsessional thinking to the structure of taboo. The totemic tribe commits itself to exogamy, but as a consequence erects a taboo against intra-tribal sexual relations.

The provenance of this theory depends on a mythology dating back to pre-literate times (although Freud attributes the notion of the primal horde to Charles Darwin, in *The Descent of Man*, 1871). The 'primal horde'—according to Freud—is led by the ruthless, envious and hated 'primal father'. He keeps all the women for himself, neither needs nor forms emotional bonds, and seeks only sexual discharge. No single individual can defeat him. Together, however, the brothers of the horde kill and eat him. The incest which the father had prevented by force must now—instead—be prohibited by a Law, enforced by the brothers, who are still under the influence of 'deferred obedience' to the primal father. A substitute for the primal father is found, in the form of a totem animal. The killing of this animal becomes 'taboo'. Through this prohibition the brothers try to 'undo' the murder.

Breach of the exogamy or incest rule recalls the earlier breach of parricide. However:

> the prohibition of incest, has a powerful practical basis as well. Sexual desires do not unite men but divide them. (Freud 1913b: 144)

The sharing of the women by the brothers divides the unity required to kill the father. Freud thus employs this fable as a representation of the origin of the moral social code, enforced through *communal agreement* rather than the might of the father. However, the need for a collective assuagement of guilt for the murder leads to a re-enactment of the crime as a celebratory ritual—the totemic feast.

A picture springs to my mind at this point—not a scene from a therapy group, but of a number of children daring each other to do something which they have tacitly recognised as very dangerous. Yet the danger *per se* represents less than the prospect of facing it *alone*, separated from the group. No son on his own could have murdered the father, but when all acted in concert they were strengthened.

Group Y #2

It is 1990 and I am in Group Y. Compared with other groups at the Centre it is unusual; all the members have been in this slow open group for less than two years. Equally surprising—and indicative of a vague hostility associated with counter-dependent feelings—is the fact that the female members attend the centre only for this small group. The group is 'their therapy'. Each of them had abusive or frightening fathers, and mothers who betrayed them, but all are unaware of any covert idealisation of their fathers or any unfulfilled dependency on their mothers. All that can be said of the men in the group is that they are far less adequate than the women...

Totem and Taboo continued

The brothers hope that their parricide will be expiated by making the women taboo, by placing certain women beyond desire. The law of taboo is used to reinforce *repression* of the desire for the women. The 'logic' of this is based upon the magical wish that if there is now no desire there can be no motive for murdering the father, and thus the parricide never occurred.

However, after the murder of their father, the sons realised that they also loved him. This allows Freud to introduce the main conceptual tool enabled by the myth: a conflict-ridden *ambivalence*. This runs as a thematic cord throughout all Freud's central texts on groups.

Filial guilt stems from the two fundamental taboos of totemism: parricide and incest. These are identical with the two repressed wishes of the Oedipus complex. The totemic meal in which the brothers identify with the primal father's strength is seen by Freud as the origin of all social organisation and moral restraint.

Totem and Taboo establishes a three-way connection between (i) the unresolved Oedipus complex; (ii) the neurotic's conflicting feelings towards the father, comprising hate, love and guilt; and (iii) the neurosis in its cultural setting, which resonates with the band of brothers' parricide, love and remorse. The sacrificial atonement for the father's murder, through an action which recalls the very deed, is a striking instance of Freud's use of a 'symbolic equation', in which one thing stands in the place of a repressed other, too psychically toxic to enter consciousness. The myth of the primal father, the rule of exogamy, the horror of incest and parricide, are painted by Freud as an ethnographic triptych of tyrant, rebellion, and co-operative totemism. In 1913 Freud had only the defence mechanism of reaction-formation as a means of accounting for incest inhibition. Later on, however, the notions of superego prohibition and identification furnish a more complete picture of repression.

Totem and Taboo illustrates that the dark, destructive forces which propelled the primal group to eat the father also exist as a swirling substrate with the potential to possess the therapy group. In Freud's text the motive for bonding is possession of the women, which also holds for the Oedipus complex. In subsequent writings the motives for bonding are more varied, and the libidinal bond extends also to an idealised version of father.

Case material from other groups

New groups are not yet groups; they are merely random collections of people with little meaning for each other, all equally interchangeable. Each person is as vulnerable as the solitary brother standing against the primal father. Each can assume the strength of the group only when the group does indeed become a group.

Five minutes into the first session of a one-year experiential group, a young lady rounds on the conductor: 'I have never met anyone as rude as you! You have not told us what to do!' Or, 'Why we are here! You are useless!' In the fifth session of another one-year experiential group, a gentle young man at last protests to the conductor: 'You just aren't right. You should wear a tie and a suit. Your hair is wrong and you aren't old enough.' These are expressions of accumulated anxiety, provoked by my unwillingness to take charge. Freud consistently maintained that a general feature of groups was their deep need to be led.

With a new group, I am not surprised if I hear: 'You never smile! Why are you so angry!' This has occurred with sufficient frequency for me to accept that my attempt at analytic neutrality merely presents as an unlikeable 'cross face'. Yet I also have to consider the extent to which these comments are provoked by what Freud alluded to as the aggressive feelings and fearful idealisation when in the presence of the father. The group's projection is: 'Our conductor does not care. His neutrality makes him unreachable.' This remote person could help but won't. It seems he does not need the group's affection any more than the primal father needs relationships. He belongs to a different order of humanity and is always threatening to attack.

Thus the neutral stance, construed as rejection, causes anger in a highly dependent group, which is then projected back onto the conductor in the form of 'he is angry with us'. The conductor's imagined anger becomes a source of group anxiety. The real anger belongs to the group, and is directed at 'the one who is supposed to know'. (This is a Lacanian notion; the 'supposed' is heavily laced with irony.) This even happens in groups which have conductors with friendly faces.

When a group begins, feelings of individuality and separateness are both at their height. Regression and irrational, primary-process thinking dominate. To contend with this, social defences are heightened and members are on their best behaviour—which is exhausting. There is no group as yet, just individuals, and, as per *Totem and Taboo*, members feel alone and powerless in relation to the group.

The proposition that the lone individual is particularly vulnerable but is strengthened when the group bonds is borne out, once the group becomes cohesive. The motive for group development, it seems, is to put at a distance the awful sense of individual isolation remembered from when the group first met.

Totem and Taboo also touches on questions concerning the technique of leadership style. The conductor's delicacy in his use of himself as an instrument for adjusting the quantity of anxiety, according to that which he judges a group is capable of containing, is vital. The conductor needs to be mindful of the new group's regressed state of dependency, and its phantasy that the conductor has the blueprint of the group's meaning and future hidden in his mind. At the beginning it is still very much the 'conductor's (father's) group'.

The Anti Group

The new group yearns for, yet fears uniformity. The desired prospect of unanimity on any subject poses overwhelming anxiety for the group. Though a group will regress on many occasions—for instance: after breaks, and after gaining or losing a member—it is at its most regressive when it is new and possesses no mutual subjective reciprocity. This is the 'no group' experience, a random scattering of individuals lacking the corporate strength of unity.

Bion proposed that a baby's perception of the absent breast—the part-object equivalent of the absent mother—is experienced as a tangible, persecutory 'no-breast' presence. This might be expressed verbally as: 'through my longing for the missing breast I can imagine it, and it hates and attacks me just as if it would if it was here.' I would venture that when the anxious group regresses, there is a 'no-group' experience similar to the 'no breast' phenomenon. It is also my sense that when the conductor makes only whole group interpretations, individual members feel a narcissistic affront. It may also be the case that the sense of 'no group' unconsciously recalls the dashed hopes and fractured desires for parental appreciation, which can brush members with a sense of existential erasure.

When this state of persecutory feeling has become chronic, due to the plethora of destructive forces, Maurice Nitsun refers to the group as an 'Anti Group' (Nitsun 1996). The group itself is felt to be persecutory and has to be attacked, though the conductor is still blamed. In this vulnerable state, issues of acceptance—who is in or out—conflict directly with anxieties about being overwhelmed by the group and loosing one's sense of self to it. The concept of the Anti Group awaits further elaboration, yet can perhaps be regarded as an accumulation of hostile projections into the body of the group, with the intention of destroying it.

Akin to Bion's theory of defensive 'basic assumption' groups, Earl Hopper has proposed that there is a constant dynamic of oscillation as the group tries to become a group. This swings between the extremes of 'massification' and 'aggregation'. My understanding of this is that massification equates with unanimity, a regressive phantasy of merging with the ideal, primary, lost love-object. Groups of this type are characterised by feelings of an undifferentiated closeness; this 'one-ness' is a consequence of projective identification, which stifles contrasts, conflicts, 'two-ness', and any sense of Other. It possesses a centripetal force, powerful enough to compromise individuality in the group.

Inevitably, however, a member of the group will dissent from this, causing collective dismay at the chasms which have suddenly opened up, and leaving members feeling isolated and stranded. This is aggregation. However, it is the oscillation itself which saves the group from the total stagnation of becoming stuck in either polarity.

Other case material

The first session of a one-year experiential group opened with complaints that fourteen members were too many. It was proposed by a highly intelligent man (who clearly saw himself as the 'dominant male') that we should split into two groups at either end of the room, and that I should stay with one group. It took quite a long time for someone to say 'and I suppose you will lead the other group?' at which point the tension dissolved. Confident that they would not find unanimity, I had merely been wondering to myself how they were going to get out of this one.

Ordinarily, I think, the neonate group regresses to primitive levels of functioning, clustered around projections and prejudice. In the light of *Totem and Taboo*, however, I would have to consider that the regression included the unconscious sense of myself as jealous primal father keeping all the women from the other men. The proposal to 'halve the supply' was a compromise offer, or a demi-rebellion, designed to mitigate my envious rage.

Considered within an oedipal context, I find no inconsistency between my actual thoughts at the time, and those which occur to me as part of my reading of *Totem and Taboo*. At one level, the group member's proposal could have been motivated by oedipal rivalry, but at the same time may have represented a call for fraternal unification. It was also a defence against the anxiety of 'not knowing'—an unfamiliar impotence—as well as an attempt to wrestle back the power he projected into me as primal father. *Totem and Taboo* relocates and dramatises the oedipal tale.

If *Totem and Taboo* were used in order to inform the leadership style, the conductor would allow himself to wear the projections of primal father whilst waiting for the group to become a group. If he gives in to a need to be liked, then no rebellion is necessary and, consequently, any banding together within the group takes longer and feels somehow incomplete. Independence cannot be granted by Authority, but must be wrested from it. The conductor understands this fight must occur in order for the group to discover its own vigour. However, if the conductor is too remote, too close to the model of the primal father, then destructive feelings will grow out of all proportion, and the fears of the group escalate into the realm of the unspeakable.

Totem and Taboo can thus be read as an historical allegory of the instinctual and oedipal themes, which Freud took up again later, in *Group Psychology and the Analysis of the Ego*.

Group Psychology and the Analysis of the Ego

In this work Freud contrasts the mob—whose archetype is the band of brothers—with two enduring social institutions, the church and the army. Whereas *Totem and Taboo* connected neurotic and childhood case material with the Oedipus complex and the myth of the primal horde, in *Group Psychology and the Analysis of the Ego* Freud uses myth and case material in order to elaborate Oedipus, libido and groups.

Freud speculates on the nature of the changes wrought by the group upon the individual. This question arises because Freudian psychoanalysis finds it cannot explain inner life without some kind of recourse to the external world. The constant re-entrance of the 'other' into inner life nudges psychoanalysis towards a more psycho-social perspective.

Freud draws on three other authors in order to establish his view that mobs and crowds are primitive organisations which cause the individual to regress. He then contrasts this state of affairs with groups that have leaders. In these groups, hierarchy exerts an influence upon group survival and stability.

Freud's reinterpretation of Le Bon's concept of group mind in *Psychologie des foules* (1895), his critique of Trotter's *Instincts of the Herd in Peace and War* (1916), and McDougall's *The Group Mind* (1920) allows him to develop his own ideas on the constituents of social ties, and to expand upon his view that inclusion in any mob will reduce the individual from a higher level of functioning to a lower level. Freud agrees with McDougall that either continuity of membership, or an internal hierarchy, promotes group survival over a given time-span, and that—to ensure this—members should know what the group is for and how it works. Also, according to this view, member relationships should be founded on custom and specialised tasks which relate to particular group functions. Cohesion is enhanced further if the group has a rival group, sufficiently similar yet different enough to cement internal bonds through external enmity. Freud referred to this as 'the narcissism of minor differences' (Freud 1930: 114).

Freud appears to favour what would later become known as object relations theory:

> ...only rarely and under exceptional conditions is individual psychology in a position to disregard the relations of this individual to others. In the individual's mental life some one else is invariably involved as a model, as an object. (Freud 1921: 69)

However, Ferenczi proposes that Freud's real motive is a selfish endorsement of his own psychology of the individual—psychoanalysis. Ferenczi wrote:

> [B]y our better understanding of the individual we had the basis for understanding the complex phenomena of the Group Mind (art, religion, myth formation) when Freud... showed us the converse, that Group Psychology was capable of solving important problems of individual psychology. (Ferenczi 1955: 371)

Even if Freud's intent was simply to extend the domain of individual psychology, his firm inclusion of sexuality and the physical instincts in a work examining man as a social being, breaks new ground for sociology. An account of social man which includes such unquantifiable behavioural determinants as 'the unconscious' became a welcome heretic in the pulpit.

Freud, certain of mankind's huge capacity for destructiveness, saw the leaderless mob as an ideal culture for the manifestation of repressed impulses, 'in which all that is evil in the human mind is contained as a predisposition' (Freud 1921: 74). Freud and Le Bon's versions of 'the crowd' are equally unreflective, uncritical, suggestible, cruel, and prone to destructive instinctual expressions normally repressed in the individual. Freud indicated that the mob knew no limits, no impossibilities, but neither was it capable of long-term survival. The mob simply provides an instinctual escape from man's struggle, made possible through its capacity for regressive trends, such as the ability to entertain contradictory truths simultaneously, a primary-process trait. The mob's need for a leader, and its desire to be led, inclines it towards illusion rather than complex reality. Being in a crowd can raise the individual's capacity for altruism just as easily as it can summon the brute in him.

McDougall emphasised that the mob's tendency to heightened affect was promoted by a 'suggestibility', which was in itself irreducible. Nothing could have upset Freud more than the suggestion that something could be both non-instinctual and irreducible! His theory rests on the notion that all psychical phenomena are reducible to the instincts, and only the instincts themselves are irreducible. Freud proposed that it was *libido* which held groups together, and that individuality was sacrificed for harmony under the principle of '*ihnen zu Liebe*'—that is, 'for their sake', or 'out of love (for others)' (Freud 1921: 92).

Relevance of the mob to group theory

I would like to consider therapy groups in relation to Freud's original contrast between groups with and groups without a leader. The contrast between the characteristics of the mob and those of the group with a leader is the first encouraging sign that we may be able to connect Freud's ideas with modern group theory.

The leaderless mob, it seems, is under the influence of such a subjective rapture of affective process that self-destruction is inevitable.

The fact that these forces are unconscious suggests that they exist *in potential* even in groups with a leader, although—usually—they will only reach a climax in groups without one.

The regressive tendency must exist as an *a priori* in every group. This includes therapy groups, but the function of the conductor mitigates its force. The conductor is recognised as an authoritative adult presence, and also as an outsider safely disconnected from group confusion. Because the conductor views the group as a whole he may be perceived as neutral and safe, as well as an indifferent and dangerous primal father.

The conductor, then, presides over a chaotic storm of unconscious destructive forces, which are especially present at the beginning every group, and threaten to re-emerge later, during times of tension.

Group Y #3

Eight of us are sitting here. Silence in the group, again. Now that we have started—we don't. But that is no surprise. A familiar lethargy creeps over us, trapping us all again. We have had to endure this increasingly numbing spell over the last year. Its impenetrable emptiness deafens us, so that no-one can think any more. Twice a week, months on end, it stuffs up and stifles all counter-transferential messages other than frustration and my wish to just walk out of the door...

I can see my wish for action here as a message telling me that I am subject to mob imperatives. Action is my familiar, ego-syntonic response to anxiety...

Relevance of the mob to group theory continued

The physical presence of anyone in the role of conductor immediately implies for the group that this as yet unknown person stands as a reassuring guard against the group's vague anxieties, which arise from regressive forces as yet outside consciousness.

These disturbances include fears of destructiveness arising from the prospect of being in a primitive leaderless mob. These are reduced from a reality to a potential only by the presence of this single person. My understanding of the primal horde suggests to me that the conductor is unconsciously subject to this state of affairs immediately on entering the group, regardless of any other anxieties which may also disturb the group. The conductor's function is, eventually, to assist the group in recognising and reconciling these forces.

If we accept Freud's analysis that primary-process behaviour is a potential characteristic of all groups, then conductors would have to include this in their thoughts about what constitutes a group's 'unconscious', instead of regarding group behaviour as determined solely by manifest, anxious unfamiliarity. The conductor's thoughts might instead be directed towards potential manifestations from the impulse-driven, unconscious, 'mob-stratum'—a group dynamic based primarily upon action. I should like to highlight that this view is inconsistent with the more general optimism expressed by many group theorists, and is more in tune with the monster that we have previously referred to as the Anti Group. Freudian theory could be more appropriately viewed, perhaps, as adjacent to Bion's version of the semi-psychotic anxieties which provoke the formation of defensive, 'basic assumption' groups.

My claim, then, is that *there is a self-destructive drive lurking in all groups*.

In its early life, when a group is not yet a group, it is still too dependent on the conductor to rebel. Nonetheless destructive processes can build up, perhaps occasioned by too many losses and additions, the first long break, or some other trauma which sours the dynamic. Under these circumstances an established group can give way to the self-destructive despair of the Anti Group. In this instance, it is the group itself which is the target; the group *as a whole* directs its attack against itself.

Ties and bonds in the group

'Group ties' is Freud's attempt to explain how the group can have such a marked influence on the mental life of individuals. Freud found that group ties to the leader rest on a phantasy of his equal love for all members. We believe that 'the General loves us all equally', and on that basis we accept orders. The primal Father—on the other hand—*persecuted* all, but equally. Regardless of whether the group's phantasy is that the conductor is persecutory or loving, members need to feel that they are held in equal regard. This raises problems for group therapy. Max Weber challenged the notion of a pure objectivity, and obliged us to recognise that parents love their children equally, but also differently. Humans categorise, select, choose and prefer, and so are partial and subjectively motivated; we love and hate at first sight. In contrast to this approach, Bion proposed that we enter each session free of the memory of previous ones. How will this approach fare when confronted with socially skilled clients, predisposed to charm and be likeable, and—on the other hand—others determined to be rejected?

Prior to the Oedipus complex, Freud suggests, all ties belonged in the domain of direct, polymorphous sexuality. The effect of traversing the Oedipus complex and entering sexual latency is to transform impulses into the affectionate mode (aim-inhibited bonds), more commonly referred to as 'friendship'. The hormonal kick-start of puberty then adds sexual ties adjacent to those of friendship.

It is thus *identification* which precedes and succeeds Oedipus. During the early stages of Oedipus, the little boy wants 'to be like daddy', a wish paving the way for empathy, which gives us the capacity to feel what is alien to us in others, the core ingredient of social humanity. Identification is the original tie to the primary love object; Klein regarded projective identification as the precursor of empathy. The capacity for object-choice belongs to a later stage, represented by the more mature wish 'to have' the object rather than 'to be' the object. Yet, after Oedipus, identification remains instrumental in the appreciation of a 'common quality' with someone else, which, as it strengthens, achieves the status of a new tie.

Because of the strictures enforced by the primal father, the brothers' only recourse was to convert their sexual impulses into friendships for each other, and so they formed the phallocentric band, which led to the undoing of the primal father. This is replicated exactly at the exit-point of the Oedipus complex, when sexual feelings become repressed and are converted into the 'affectionate' current. Parricide hammered the final wedge between affectionate and sexual love, nudging forward the brothers' embryonic democratic legislation for enforcing totemic exogamy as the instrument of incest prohibition.

Group Y #4

We return, and I am still confused. A recent feature has been that the male referrals are far less able than the women. Nor do they survive; their group life-expectancy is from three to six months. The women are never absent and do not leave; arch politeness towards one another, accompanied by distance, poisons the atmosphere. The genders are reversed in relation to the primal father myth. The men are not even bonded together by their mutual terror of the women. I wonder at my own position, as a man, supposedly in charge of a group which oppresses me. Yet I sense that I am also the lynchpin of its problems, trussed for a lynching...

Horizontal and vertical group ties

Conceptualising group bonds in terms of 'vertical' (hierarchical) and 'horizontal' (fraternal) ties, Freud viewed the tie to the leader as founded upon *idealisation*. He placed much more emphasis upon vertical idealisation than the horizontal ties between members. It is also primary in the sense that the formation of horizontal ties *depends* on the vertical link with the leader. The horizontal group forms upon the realisation that group members share the same idealisation and relative position with respect to the leader.

As children, we were motivated to form social bonds with our peers through the agency of a teacher or parent. Relating to the conductor causes a regression to peer identification. The paradox, however, is that regression also impels the group to idealise the conductor as an *alternative* to an object relationship. In practice, the conductor of a therapy group invariably enjoys only a mixed response from the group, and should become concerned about group dependency only if a uniform idealisation becomes entrenched, rather than the more usual move towards greater differentiation amongst group members.

This observation allows us to speculate on the dynamics which precede the formation of groups. In church, army, psychoanalytic training institute, or therapy group, the individual is bound both vertically to God, General, training analyst, or conductor, and horizontally to fellow peers. The double vertices of these intense bonds provide 'an explanation of the principal phenomenon of group psychology—the individual's lack of freedom in the group' (Freud 1921: 95).

Freud observes that:

> the loss of the leader in some sense or other, the birth of misgivings about him, brings on the outbreak of panic... the mutual ties between the members of the group disappear... at the same time as the tie with their leader. (Freud 1921: 97)

These comments direct us to an unconscious level of *group anxiety*, voiced as concern for the conductor's well-being, or anything which spoils the group's idealised image of him. We usually interpret this anxiety as individual dependency, rather than concern for the survival of the group as a whole.

Affectionate ties bind the group horizontally. They fail, however, due to a break in the vertical tie, which causes panic and results in group disintegration. Panic stems from the anxiety that, once the bonds have been severed, man is alone with his chaos and danger. Fearing abandonment, his worry is 'that the centre will not hold'. This suggests that the anxiety in relation to external danger is illusory, because the fear is actually motivated by the feeling of being alone and unprotected by comrades.

I take this fear of vulnerable isolation as support for my proposal that what impels group development is the avoidance of a regressive return to the no-group experience. The dilemma of this, as posed by Freud, is that being in a group entails a sense of inhibition and restriction. People are inevitably bound and bonded through social relations, yet this provides the individual with a sense of safety; inclusion in a group lends the individual a sense of power.

Those keen playground memories of inclusion and belonging, versus exclusion and isolation, direct us to a more personal appreciation of the significance Freud attached to the building blocks of social humanity, the ties of affection between peers. This primitive level of existential well-being and psychic survival is evident in such everyday events as going to a new school, or starting in a group. Teacher enters the class and the lonely, anxious, new child, equally hopeful and fearful, intently searches the adult's face for reassuring clues. We meet the adult edition of this in fairly new therapy groups, voicing the impression that 'it's a bit like starting school', which soon generates a chorus of recollections. I judge these as adjacent to first impressions. The group members are far too new to think yet of 'we' but, as they warm themselves to the themes of 'beginning and belonging', they seem encouraged that the topic is the 'right thing' to talk about, because it can include everyone.

Anti Group formulae

Nitsun, writing on the topic of the Anti Group, argues that therapy groups which threaten to self-destruct do so due to internal causes— that is, due to the weight of destructive projections. He offers the flexible concept of a 'group object relation', which is an internal representation of the group, specific to the mind of each member.

Members and conductor come to feel equally persecuted by the Anti Group, and are thus equally hostile towards the group itself. In harbouring the same persecutory images of the group as the group members, the conductor's belief in his own perceptions is undermined.

If we do not know how often Anti Group phenomena make their appearance, this is because of our unwillingness to make our failures public. Supervisors who come across groups which self-destruct share this failure with their supervisees, and thus even they are reticent on this theme. I am not sure if Nitsun shares my view of a universal layer of Anti Group sentiment within every group, but the aggression Freud discerned in the primal family and the mob has—it seems to me—the potential to arise also in therapy groups with leaders.

Group Y #5

Personal material still finds its way past our individual suffering into the group. Occasionally members recall earlier painful events, as if they are try-ing to impersonate a group. I wonder why they have not been deterred by the brief responses, hollow imitations of interest. When the group's most pressing concern is itself, in the here and now, it does not matter how shocking past memories may be, or the dramas of group members' everyday lives. The group will be unable to settle on anything until the main, here-and-now, 'whole group' preoccupation is addressed...

The tie through reaction-formation against envy

Freud made the case for a primary, vertical tie to the parent based on idealisation, and horizontal ties of affection to peers. He subsequently developed a notion of a universal social bond, arising from a conjunc-tion of the two ties, which provided me with the best clue for under-standing Group Y...

Children fear being alone. They can only be comforted, at first, by their mothers, and then later by familiar figures. Group feeling is pro-voked by the presence of competitors—for example, a new baby in the home, or other children in the nursery—and thus it takes its form as a response to *envy*.

The envious child cannot openly put into action its plans to use the baby for interesting experiments into the laws of physics—testing if it floats in the bath, or how high it will bounce if dropped, etc. The child sees that his rivals are also loved and—if he acted on his envy—he would loose *all* love. Self interest, and acknowledgement of the longer term consequences of his actions, enter into a compromise with envy. This results in a reaction-formation—'I *love* baby'—which leaves the child little choice but to identify with the others.

This presentation, typical of Freud, possesses a Dickensian quality, with its intimations of childhood miseries, lightly touched upon, of absence and lack as a means of opening *necessary* wounds, without which future development would perish from lack of incentive. The birth of individual socialisation—suggests Freud—is marked by a reaction-formation arising from a clamouring for fairness, a plea that all be loved equally by the leader. The child has given up the demand that he be loved most of all. Thus the maintenance of justice—an axiom of our adult lives—is based on the wish that no one else is made the favourite.

For Freud the fans gathered around their matinee idol would prefer to tear out each other's hair. However, they form a compromise, and tear out their own hair instead. Really, they want him for themselves. Peering more deeply into this social phenomenon, Freud notes that the real wish is: 'if I cannot have him, neither will you'.

In this way, then, reaction-formation converts destructive envy into social identification. Rivals turn themselves into a fan club. Sacrifices are made—or rather, we deny ourselves so that others might be equally deprived:

> What appears later on in society in the shape of... *esprit de corps*, group spirit, does not belie its derivation from what was originally envy. (Freud 1921: 120)

Group Y #6

We are now in a pattern of fifteen minute silences at the start of every session. The atmosphere is thick and even Anthony, one of the least sensitive people I have ever met in a group, reacts to it by telling us what a remarkable chap he is, how wonderful it is to be as free as he is, to come and to go as he likes. When the group tells him that he never has a penny to spend on his freedom he says 'but that is freedom!' The group then reminds him that it would be better if he 'freed' all the cassette tapes he stole from the centre and gave them back. He has a limp and uses crutches, because a year ago he stuck his legs under a double-decker as it pulled into a bus-stop. He gives a passport photo of himself to the youngest female in the group. She returns it to him, saying 'you should give this to someone who likes you'. The group are variously amused or indifferent. No-one likes anyone else in here. I feel like the 'old woman who lived in a shoe'...

The tie through reaction-formation against envy

Freud's understanding of groups rests on the notion of the group's 'libidinal constitution', of which he ventures this definition:

> A primary group of this kind is a number of individuals who have put one and the same object in the place of their ego ideal and have consequently identified themselves with one another in their ego. (Freud 1921: 116)

Though the object Freud refers to is the leader, group theory places a much greater emphasis on the group itself as the common quality. Freud's language conveys something of the nature of the bonds between group members—aspirations of proud loyalty. These bonds conjure feelings of warmth, security and—perhaps most important of all in this era of anomie—a sense of *belonging* to one another. Group meanings are internalised by the members into group representations.

Finally, too late, I understand Group Y...

Now it has become clear that the women of the group had been motivated by the mandate: 'If I can't have him [me] neither will you'. To achieve this they each had to prevent the others from using the group constructively and being most favoured by me. I was forgotten as they fought to stop any individual reaching me. They reduced the risk of my condemnation of any one of them by acting equally badly. Hindsight tells me that it was my photograph which was desired, not the unfortunate Anthony, who was himself free of their oppressive needs. 'All the members must be equal to one another, but they all want to be ruled by one person' (Freud 1921: 121).

Falling in love and group boundaries

On the assumption that it was the prohibition of direct sexual expression which forced the brothers to form affectionate relationships and cemented the band, Freud surmised that a couple in love *reduces* the quota of affection available for group ties. A loving couple ignores earlier bonds:

> Two people coming together for the purpose of sexual satisfaction, in so far as they seek for solitude, are making a demonstration against the herd instinct, the group feeling. (Freud 1921: 140)

In this way, loving couples *disable* group formation. Exogamy forces the men to look *elsewhere* for partners. The conductor, then, acts in a similar manner to the primal father, by insisting that as much libido as possible be retained within the group, for the purpose of group cohesion.

For instance, we ask our out-patient groups not to meet outside the centre. When a sexual relationship occurs in the group this is regarded as an 'acting out'. I define this as an alternative to *knowing* about repressed memories, which the 'action' keeps hidden. The group—I insist—has to put into words what its behaviour is telling it.

However, knowing all along that the analytic guidelines are impossible—that is, the injunction to free associate—we listen to the breaches of the rule, the hesitations and diversions. In the case of a sexual relationship, the conductor is placed in the invidious position of interpreting and thus *pathologising* an event which would usually bring a happy smile to most faces. However, it would be hypocritical to condemn an event which is actually expected. Our function is to interpret so as to evoke further material. As the relationship occurs in a group context, there are two broad views of it which we can adopt: firstly, as an oedipal challenge to a same sex conductor; secondly, as an expression of anger, due to a frustrated wish for intimacy with an opposite sex conductor.

Freud's existential bias provides us with a glimpse of his strong commitment to the individual within the group:

> Even in a person who has in other respects become absorbed in a group, the directly sexual impulsions preserve a little of his individual activity. If they become too strong they disintegrate every group formation. (Freud 1921: 141)

This is no longer a popular view. An inability to cope with being a member of a group is now taken as socio-phobia, or an adolescent fixation.

Group Y #7

Nothing I say can turn the group to the 'here and now'. I refer to the trouble which we are all having, the discomfort of sitting in here, and that it might help if we explore not just how we feel in here, but also what we feel we are doing to each other and what is being done to us. Eventually, as no one seems to have heard, I repeat myself a bit louder. 'Why can't we do this?' There is a period of silence, during which I resolve to remain silent also. Not another word, and no more cajoling... I can be mulish too... But then I end up saying: 'maybe the group feels too wrong to ever get it right again'. They look at me as if I have taken leave of my senses, and I know that I was way off target. I had spoken for myself, and they were still expecting me to get it right...

Groups and neurosis

Foulkes' much-quoted aphorism on the basic laws of group dynamics, that the group collectively constitutes the norm from which, individually, members deviate, refers to neurotic behaviour and social expectations.

A pressure towards conformity is exerted upon individual, isolationist behaviour. Freud asserted that the poorly repressed sexual impulses of the neurotic lower the libidinal bonds available to the group. As neurosis disobeys aim-inhibition, the presence of neurotics in a group has the same counterproductive effects on cohesion as a group of loving couples. Obviously, this constitutes a problem where groups are set up expressly for people with neuroses. However, it is only when cohesion of the group has been established that effective 'working through' can occur. Cohesion connotes stability, but this becomes 'stodginess' if hostility is avoided. In both individual and group psychotherapy, a balance has to be struck between a safe but moribund therapy, and one in which the parties are so persecuted by hostility towards one another that no insight can slip in between the locked horns.

Freud identifies and unravels an apparent contradiction:

> where a powerful impetus has been given to group formation neuroses may diminish and at all events temporarily disappear. Justifiable attempts have also been made to turn this antagonism between neuroses and group formation to therapeutic account. (Freud 1921: 142)

The neurotic, preoccupied with internal conflicts, has no room for intimacy and fills in the gaps caused by social isolation with a network of symptoms.

Freud's evidence for this is based on the phenomena of religious beliefs, which operate as a *collective* repression of instinctual impulses.

Freud describes religion as, in effect, an *ideological* neurosis, which saves the individual from having to construct a personal neurosis. This entails that a fundamentalist society might be 'neurotic', but not its individual members.

How do we 'provide a powerful impetus to group formation', as described by Freud? At first glance, Freud's comments on the effects of the neuroses in groups seem quite distant from what happens in therapy groups. However, closer consideration reveals that, in fact, we *already* follow Freud's edict concerning the scrutiny necessary in the selection and preparation of 'core' members of any new group—for instance, in the way in which 'fragile' referrals are placed in well-established groups.

The second issue raised by Freud is more troublesome: that people may be able to replace their individual neuroses by joining a neurotic group. However, Freud's aversion to primitive group processes is palpable. The kind of group to which Freud is referring is perhaps more appropriately exemplified by 'wild' groups such as Jones Town, Heaven's Gate, or other extreme cults—rather than by our own therapy groups! Freud's anxiety concerning primitive group processes, then, need not be regarded as sufficient reason to disregard the more mature, individual emancipation from neurosis which is sought for through the therapy group.

Civilization and Its Discontents

Restricted by his first topography of the psyche, Freud had available only terms such as 'conscience' and 'ego-ideal' to account for *guilt*. His later, structural theory, as outlined in *The Ego and the Id* (1923), linked the dissolution of the Oedipus complex with the formation of the superego—the agency of 'social humanity'. Freud's structural theory enabled him to posit guilt as the crucial ingredient of social humanity, and also the motivating force of the neurotic's need for punishment. He set out the social implications of these ideas in *Civilization and Its Discontents* (1930). This dark and sombre text returns to the topic of social ties, and fuses the very notion of them with the cultural function of guilt.

Unhappiness, in this text, is regarded by Freud as a tangible reality. The nature of unhappiness is bound up with the nature of time, and our sense of isolation and of 'being lost in the world'. A group setting—it might seem, then—is an ideal place in which to address existential misery. Freud's answer to his question 'why is man unhappy?' is that bodies age and die, the natural world threatens us, but—mainly—our relationships cause us pain. His conclusion was that 'the intention that man should be "happy" is not included in the plan of "Creation"' (Freud 1930: 76). Mankind on its rack, Freud suggests, will seek any relief—alcohol, work, or religion to relieve the pain of existence. (R.D. Laing would have held that madness was another option, although this assumes that the unconscious possesses some degree of intentionality.)

Freud suggests that existence entails a measure of pain, and that happiness amounts only to an absence of un-pleasure. Freud was already aware of the way in which the conflict between impulse and the constraints of the social world led to the creation of the superego as an agent of socialisation

At birth, a pure pleasure-ego exercises narcissistic dominion. Frustration at Mother's absence explodes the illusion of primary narcissism, and the baby now suffers as much from impotent pain as it had once enjoyed omnipotent control of its mother. This impingement of the external world is experienced as frustration, and breaches the pleasure principle. Loneliness and neediness provides a sufficient gap for the first insertion of the reality principle, which is installed by the first contrast we ever make, between 'me' and 'not me'.

Religious, mystical, oceanic feelings of being 'at one with the world' are now reinterpreted by Freud, in the light of these hypotheses, as regressive phantasies which deny the reality principle and attempt a return to a state of primary narcissism and omnipotence. If life is too hard for us, Freud suggests, we begin to question its purpose, and only religion has the temerity to venture an answer. Freud's challenge is that there is no purpose to life, yet human behaviour suggests that we assume the purpose of life is 'to be happy'. This begs the question: what do we want? Is it love? Is it the impossible?

Group Y #8

I recall an event which took place some years after the group ended, which led to my new understanding. A woman who had dropped out shortly before the end told me, a few years later, that although the group was awful, the final blow had arrived when she had seen a woman (my wife, as she correctly guessed) give me a lift in a car. She could not banish either this image or her feelings of guilt. A competitive group, such as Group Y, could tolerate only the one self-destructive, self-preservative compromise, that which is based upon the sado-masochistic logic of 'we will kill the one we love, so that no-one else can benefit'. This became 'the purpose' of life in the group...

Civilization and Its Discontents

In our helplessness we seek in vain for father's protection. Freud theorised that it is in the absence of this that we behave as if the purpose of life was to be happy. Yet the more we seek the protection of father through the security afforded by civilization, the greater the demands of civilization and the restrictions it imposes upon the individual. The balance-sheet reads: individual hedonism is sacrificed in favour of egalitarian justice and state protection. Yet the individual still continues to kick feebly against the constraints of society.

The final revision of Freud's instinct theory broke new ground. The libidinal power of Eros, the force behind infant curiosity and object-seeking, binds mankind in ever-expanding unities, working as a hidden advantage in groups. Aggression, the derivative of the death instinct, shares and competes in the world with Eros. The hostility of people towards one another opposes unity and civilization.

The opposition between the libidinal and the aggressive instincts is muted by fusion. The opposing instincts can be seen as two sides of a zip fastener. If the zip is almost fastened, the opposing instincts are fused or neutralised. However, the manner in which the zip is secured varies in each person. The less fastened, the more the instincts are defused, the greater the pathology. Both Freud and Klein believed that the particular configuration of instinct fusion determined individual personality.

Civilization controls aggression by encouraging the individual to introject their aggression into the unconscious part of the superego. Now fuelled with aggression refined from crude death instinct, the superego attacks the ego as aggressively as the ego had wanted to treat other people. The child needs love and fears its loss, but it cannot protest 'it isn't fair' without risking abandonment. An inevitable cause of psychic distress is the way in which the human infant remains dependent upon its mother for far longer than any other mammal. More evidence for an invisible battle between superego and ego is found in the formation of painful neurotic symptoms, and the attendant need for punishment. The latter arises because, in the conflict between psychical agencies, an aggressive wish is judged as bad as a destructive deed. The judge, the superego, because it is itself part of the psyche, sees all and responds severely, to even the most repressed images.

The legacy of parental authority causes us to treat bad luck as a just punishment. In the face of misfortune, our conscience searches for the crime we have committed. Freud went to hear Mark Twain talk about the first melon he ever stole, and his subsequent discovery that it was unripe. Twain paused, and asked himself: '*Was* it the first?' (Freud 1930: 126 n2).

Case material: Mr. E

In therapy groups, inter-agency conflict appears in the members' relationships to one another, to the conductor, and to the group as a third entity. I have in mind one very angry group member, Mr. E, who often asks me if I am 'all right', and is reluctant to enter the room without that reassurance. It frightens him to be mistrustful and angry with me. His question tells me that he has repressed and projected these feelings, which means he believes that I want to punish him. 'Are you all right?' equals 'am I angry with him?'. Mr. E has impossible moral standards and a vicious, primitive superego. I find him a good and loyal man, who unconsciously indicts himself for the worst betrayals.

The formula of aggression introjected into the superego, leading to conflict, anxiety, guilt and self-punishment, can be used to understand childhood responses to parental rejection. Indeed, Mr. E was intensely loyal to his psychotic father and raging mother. The dependent child forms an identity based on a conviction of its own 'badness', in order to restore a credible parental authority, whilst struggling to repress the more painful reality. The child's conviction that he is a bad person derives from his attempt to exonerate, idealise and protect his parents from the accusations he silently formulates. Freud's idea that socialisation begins when the child realises that its protest against receiving less love than the new baby will result in loss of all love, illustrates well the danger of protesting 'It's not fair', even when it *really* was not fair. In effect, the child revises 'It's not fair' to 'It must be fair, so *I* must have done wrong'. This is aggravated when parents actively distort the child's perceptions of external reality.

Mr. E's volatile mood swings became apparent on his entry into a colleague's group, three years previously. The group was too small to contain the swift, violent negative therapeutic reaction which spread from the conductor to the other four members, all roundly attacking one another.

In such a fragile group, both conductor and supervisor can become protective of the rest of the group. The member projects his hostility into the group and, now devoid of hostility, feels victimised. In actuality, he is trying to provoke from the external world a response which in his paranoid fantasy he imagines already exists. The motive is to force the persecutors out in to the open because, like a castle, our best defences (our 'projections') face outwards.

Risking his further ire, I removed him from the small group so that he only attended the twice-weekly large group, more able to contain his frequent 'blow ups'. This group now had to cope with his self-justifying assaults upon a real or imagined enemy, then his brooding isolation and counter-attack against the community, and finally his fear, suicidal feelings, and eventual return to anxiety. When this borderline 'victim' attacked, it was with greater force than the whole group put together. He would say: 'So it is all my fault, isn't it?' I had still not seen this as a *real* question directed towards his superego, but more as an ironic retort. His intense, defensive attacks took him beyond guilt and fear, and he also began attacking me. The level of unremitting, paranoid accusation divided the staff team, reflecting his own internal splitting of us into good and bad. It is consistent with the effects of this primitive splitting that we adopted the absolutist mentality of the paranoid-schizoid position: 'you are *all* bad so I am *all* good'.

Groups will do anything to avoid anger. The reasons for conflict remain hidden, and consequently the group seems masochistic. I watch a group struggling to understand, to forgive, but not to *confront* the threatening behaviour of one asocial member. It often seems that this person has unconsciously re-created an ego-syntonic scenario in which he is the victim, repeatedly cornered and fighting for his psychic life in the group. This 'injured and innocent victim' is unaware that he is perceived as persecutory, because all his hostile feelings are projected into the group. But at the same time the group denies its dislike by adopting a conciliatory stance. The 'victim' then becomes increasingly paranoid, and escalates his attacks on the group in an attempt to provoke a 'truth' from it which will confirm his persecutory feeling. If we accept that his worst fear is to realise the falsity of his perceptions—which is akin to madness—then we can understand his urgency to provoke the group to attack him in reality. But his provocation is only met with 'understanding', because the group's reciprocal imperative is to deny knowledge of its persecution and hatred of the attacker. Thus, even more inaccessible to expression is the collective 'rationality' of the group which prompts it to sense and sympathise with the attacker's delusion. The group knows its confrontation with the reality of the situation would leave the attacker isolated, with a new hatred fuelling even earlier unconscious injuries, cramming a regressed and hostile superego.

Freud, in his search for the origins of conscience, returned to the tribal myth first outlined in *Totem and Taboo*. The brothers hated and then killed the primal father but, after satisfying their hatred, they found a door which opened onto love, remorse and ambivalence, setting up an identification with the father and generating the superego.

The father's power is relocated in the superego in order to ensure that the impulse and the deed never return. But they do... Not really the deed itself, however, but aggressive wishes and guilt which appear in each generation, threaded onto a continuing strand of ambivalence. The eternal conflict between Eros and destruction ensures guilt is carried forward by everyone born to every society which has the family as its basic social unit. Guilt spreads in ever widening circles, infusing society:

> Since civilization obeys an internal erotic impulsion which causes human beings to unite in a closely-knit group, it can only achieve this aim through an ever-increasing reinforcement of the sense of guilt. What began in relation to the father is completed in relation to the group. (Freud 1930: 133)

At this point we can appreciate the huge role which Freud awarded to the Oedipus complex. A dynamic within the family provokes a structural change in the ego. The child takes something from a parent into its psyche, and the encroachment of instinct is countered by this 'superego' which is, in part, a social structure. The vexed question of which is primary, the individual or the group, is answered by the paradox uncovered by Freud: that the individual's life-long aim is to be happy, yet happiness itself depends on the individual's entry into and successful adjustment to the company of others. The wish for happiness is egoistic, whereas the benefits of community life are only gained through sacrifice. Civilization regards individual happiness as secondary to its goal of uniting individuals. Freud thought it was only 'in so far as the first of these processes [that is, "to be happy"] has union with the community as its aim that it need coincide with the second process [that is, "adjustment to others"]' (Freud 1930: 140-1). The struggle between the individual and society is, at this point, no longer based on the death instinct, but on choices between different amounts of libido directed to the self or to others—the very 'stuff' of groups.

Conclusions

The thesis of this paper is that there is a substrate to all groups, derived from the self-destructive primal horde. This suggests that the collective is parricidal in nature, and is kept in check by authority and institutionalised taboo. This is initially represented in the therapy group by the conductor's authority, which is later superseded by the authority of the group itself. Projections of authority on to the conductor modify unconscious destructiveness by making the group safe enough for a sense of 'group-belonging' to emerge. The phantasy that the leader loves us all equally—the 'vertical bond'—promotes a regressed relationship to the conductor based on idealisation. Members sense the similarity of each other's position in relation to the leader, which then inclines them towards an identificatory 'horizontal bond' with one another.

It is clear that Freud envisaged the leader's function as an essential component in determining the difference between the chaotic, affect-driven mob, and the enduring group. For instance, according to Freud the army might panic not because of the overwhelming odds it faces, but due to an anxiety that 'the centre does not hold', that the leader might fail. If this were to occur, the army would regress back to a mere aggregate of frightened individuals.

Freud directs us towards the darker side of those unconscious forces which influence social humanity. Sociology tends to emphasises those considerations which have a bearing upon the superego, internalisation, and the ego's adaptability, whilst remaining suspicious of 'instincts' and ignoring intra-psychic conflict. We now prefer to think of instinct as subsumed by the juggernaut of culture, rather than to follow Freud into that problematic arena in which instinctual energy is in endless conflict with reality.

There remains the problem that a 'neurotic' group affords the opportunity of a collective neurosis in order to disguise individual neuroses—as in religious institutions. Neurotic individuals who are 'well-adjusted' to a delusional group feel normal within the confines of that group. However, this idealised group lies outside society and is neurotic in itself. This leads to the question of how we might 'earth' such groups, ground them in some wider reality, and thus prevent the growth of a delusional ideology. (Perhaps the answer lies in the notion of transference, which implies working with phantasy material that shares a common border with delusion.)

Freud's ideas challenge group theory by tracing the relationship between humanity and civilization, which is conceived as a set of hostile social regulations that curb impulse, and become internalised by means of the Oedipus complex. The totemic horde, Freud asserts, sacrificed individual satisfactions so that there should be justice for all, rather than the right of might for the one. Civilization, then, exchanges fear for neurosis. Even so, parts of the original 'uncivilised' personality continue to insist on their insertion into the equation; individual libido fights against the authority of the group.

However, these problems vanish when the group has attained a more sophisticated level of culture than its individual members, allowing them to internalise the group's more mature ego-ideal. The conductor's technique and maturity is a crucial factor in the achievement of this by the therapy group.

Controlling aggression is regarded as the central problem which confronts civilization. In his abandonment of social remedies, due to his conviction that social problems were caused by human nature, Freud revealed his low opinion of the mental functioning of groups. He hoped that the remedy for violence was internalisation of aggression into the superego, and the replacement of instinct by intellect. Writing to Einstein on this topic, he toyed with the idea of a society founded on a 'dictatorship of reason' (Freud 1933a: 213). His devotion to reason and science entailed the substitution of 'knowing' in the place of repression or magical thinking. Reality had to dominate if man was to progress. Thus Freud was—overall—a reflective pessimist, who remained fatalistic on the issue of relations between society and the individual.

Perhaps a more optimistic version of Freud's outlook—however— is that therapy might offer a 'best mother', remedial experience, in order to improve on a poor original. Freud's technique rests upon a model of tolerable deprivation, which is designed to expose analysands to their own repressed, unwanted thoughts and experiences—which have made them neurotic in the first place—and to interpret the consequences of these.

I find it a cause for regret that Freud's ideas have not had a greater influence upon group theory, due to our fear of the notion of instinct, and the attraction of the more 'user friendly' theory of object relations. Inevitably, the theme of this paper raises more questions than it can be expected to answer. However, Freud, it seems, offers a theory of social relations which suggests that society—and, by inference, the group—is determined by unconscious processes to a greater extent than we might wish. Freud's commitment to what he regarded as the fathomless influence of oedipal forces, opened the door to an understanding of those powers which act upon the psyche in the presence of 'others'.

FOULKES AND GROUP ANALYSIS

Robin Cooper

I perceived ever more clearly that the events of human history, the interactions between human nature, cultural development and the precipitates of primaeval experience (the most prominent example of which is religion) are no more than a reflection of the dynamic conflicts between the ego, the id and the super-ego, which psychoanalysis studies in the individual. They are the very same processes repeated upon a wider stage.
- S. Freud

It looks as though we must reverse our traditional assumption, shared also by psychoanalysis, that the individual is the ultimate unity, and that we have to explain the group from inside the individual. The opposite is the case. The group, the community, is the ultimate, primary unit of consideration, and the so-called inner processes in the individual are internalisations of the forces in operation in the group to which he belongs.
- S.H. Foulkes

In psychoanalysis nothing is true except the exaggeration.
- Theodor Adorno.

Background

S.H. Foulkes inaugurated a distinctive school of group psychotherapy, which he referred to as 'group analysis', or 'group-analytic psychotherapy'. He was trained as a psychoanalyst, but came to regard the development of group analysis as his life's work. He wrote several books elucidating his view that group analysis—informed by psychoanalysis—offers enormously important, and—for the most part—overlooked therapeutic possibilities. Furthermore, he asserted that his group-analytic perspective called for a revision of some of the basic assumptions of psychoanalytic theory.

Foulkes started reading Freud in the early years of his medical studies, in Heidelberg. At once it became clear to him that he wished to pursue a career in psychoanalysis. He refers quite unequivocally to Freud as the greatest influence upon his professional life. When he came to England, at the invitation of Ernest Jones, the British Psycho-Analytical Society became his second home, and he continued to practice psychoanalysis throughout his life. However, according to Foulkes, Jones and other senior figures within the Institute of Psychoanalysis regarded his interest in groups as a 'breach of faith', although he never saw himself as a dissenter.

With regard to the evolution of group analysis, one formative phase in Foulkes' life particularly deserves mention—the Frankfurt years. The Frankfurt in which he lived between 1921 and 1933 was a centre for radical and critical thought, bridging the disciplines of social philosophy, sociology and psychoanalysis.

Firstly, a centre for research in Gestalt Psychology was set up by Max Wertheimer (one of the founder members of the movement), and Adhemar Gelb. Associated with them was Kurt Goldstein, the Director of the Institute of Neurology. Secondly, the Sociological Research Institute of the University was established in 1924. From this emerged the widely influential 'critical theory', associated with the names of Max Horkheimer, Theodor Adorno, Erich Fromm, Herbert Marcuse, Friedrich Pollock, Leo Lowenthal, and—in more recent years—Jurgen Habermas. Behind them loomed the formidable intellectual figure of Walter Benjamin. In 1929 an Institute for Psychoanalysis was founded within the Institute for Sociological Research. Unlike the Berlin Institute, the Institute for Psychoanalysis at Frankfurt was not initially designed for the training of analysts, but to develop the *theoretical* interests generated by the Frankfurt School. Joint seminars, attended by Foulkes, took place between the two institutes.

This collection of original thinkers, and the cross-articulation of ideas between the disciplines of economics, politics, psychoanalysis, medicine, history, philosophy, cultural theory and anthropology, provided a stimulating milieu within which some of Foulkes' own ideas began to take shape. Looking back at the Frankfurt School, we cannot fail to be impressed by the rigour, intellectual restlessness, and passion which informed its critique of bourgeois individualism, and its persistent aversion to foreclosure within philosophical systems. To this end, much of its attention was directed towards Marxism, the phenomenology of Husserl, and psychoanalysis—the dominant cultural/intellectual influences of the day.

It would take a great deal of space to spell out all the themes addressed by this community of scholars, the clinical implications of which were taken up and developed by Foulkes. However, especially important in this regard is the Frankfurt School's study of *authority*, and of the *family* as the vehicle which transmits the individual's susceptibility to the structures of authority. Other highly important Frankfurt influences upon Foulkes, outside the immediate parameters of the 'critical school', include the work of the psychoanalytically informed sociologists Karl Mannheim and Norbert Elias, the Gestalt psychologist Gelb, and the highly influential neurologist Kurt Goldstein. The influence of the 'figure-ground' motif, as explored by the Gestalt psychologists, and of Goldstein's sophisticated 'holistic' approach to neurology, is apparent throughout Foulkes. 'What Goldstein could demonstrate', writes Foulkes, 'was that the organism always reacts as a whole, that the central nervous system is an interconnected network which reacts as a whole' (Foulkes 1975: 15). This idea is transposed more or less directly into Foulkes' conceptualisation of the individual as a nodal point within a network. (Goldstein's work, incidentally, is taken up at length in the earlier works of Merleau-Ponty.)

Foulkes' first experiences with psychoanalytic groups were in 1939, in Exeter, where he was working as a psychotherapist in a psychiatric practice. He wrote his first paper on group analysis in 1942. That same year he was posted to the Military Neurosis Centre and Psychiatric Training Centre at Northfield, where he remained until the end of the war. During these years, which have been much written about, he witnessed the introduction of group psychotherapy into British army psychiatry.

Subsequently, Foulkes gathered around himself a small circle of colleagues who were interested in furthering their understanding of groups, and of the emerging analytic group psychotherapy. This was the forerunner of the Group Analytic Society, which was founded in 1952. The training body, the Institute of Group Analysis, was set up twenty years later.

Foulkes' project proceeded on two, inseparably interwoven fronts. Firstly, the discovery and promotion of the group as a therapeutic device, as a therapeutic situation. Foulkes addressed—often in very practical terms—the potential of the group for therapy, and the circumstances under which a group might be therapeutic. Secondly, he explored the implications of this for psychoanalytic theory. There are innumerable passages in Foulkes where he speaks of these two aspects at once:

My reasons... for 'labouring in the vineyard' ...and taking such an active interest in groups were twofold: firstly, the theoretical gain which this new field of investigation promises. The group situation is a new situation, offering great scope for research and study. Secondly, the clinical impression formed of the great therapeutic power of the group. (Foulkes 1990: 138)

The Group Analytic Situation

Foulkes did not tend to make pronouncements on the nature of groups in general—nor upon the therapeutic usefulness of groups—beyond his recognition that we are irreducibly group creatures, and that we 'belong' to groups and groupings of one sort or another. He had a great deal to say, however, about very *specific* groups, groups constituted under very specific conditions. 'Our domain', he wrote, 'remains the small group' (Foulkes 1990: 179). By 'small' he meant a group comprising eight or so members, plus the therapist. Such a group is 'large enough to be representative of its community. Yet it is intimate enough to trace the ramifications of the reactions in the individual member and to explore their roots inside the individual' (Foulkes 1984: 55). His 'domain', then, is not just the small group, but the small group under very specific conditions:

> When I say 'the group', I mean in this case the group-analytic group—that is to say, a group of patients under specific conditions set by us, with therapeutic intention, and under the specific leadership of a group analyst. We have to specify this because it is one of the fundamental insights to keep in mind that there is no such thing as 'a group' in the abstract. We need to know many things about the group's composition, its situation, its aims and so forth, before we can pronounce at all on its character or behaviour. (Foulkes 1990: 210)

> What distinguishes our analytic groups is not the presence of certain unique factors, but the particular combination of the several factors which we have already enumerated. (Foulkes & Anthony 1984: 59)

Although Foulkes' writings can at times become rather convoluted, much of what he says about the therapeutic potential of groups takes the form of very simple, practical, and down-to-earth 'guidelines'.[1]

One of the most basic considerations, to which he returns again and again, is the 'setting'. This term refers, in its broadest sense, to the total environment within which the group meets and performs its task, and may include issues relevant to the cultural and political context within which the group takes place. Of course, the group can never be hermetically sealed off from the rest of the world, so these dimensions of life are inextricably interwoven with what happens 'inside' the group. However, when Foulkes refers to 'setting', he usually has in mind more specific factors to do with the group's immediate, lived environment—such as its space, its time, and its boundaries. The last of his books, which is devoted to 'method and principles', discusses in great detail these aspects of running a group. The therapist, as 'dynamic administrator', is concerned—Foulkes suggests—with the 'conditions set'. It is the therapist who sets the time and place, and frequency of meetings (usually once or twice weekly). Group analytic groups are, almost invariably, 'slow open'—that is, its members stay within the group for periods commensurate with any other analytic therapy, and in accordance with their own time, needs and desires. Indeed, the membership may remain unchanged for long periods. The lifetime of such groups is indeterminate. I know of two in London which have been meeting for more than 21 years, each with its original conductor, one group meeting once per week, the other twice-weekly.

Foulkes' guiding principle for running a therapeutic group—it might be argued—is: create, maintain and look after the setting:

> Our answer to the question how group concepts are applied to the individual in the group has been so far: by exposing him to the particular dynamics which prevail in the condition created by us and which act upon him and through him. If we look after the group, we implied, the individual will look after himself. (Foulkes 1984: 160)[2]

One might wonder how 'exposing' a person to any particular dynamic is in itself therapeutic, let alone analytic. Foulkes appears to imply that participation in an analytic group is a very passive experience—however, this is not at all what he wishes to convey. On the contrary, he states elsewhere that: 'active participation on the part of the group members is the conductor's first aim' (Foulkes 1983: 140).

Foulkes places such emphasis upon 'looking after the group' because the group itself, he tells us again and again, is the 'active agent for change' (Foulkes 1975: 107). The group, he says, 'is and remains the active agent and the decisive context' (Foulkes 1975: 110). However, in the first instance it is perhaps not so much a question of the member being 'exposed to dynamics' as being invited to enter a culture, with its characteristic rituals and traditions. As an example of 'culture', in this context, we might think of Foulkes' discussion of group rules, or what he calls 'principles of conduct required'. This refers to such things as attendance, punctuality, meeting outside the group, and so on. 'In the slow-open group', Foulkes writes, 'the newcomer absorbs the established custom and behaviour of the group: a self-propelling tradition is the most powerful factor here' (Foulkes 1990: 171). So, for example, with regard to infringements such as latecoming or absence, Foulkes prefers 'to demonstrate the reasons for these rules *in flagrante* as it were' (Foulkes 1990: 171). He prefers, that is to say, to inculturate these rules by showing their significance, and thereby foster an ambience whose emphasis is more upon attentiveness than blind attendance:

> Whenever possible we should avoid laying down rules but allow the rules to develop by tradition and by convincing the group, whenever warranted, of the undesirability of certain behaviour, preferably on the very first occasion it occurs. A simple example: regularity and punctuality. I do not tell people that they are expected to be regular and punctual; I take it for granted. When anyone is late or absent the significance of such actions is made clear to the group by purely analytical means. (Foulkes 1990: 290)

This is a complicated statement. The principle of 'showing' by 'purely analytical means' can, of course, easily become a mystification—subtly tyrannical, as much as any laying down of rules.[3] As it happens, Foulkes is fully aware that circumstances arise with groups where it is necessary for the rules to be made quite explicit.

Free Group Association

The concept of free association is quite central to the analytic enterprise. Free association requires that the patient give voice to all thoughts which enter his mind, as they occur to him, and, so far as is possible, omitting nothing. Effectively, free association asks the patient to let his thoughts wander, and think these thoughts out loud.

Impossible enough at the best of times, the fundamental rule requires some modification with respect to group analysis.

Rather than a chorus of free associations, or a free-for-all collective monologue, Foulkes encouraged 'free floating discussion'. By this is meant a collective discourse in which each may have his fullest say, and which suspends, so far as is possible, the ordinary inhibitions which stand in the way of voicing whatever comes spontaneously to mind.

The equivalent, therefore, of the psychoanalytic recommendation to 'free associate' becomes 'associate freely', to or with one another. Members of the group are encouraged to converse with one another as freely as possible, to relax 'censorship' as far as they are able, and to enter a conversational mode whose keynotes are informality and spontaneity. This culture is encouraged, of course, not by decree but, as Foulkes suggests, by 'the way in which the communications are treated'.

Foulkes makes two important points, first of all he proposes that a collective 'free associative' process can be recognised within the spontaneous conversation of more or less any small group, if one listens with a sufficiently attentive ear for the links and connections between what people are saying. These links constitute (often quite unconscious) associations to what each has been saying, and to the situation of the group as a whole. 'Even in quite ordinary life groups', writes Foulkes, 'one can discern these associative components' (Foulkes 1984: 176).

Secondly, these associative processes can be particularly enhanced by the establishment of a conducive *culture*. 'The keynote in group analytic sessions', he suggests, 'is informality and spontaneity of contributions which leads to what I have described as free-floating discussion' (Foulkes 1984: 40). There are conditions, then, which favour the emergence of free group association—for example, when there are no dependencies 'in actual life' between the participants, who are therefore able to speak uninhibitedly with one another without fear of extragroup consequences. 'Under such conditions the spontaneous ideas of the patients become the group equivalent of free association' (Foulkes 1984: 176). Another example is when the therapy group is given no collective task to perform, when it has no 'occupation' and so aspires, as far as possible, to 'aimlessness'. The more the group is 'occupied' or has an 'aim', the less freely can group association emerge:

A strictly functioning work group, or a very conventional social gathering will strongly repress and disguise underlying latent feeling, fantasy and impulse, but a group under relaxed conditions... will disclose much more of this, though largely debarred from conscious recognition on the part of the participants... In the group analytic group, the emergence of a more primary type of communication is particularly favoured by the prevailing conditions. (Foulkes 1984: 73)[4]

In his illustration of how free association is achieved, Freud suggests that the patient should say whatever goes through his mind. 'Act', he says, 'as though, for instance, you were a traveller sitting next to a window of a railway carriage and describing to someone inside the carriage the changing views which you see outside' (Freud 1913a: 135). Foulkes, at several points in his discussion of free group association, uses more or less the same image of travelling in a carriage, with the difference that there are now a number of people within it who are casually chatting to one another. In these circumstances where people are 'casually thrown together', such as in a railway carriage, says Foulkes, 'the ongoing conversation approximates to free group association, the unconscious meaning readily shows itself' (Foulkes 1984: 118). 'I could observe', he writes of one such experience of observing people under these circumstances, 'that conversation was very disclosing as to the personalities, their relationships, interaction and the little group as a whole, references always being tangential, and I think for the most part unconscious' (Foulkes 1984: 73).
'Free association', concludes Foulkes:

works out in a different way in the group situation from the individual situation—just as it works out differently in the analytic situation from the procedure of self analysis. Free association is in no way independent of the total situation. (Foulkes 1983: 71)

Freud himself suggested that:

The patient remains under the influence of the analytic situation even though he is not directing his mental activities on to a particular subject. We shall be justified in assuming that nothing will not occur to him that has not some reference to that situation. (Freud 1925: 72)

The fundamental attitude of the group analyst, asserts Foulkes, remains the analytical attitude, corresponding to that of the psychoanalyst in the individual situation, 'but with the very great and essential difference that he is aware of operating in a group situation and that his total role is correspondingly different'. It seems to me that what is important here is not just that the *situation* of free association has changed, but that Foulkes has adopted a particular *orientation* towards this situation, illustrated here by the shift of inflection from perception to production: 'I discovered', writes Foulkes, 'that if I listened horizontally or laterally, I could perceive or, if you like, produce links between what they said' (Foulkes 1990: 290). Indeed, this shift of emphasis is illustrated in many other statements he made:

Everything can be taken as an associative response, a reaction against, or an unconscious interpretation of what was happening. (Foulkes 1990: 172)

The contributions of the individual participants also assume the function of unconscious interpretations. The group analyst at any rate has the right to look upon them in this sense, and in this way can help the group understand what they themselves are unconsciously saying and indicating. (Foulkes 1984: 176)

It is possible to consider the group's productions as the equivalent of the individual's free association on the part of the group as a whole. (Foulkes 1984: 117)

What the patient says *in fact* becomes the equivalent of free association through the way it is received and how it is understood. (Foulkes 1975: 96)

However, it is also *by necessity* that Foulkes adopts this orientation to the group:

Years of study and observation have taught me that it is necessary for the conductor to treat the productions of the group as interconnected communications, which they always are, if they are to operate as free associations in the group. (Foulkes 1984: 73)

It would be quite impossible for the therapist to follow each individual separately... he focuses on the total interactional field, on the matrix in which these unconscious reactions meet. (Foulkes 1990: 157)

The group analyst... orients himself as to his own interpretation in an otherwise bewildering situation by his awareness of the group context. (Foulkes 1990: 181)

Here it is important to add that Foulkes insists that awareness of the group context should not be taken as a warrant for subjecting the group to endless 'group' interpretations. 'We observe these dynamics for our *orientation* in the first place', he states, 'not necessarily to point them out to the group' (Foulkes 1984: 164).

The Group as a Whole

Foulkes repeatedly claims that an analytic sensibility is necessary, but not sufficient, for a group analyst, who will be required to develop a 'different frame of reference' from that of the individual analyst. Here we think of the notion of the 'group as a whole'. Translated from Foulkes' language, the 'group as a whole' is the background (elsewhere he uses the word 'horizon') against which everything is heard. 'It is axiomatic', writes Foulkes, 'that everything happening in a group involves the group-as-a-whole as well as each individual member' (Foulkes 1984: 49). 'Every event involves the whole group' (Foulkes 1984: 163). This idea is elaborated throughout his writings:

The whole is more elementary than the parts. With this insight we have arrived at one of the basic concepts in group psychotherapy, without which all other observations are misinterpreted or insufficiently described, namely, that what we experience in the first place is the group as a whole. (Foulkes 1990: 154)

Whilst having an eye on each individual member and on the effects they and their utterances have on each other, the Conductor is always observing the group as a whole. The 'Group as a Whole' is not a phrase, it is a living organism, as distinct from the individuals composing it. It has moods and reactions, a spirit, an atmosphere, a climate... One can judge the prevailing climate by asking oneself: What sort of thing could or could not possibly happen in this group? What could be voiced?... In fact it is the group as a whole with which the Conductor is primarily in touch and he experiences its individuals inside this setting. He should sense what the group needs at any moment. (Foulkes 1983: 140-141)

We concentrate on themes, motifs, meanings which concern the whole group, all of the members, which seem to underlie their communication... We do so for our orientation in the first place, not necessarily to point them out to the group, as some workers do... but as a background, a framework for our interpretations. (Foulkes 1984: 164)

The basic conviction that group is a more fundamental unit than the individual... goes beyond the more usual emphasis on inter-personal relationships and reactions. This refers to the practical conduct of groups, as well as to theoretical thinking. In both, the group as a whole is put into the centre. (Foulkes & Anthony 1984: 235)

In some ways his use of this term is unfortunate, insofar as it might suggest a reification of the group. In fact, the view that a group has properties over and above the individuals who make it up and their inter-relation, can be very misleading. Speaking of the group as a 'living organism', as Foulkes sometimes does, encourages the confusion.

Foulkes employs the notion of group as a whole, as *context*, as *background*, in therapy. Sometimes he suggests that the concept is rather like that of horizon, which frames everything but cannot itself be framed (Foulkes 1990: 230). Looking at it another way, the group-as-a-whole is simply a *latency*.

Whilst belief in the 'group as a whole' can be quite illusory, we might, like Bion, regard the idea that the members of the group are all part of a single, integral body as a *regressive unconscious fantasy*, which is generated within the group. Indeed, a very important aspect of the 'group as a whole' is to do with its unconscious phantasy-generating implications. How might the group-as-a-whole be experienced, either differently or collectively, by the group members. What does it unconsciously represent to them?

The whole group can serve as an imago, a reflection of phantasies of the group which are in everybody's mind. (Foulkes 1984: 164)

Pregenital regressions are readily observed in terms of the group as a whole. Especially pronounced is the oral level and correspondingly earlier intellectual development—dependency both wished for and feared and defenses against it—the hatred of dependency, unconscious material related to birth, early anxieties, separation, insatiable demanding, anger, rage and frustration, clinging, belief in magic, archaic images, primary process thinking, primary identification etc. (Foulkes 1990: 242)

On a very deep, archaic, level...the group represents the mother. At other levels it represents all sorts of things at different times and for different patients. (Foulkes 1975: 128)[5]

Foulkes was emphatic that, whilst the 'group as a whole' is the background, the individual is in the foreground. It is the individual who is being treated in group psychotherapy and not—as it sometimes is misunderstood—the group. 'Our ultimate object is the individual, our focus is the individual-in-the-group' (Foulkes 1990: 179). A good group, he claims, 'breeds and develops, creates and cherishes that most precious product: the human individual' (Foulkes 1984: 170). Group analysis is *psychotherapy of the individual*, in the group, through the group. 'The truest account of what I do', writes Foulkes, 'is that I analyse in the interest of each individual, but in the group context' (Foulkes 1990: 229). To understand Foulkes, then, it is crucial to understand the emphasis which he places upon the therapist being able to *make the fullest use* of this group context.

Leadership

Foulkes frequently refers to the group analyst or therapist as the *conductor*. He does so partly to avoid some of the misunderstandings which may be generated, in this context, by the term 'leader'. He recognises, also, a similarity between the group therapist and the conductor of an orchestra. The conductor is not producing the group's ideas, but interpreting them and helping bring them to light. He does not lead the group or the individuals, but directs the procedure, by following the process.[6]

Why did I call it conducting? There was at first an element that made me choose the term from the point of the musical conductor... I was not producing; indeed I was refraining from producing the group's ideas, influencing them as little as I could, but I was nevertheless doing something. I was not the composer who wrote the music but the conductor who interpreted it, who brought it to light. (Foulkes 1990: 292)

We might also discern a Frankfurt influence here—namely, Adorno's work on the social facets of music and, for example, the conductor's relation to the orchestra, and the musician's attitude to the conductor, which Adorno describes as 'ambivalent'.

Foulkes' conception of the place of the therapist-conductor is elaborated in his discussions of the phenomenon of group leadership in the analytic group, particularly in his paper 'Concerning Leadership'.[7] Here, Foulkes draws a distinction between the manifest and latent levels of the group. On the *'manifest'* level, the therapist—the 'natural leader' of the group—declines from assuming 'active leadership'. He *conducts* the group, and thus

puts the group as a whole into the centre and submits his own function completely to the interests of the group... he lets the group speak, brings out agreements and disagreements, repressed tendencies and reactions against them. He thus activates and mobilises what is latent and helps in the analysis and interpretation of content and interpersonal relationships... He encourages the active participation of the group and uses the contributions of its members by preference to his own... He treats the group as adults on an equal level to his own and exerts an important influence by his own example. He sets a pattern of desirable behaviour rather than having to preach to the group... The conductor represents and promotes reality, reason, tolerance, understanding, insight, catharsis, independence, frankness, and an open mind for new experience. (Foulkes 1984: 57)

Foulkes proposes that the conductor attempt to foster a 'tolerable imbalance' between constructive and disruptive inclinations, as the members struggle between their own egotistical needs and impulses, and the restrictions imposed by the others. More explicitly, the individual learns that he needs the group's authority for his own security, and for protection against encroachment by the others. And so, in return for this sacrifice of his own 'unbounded activity', he expects the group's support of his own individuality. His conflict, then, is that: 'he must tolerate the wishes and desires of others if his own claims are to be tolerated and he must restrict in himself what he feels he cannot tolerate in others' (Foulkes 1984: 59). The negotiation of this conflict zone, where each individual member is actively brought up against his relation to others, and to the group as a whole, constitutes what Foulkes calls 'the first basic problem'. It calls for the constant discernment of the conductor, and it is made possible only insofar as the conductor does not play the part of a leader.

At the *latent* level, Foulkes refers to the therapist's being put in the position of the primordial leader who is 'omniscient and omnipotent'. The group on this level shows a need and craving for a leader in the image of an omnipotent, godlike father figure, from whom they expect 'magical help'. The negotiation of this constitutes the group's 'second basic experience'. It is helped by the therapist accepting this position consciously, without exploiting it for his own needs or taking it personally. He behaves, then, 'very much in the same way as the psychoanalyst does in the transference situation', giving the group 'the security and immunity emanating from his authority as leader as long as the group is in need of them' (Foulkes 1984: 61). He must, furthermore, accept this position as leader in order to be able to liquidate it later on; unless this position is taken on, the group 'cannot be weaned from the infantile need for authoritative guidance' (Foulkes 1984: 61).

These two levels—of course—intersect. The conductor, by not taking an active leading role at a manifest level, makes possible the group's 'growing maturation' through 'analytic and integrative processes', thereby 'digging his own grave' with regard to their dependence upon him as 'primary' leader. At the same time, however, without being in a position of 'basic authority', without the 'primary leadership', the therapist's contributions would lack weight, and his example would not have the significance necessary to effect change. Foulkes speaks of a 'crescendo move' in the maturity of the group, and a 'decrescendo move' in the authority of the leader. 'Dependence upon authority is replaced by reliance on the strength of the group itself' (Foulkes 1984: 63). Looking at it another way, the group at first borrows strength from the leader's authority and integrates through him; this is a 'preliminary integration' resting on immature, infantile grounds. As the group becomes stronger and develops 'more mature integrations', it has less need to borrow strength in this way. The decrescendo move in the authority of the leader, then, encourages the integration of the group. The conductor watches this process 'on both levels', aiming for the right balance between upsetting factors and the tolerance of the group to cope with them.

Identification

It is striking that, throughout his entire chapter on leadership, and especially in those sections which address unconscious aspects of leadership, where—as Foulkes states—his interpretation rests particularly upon Freud,[8] there is no mention at any point of the concept of *identification*. There is, moreover, only a faint reference to *transference*. Foulkes writes that the group analyst, who 'accepts whatever position the group chooses to confer on him', neither actively assuming it nor acting upon it, nor denying it, 'behaves in this respect very much in the same way as the psychoanalyst does in the transference situation' (Foulkes 1984: 61).

Although Foulkes does acknowledge the importance of Freud's essay, *Group Psychology and the Analysis of the Ego*, he indicates elsewhere that it is not especially relevant to his own group-analytic concerns, insofar as Freud is merely using 'the group model' to illustrate processes to do with 'the individual patient in isolation'.[9] Foulkes, at a number of points in his discussions of 'leadership' insists, on the contrary, that it is the *group* situation which will throw more light on *psychoanalysis*, or upon 'the mechanisms operating in individual psychoanalysis'. The issue here, for Foulkes, concerns the *identity* of group-analysis. It is reminiscent of the way in which the identity of psychoanalysis was at stake for Freud, who—in *Group Psychology and the Analysis of the Ego*—sought to distinguish analysis from hypnosis.[10]

Clearly, Foulkes takes from Freud's essay what he wishes. He quotes with evident satisfaction,[11] for example, the following statement:

> We must conclude that the psychology of the group is the oldest human psychology; what we have isolated as individual psychology, by neglecting all traces of the group, has only since come into prominence out of the old group psychology by a gradual process which may still, perhaps, be described as incomplete. (Freud 1921: 123)

What he then leaves out, however, is what Freud goes on to say two lines later:

> Further reflection will show us in what respect this statement requires correction. Individual psychology must, on the contrary, be just as old as group psychology, for from the first there were two kinds of psychologies, that of the individual members of the group, and that of the father, chief, or leader. The members of the group were subject to ties just as we see them today, but the father of the primal horde was free. (Freud 1921: 123)

In fact Freud's discussion of group-formative processes, concerning leadership, the relationship between the psychologies of the bound and the free (the subject and the subjected), culminating in the myth of the primal horde, can be seen to have had a greater relevance to analytic groups than Foulkes seems to have recognised. 'There must be a possibility of transforming group psychology into individual psychology', wrote Freud (1921: 124). How does an individual become *possible* in a group?

Foulkes may not make much explicit reference to identification, but throughout his discussion of leadership he is evidently aware that much of his argument pivots around this concept. First of all, the encouragement of identification is very much taken for granted. Foulkes readily concedes that the conductor 'exerts an important influence by his own example', that he 'sets a pattern of desirable behaviour' and 'represents and promotes reality, reason, tolerance, understanding, insight, catharsis, independence, frankness, and an open mind for new experience' (Foulkes 1984: 57). This is by no means the only place in which Foulkes informs us that the therapist is there to be taken as a model.

However, Foulkes also maintains that the politics of psychoanalytic practice are—ostensibly—anti-authoritarian. The tendency to make the therapist into a leader (in the sense of a 'model person') says Foulkes, 'is one of the greatest resistances' (Foulkes 1990: 293). He is fully aware, accordingly, of the need to proceed carefully:

> He must be very careful in his interventions, in what he is, does, and represents, because he is likely to be taken as a model, and it is difficult but important to free the members of the group from using this model function of the therapist as a guide for their

own development. The tendency, more or less strong in individuals, to behave like him in the ongoing process is a definite resistance and has to be continuously analysed. (Foulkes 1975: 110)

By refusing to be the ego ideal or to be put into that position, one counteracts the members' tendency to learn by imitation, by identification, and so forth, and to make the mistake of thinking that the ideal behaviour would be that of the group therapist. Not only may his way be far from ideal, but how he behaves in his model as a therapist is certainly not a model for life. (Foulkes 1990: 293)

But 'refusing to be put in that position' does not seem to be an option, according to Foulkes' own account. What, then, would be a resolution of this question: how does the therapist use his authority in order to wean the patient *from* this authority?

Foulkes' answer is, in part, the familiar one: that this weaning is only partly possible, and then only through (continuous) analysis—that is, the group leader/conductor assumes an *interpretative* leadership. However, at this point we must also note a crucial and distinctive feature of Foulkes' approach to groups. The group members, in part—he asserts—assume this analytic, interpretative role *themselves*. 'Collectively', he suggests, 'they can do what individually they fall short of, acting as each other's therapist' (Foulkes 1983: 170). Furthermore:

A well conducted group learns to do even that work by itself, and the more the group does it, the more that comes from inside the participants, the more effective and convincing it is, and the less authoritarian. (Foulkes 1990: 293)

What is particularly important in Foulkes' discussion, then, has to do with the *group-specific* factors which contribute to this resolution. For here, as Foulkes writes, '[d]ependence upon authority is replaced by reliance on the strength of the group itself' (Foulkes 1984: 63). Putting this another way: 'the ego thus becomes freer, while also being strengthened in identification with the rest of the group' (Foulkes 1983: 134). The difficulty with this, from the point of view of Freud's formulation, is that it is precisely their dependence upon the leader's authority which holds the members of the group together. They identify with one another *through* 'having put one and the same object in the place of their ego ideal' (Freud 1921: 116).

'As the group progresses, becomes more mature and better integrated', writes Foulkes, 'it brings the conductor down to Earth' (Foulkes 1986: 144). But how far, I wonder, is this is consistent with the actual experience of group analysts? There is a story of one occasion when Foulkes did not utter a single word throughout an entire group-therapy session (usually an hour and a half). Would this be an example of the group doing the work by itself? Of a 'decrescendo' in the leader's authority? It may indeed be the case that the conductor 'wants to replace submission by co-operation on equal terms between equals'. But is there not still a confusion here between the person and the position? Let us for a moment turn to a statement by Foulkes which does make this distinction clear.

> One of the important points regarding the leader at which we as analysts may look differently is that he is not equipped with certain mysterious personality qualifications that predestine him to be a leader, just as a hypnotist is not so equipped. We know—in fact it was Bernheim's great contribution in this field—that hypnosis and similar relationships rest on suggestion. One can also turn this around, as Freud did, and say: if you are in a certain position in relation to another person or persons, then what you say, whatever you say, is a suggestion—i.e., it is taken in and believed firmly by those whom you address. It is the position in the group that makes a person into a leader and gives him these qualities. That some persons may be more liable to be put into such a position than others need not be questioned. However it is the transference position in the sense of the delegation of the ego ideal to a person who probably inherits the very early or primordial authority of 'the father'. It is that position which makes him into a leader. (Foulkes 1990: 288)

This, says Foulkes, is Freud's formulation. It is at this point in his discussion of *Group Psychology*, concerning the issue of the group member putting *himself* in the place of his ideal, that Foulkes parts company from Freud. He proclaims that Freud's *direct* contribution to group psychology does not seem to him to be very important. Furthermore, the sort of 'group' of which Freud writes, he asserts, has 'nothing to do with our idea of a group: one might say it is its opposite' (Foulkes 1990:

289). What Freud has to say about these (highly organised) groups is drawn 'largely from the descriptions of others and from the writing desk'. In other words, Freud doesn't quite know what he's talking about—at least, with regard to the small, intimate face-to-face gatherings with which group-analysts are familiar.

Foulkes concludes 'On Leadership' with this paragraph:

> there will remain a nucleus, not at present reducible by science, more nearly expressed perhaps by art and religion, bound up with his own personality, a primary rapport (charisma Max Weber called it) based on love, respect and faith. Without these, he cannot awaken or bind the spell of what the poet called 'the old enchantment'. (Foulkes 1984: 65)

Foulkes is writing here of an irreducible nucleus of primary rapport, where the patient is spellbound. This seems to gesture again towards hypnosis—the unwanted guest, or host, of psychoanalysis. As is made clear in Borch-Jacobsen's analysis of *Group Psychology*, hypnosis will not go away. 'Hypnosis', writes Freud in that essay, 'is not a good object for comparison with group formation, because it is truer to say it is identical with it' (Freud 1921: 115). Foulkes has no more to say specifically about hypnosis, although he recognises that the phenomena of conformity and suggestion deserve very serious attention.

The 'astounding' degree of the conformity of the group with its leader, he states, can hardly be overrated. The group, he suggests, continuously says and does what the therapist expects and wants to hear. He refers to the 'astonishing phenomenon of conformity of, in a sense, complete submission to the conductor's conscious and unconscious opinions' (Foulkes 1990: 211). 'This factor seems so important to me', he goes on to say, 'that I think that any true theory of group behaviour or of the behaviour of individual people in groups should start from this phenomenon' (Foulkes 1990: 211).

He insistently reminds us that the power of suggestion is usually underestimated:

> We can hardly overrate the great power of suggestion, conscious or unconscious – also on our own part, which enters into the effect we have on the group... The group hands over the suggestive power mostly to the leader. (Foulkes 1990: 212)

He goes on to assert:

> There is no question in my mind that, in our own way or any
> other method, far more of the effects we can observe are due to
> suggestion...than we like to think and which we tend to ascribe
> to our specific operations. (Foulkes 1990: 212)

> As to the ways in which this influence might be 'dis-spelled',
> Foulkes has to console himself with the thought: 'I am satisfied
> that I can reduce this element of suggestion to a minimum'.
> (Foulkes 1990: 294)

Transference

'The group-analytic group', wrote Foulkes, ' is essentially a transference group' (Foulkes 1984: 74). He insists that 'the phenomenon of
transference is of fundamental importance for all psychotherapy', but
at the same time repeatedly suggests that concepts derived from what
he calls 'the psychology of the isolated individual' (that is, psychoanalysis) have different implications within the group.

Foulkes' discussion of transference in groups is at times quite muddled. One of his aims, however, is to make a distinction between 'classical transference' or 'transference proper', and 'the more general use
of the term', referring, in the case of the latter, to all relationships within the situation—that is, between members of the group. These are
treated 'as if they were transferences', that is, 'accepted and subject to
interpretation and analysis' (Foulkes 1984: 285). According to Foulkes,
'true transference neurosis' can be analysed in the group, although it
'does not develop in the same pure style as in the individual psychoanalysis', and so 'cannot be analysed and worked through in the same
detail' (Foulkes 1984: 177).

> The individual patient's transference relationship to the conduc-
> tor or to any other member of the group cannot develop to any-
> thing like the same extent as in psychoanalysis and be analysed
> *vertically* (as we call it) to anything like the same degree. Instead,
> transference in depth and in its regressive character is more in
> the background, and the *horizontal*, contemporary plane presents
> itself for relational purposes. (Foulkes & Anthony 1984: 51)

The 'vertical' dimension offers the possibility of a deeper analysis of transference, and of the 'intra-psychic dynamics' of the personality. Analysis on the 'horizontal' plane too, Foulkes argues, offers a number of advantages, referred to throughout his books. The group situation, for example, 'affords a much broader and richer insight into the patient's various modes of action and reaction to different people in different and unforeseen situations under conditions much closer to ordinary life'. (Foulkes & Anthony 1984: 42) It offers an opportunity, also, to explore what Foulkes refers to as the 'social unconscious',[12] unconscious social or interpersonal influences, or, in the context of the group, 'the influences exerted on the individual by other individuals in the group and by the group as a whole', of which the individual may be unaware. (Foulkes & Anthony 1984: 42)

Foulkes' style tends to be pragmatic. As he himself puts it, he is much less concerned with how people have become how they are, than with what is preventing them from changing. It is his repeated claim that the group analytic situation, characterised by an intricacy of inter-personal interactions, and the challenges of working through their problems, proves itself particularly fruitful in this regard. It is in this sense that Foulkes sees an affinity between group analysis and 'the existentialists':

> It is characteristic of all modern development to emphasise the experience which is made in the therapeutic situation itself. This is the experience of the 'here and now' of existential psychother-apy, which at long last hopes to come into his own. (Foulkes 1984: 145)

Foulkes—to my mind, quite rightly—is critical of the guiding prin-ciple of depth psychology—that 'deeper is better'—and argues that a psychoanalysis which proceeds on this assumption often does more harm than good.[13] He is repeatedly critical of an analytic tendency to 'plunge into' the depths. Group analytic psychotherapy, he says, ' is not a hunt for unconscious meanings' (Foulkes 1990: 210). In another passage, he suggests that:

> a therapist with a sense for depth may agree that, in the general run of our profession, there is a false idea of depth and surface. Depth is always there: it is always possible to get hold of it on the surface, it is there all through, visible and tangible. It depends on

who is looking, who is listening; one need not jump from what
is going on to what is behind it. (Foulkes 1990: 280)

'Everything', he says, 'including the so-called depth, is always present if we have eyes to see it.' (Foulkes 1984: 287)

Norms and the Basic Law

Whilst Foulkes is quite right to insist (and to demonstrate) that the
group situation has specific features which can very profitably be
made use of, it is also appropriate to point out his tendency, in this
regard, to make somewhat exaggerated claims, and at times to *idealise*
the group.

It is worth remembering, in this context, that Foulkes—a Jew—left
Germany in 1933. Only the year before, he had been holding a joint
seminar on Freud's *Group Psychology and the Analysis of the Ego* with
Landauer, one of the founder-directors of the Institute of
Psychoanalysis, as mentioned earlier. Foulkes found this work highly
productive, but it came to an abrupt end when the Nazis came to
power. Landauer was subsequently arrested, and died in Bergen-
Belsen. Although Foulkes would be the first to point out that there are
all sorts of distinctions to be made between mass-movements and
small groups, nevertheless he claims—without any evident disquiet—
that the group, like the broader community of which it is a miniature
edition, 'itself determines what is normal, socially acceptable behaviour'.

This touches upon the important question of Foulkes' 'normative
criterion of health'. Consider, for example, what he refers to as the
'Basic Law of Group Dynamics':

The deepest reason why these patients, assuming for simplici-
ties' sake, psychoneurotics, can reinforce each others' normal
reactions and wear down each other's neurotic reactions is that
collectively they constitute the very norm from which, individually, they deviate. (Foulkes 1983: 29)

First of all it is important to bear in mind, as we read this, that Foulkes
did not regard the group norm as some fixed thing, as immutable. On
the contrary, he asserts that 'valuations and norms are restated and
modified by comparison, contrast and analysis'. (Foulkes 1990:

155)'Even what is normal or not', he writes, 'is a question of values which might be shared or not and which should indeed be critically considered even though these values may be generally accepted by the group'. (Foulkes 1975: 129) Nonetheless, Foulkes' 'basic law' remains a problematic statement, and requires that we investigate it further.

Foulkes proposes—in effect—that the neurotic position is in its very nature highly individualistic; it is, as he puts it, 'group destructive' in essence. The neurotic is disarticulated from his 'group' so that— instead of 'communication'—we have the formation of the symptom. The symptom 'speaks' of this disarticulation. The work of therapy consists of translating this 'autistic' symptom into 'socially acceptable articulate language'.

So, in the group, Foulkes proposes, the disruptive, anti-social and destructive aspect of neurotic behaviour is forced to come into the open, where it is felt as a disturbance by each of the others and is not 'shared' by the group as a whole. For this reason, by a process Foulkes describes as 'inevitable', the individual in his neurotic aspect is set upon by the others. This is a process in which the individual himself participates quite actively, by attacking in his turn the other person's neurotic defences. By contrast, the individual 'in his healthy socially adjusted aspect' is supported and allowed to develop and flourish in the group. Group destructive energies can, therefore, be harnessed for undermining the neurotic propensities of the members of the group. The constructive forces in the group, meanwhile, work to combine and support the group members. In other words, Foulkes suggests that disruptive forces are *consumed* in mutual analysis, and constructive forces are utilised for the synthesis of the individual and the integration of the group as a whole.

By this line of reasoning we arrive at the basic law: that although each member of the group may represent some form of deviance from the social and cultural norm, when taken together the group members have what one commentator on Foulkes has referred to as a 'built in developmental thrust' towards regaining that norm. In Foulkes' own words:

> The sound part of individuality, of character, is firmly rooted in the group, and wholly approved by it. The group therefore respects and supports the emergence of and the free development of individuality... Neurotic symptoms disappear into the common pool as soon as they become communicable and their

individual ingredient is now free for group syntonic, socially acceptable employment. That is the reason why neurotic behaviour tends to diminish in the group and normal behaviour to be supported. (Foulkes 1983: 30)

As they stand, these claims may leave us quite perplexed on a number of points. I shall examine some of the questions that they raise.

First of all we are left—notwithstanding Foulkes' quite explicit repudiation of *adjustment* as the goal of group analysis—with the uneasy equation between the 'sound part of the personality' and 'social acceptability'. Even where groups are made up of 'isolated, unacquainted individuals meeting for the purpose of treatment', argues Foulkes, 'there is agreement as to what is desirable normal behaviour, what is sick, good, bad and so forth'. Is this really the case?

Secondly, Foulkes is using the rather worn out language of confrontation between the 'healthy' parts and the 'unhealthy' parts of the personality/group. In the passage I have quoted above we encounter this model: disruptive, neurotic behaviour is forced into the open territory of the group where it is set upon by the others, who attack the defences, and so on. Now, of course there is in the therapy group—as within almost any other sphere of human life—scope for confrontation. Much of the vitality of a group will be to do with the way in which its members challenge, provoke and arouse one another. However, to place at centre stage this image of embattlement between the forces of good and bad is lamentably simplistic.

Thirdly, at a number of points in the passages quoted in this chapter, I think we are entitled to ask simply: *is this really so*? *Is it the case* that the sound part of character is really, wholly approved by the group? *Does* the group necessarily respect and support the emergence of and the free development of individuality? *Does* neurotic behaviour tend to diminish in the group, whilst normal behaviour (however this notion is nuanced) is reinforced?

One possible way of approaching these questions would be to try to sketch out some of the conditions under which these claims (or, perhaps, a rephrased version of them) might hold true. Ironically, despite the sweeping generalisations Foulkes makes in certain areas of his writing, in other places we encounter prolonged reflection precisely upon the conditions under which a group can be said to be 'therapeutic'. These conditions have to do with its setting, composition, and leadership (its style, spirit, and integrity), the interventions which are made, and the values which come to prevail, and so on. The simplistic assertion of the basic principle does not do justice to the intricacy of these variables.

'Normality' is a statistical notion. If we insist upon a normative guiding-principle in our approach to group dynamics, then let us re-phrase it. Rather than proposing that within the group there is a developmental thrust towards health, let us define the health—the well-being—of the group as its capacity to embrace its variations. Thus, it might be proposed that a healthy group, like a healthy ecosystem, contains within its wholeness its own disorders or disorderings. That is, it is 'in order' or it 'works' not when its disorders are removed, but when they are included within an interplay of ordering-disordering. This ordering process is dependent upon its complementary disordering—as the mean is dependent upon the variations around it.

Person

There are other places in Foulkes' work where his enthusiasm for the group causes him to become muddled. For example, he makes an analogy with Japanese paper flowers to describe how the individual only 'blossoms' in a group.

> In order to make them show what they were, in order to develop them one had only to throw them into water, when they would spread out and develop into beautiful flowers, leaves and stems. This fascinated me as a child, and I have often thought back on it by way of comparison. The individual out of the group, in isolation, is almost like such a Japanese flower before it is in water. Only in the group situation can he spread himself out, show himself as what he is, what his symptoms mean; what he can do and what one can do for him. (Foulkes 1984: 100)

> The human being is a social animal, he cannot live in isolation. In order to see him as whole, one has to see him in a group, either that in which he lives and in which his conflicts arise, or on the contrary, in a group of strangers where he can re-establish his conflicts in a pure culture. (Foulkes 1990: 272)

Foulkes is quite right to emphasise the irreducibly social nature of human life, and the priority of human *belonging*. But the claim that 'only in the group situation can he... show himself as what he is' is questionable in a number of senses. One does not need to have had the experience of running a group to appreciate that circumstances arise where particular individuals conspicuously *fail* to thrive in groups. Perhaps nowhere as much as in a relationship with *one other person* might an individual 'show himself as he is'.

'In order to see [a person] as a whole, one has to see him in a group', writes Foulkes. What *is* this 'as a whole'? *Which* group? For Foulkes has already reminded us that there is no such thing as a group in abstract. We are commonly told how differently people behave within a group from one another. Foulkes himself is very clear on how different group conductors elicit different behaviours.

Foulkes is—quite rightly—insistent that what we call 'mental illness' does not reside within one individual, but is to do with what goes on between individuals. As he puts it, 'it is the common product of a number of persons who co-operate to bring it about and to maintain it'. (Foulkes 1984: 133) At other times, however, his argument seems to be that it takes a number of people to *drive* someone mad, so it takes a group to cure him. Now, this certainly does not follow logically, although of course it is empirically true that some people are *particularly* helped by groups, or by living in certain kinds of therapeutic communities.

'From the mature, scientific point of view', writes Foulkes, 'each individual is... an artificial, though plausible, abstraction'. (Foulkes 1983: 10) Elsewhere he comments that to speak of the individual is an abstraction 'as far as the psychology of the total person is concerned'. (Foulkes 1990: 230) Now, of course, we can speak about individuals, or persons, or for that matter groups, *abstractly*—but this does not mean that to speak of an individual is to speak of an *abstraction*. When Foulkes proposes that the individual is an abstraction 'as far as the psychology of the total person is concerned', perhaps he is reminding us that we should properly consider the person in the fullness of his social, interpersonal milieu. But this, surely, is entailed precisely in the concept of 'person'. This is part of what we *mean* by 'person'. Persons are constituted by their mutual relations to one another, which are articulated into a common world.

This takes us back to the question which we touched upon earlier— what is at stake for Foulkes? What are the implications for psychoanalytic theory of the themes he addresses? He claims that they are many, and that they are far-reaching. Again and again he claims that Group

Analysis is the basis for a new theory of psychoanalysis, and of a new understanding of human life. He writes, for example:

> I am convinced... that the study of mental processes in their interaction inside the group-analytic situation will teach us much that is new and help to solve the theoretical, conceptual problems which are self-perpetuating in the psychoanalytic situation. Therapeutic group analysis is the foundation upon which a new science of psychotherapy can rest. (Foulkes 1984: 14)

An example of the self-perpetuating 'conceptual problems' within psychoanalysis might be the tendency towards 'Cartesian Isolationism'. Psychoanalysis, Foulkes argues:

> is based on the individual in Cartesian isolationism: one body, one brain, one mind. The world is built up from bodily needs and sensations, although an outside reality, impersonal and objective, is recognised. Social relationships are secondary... (Foulkes 1984: 124)

Again, the psychoanalytic view, according to Foulkes:

> inevitably supports the idea of the individual as the elementary unit, who must form relationships with others in a roundabout, often very complicated way. He is forced to do this by his needs, for which the others are 'objects'. As we have each our own body, our own eyes, our own brains, so we have our own mind. (Foulkes 1990: 272)

> The psychoanalytical view takes the individual mind as the unit of observation and tries to understand all mental processes in terms of this individual mind. (Foulkes 1990: 226)

First of all, we might take issue with what Foulkes, who adheres 'to the classical line of development of Freud's work' (Foulkes 1984: 123), takes to be the 'psychoanalytical view'. If we do not *start* with some of the assumptions he describes—the assumption that the human being is some sort of monadic system of self-enclosure, the self-possessed subject of post-enlightenment psychological man—then we have no need to seek, in group analysis, the foundations of a new, more social, science of psychotherapy.

However, even though we might readily accept that—notwith-standing its various post-Freudian developments—there remains within psychoanalytic theory a stubborn tendency towards 'Cartesian isolationism', towards solipsism and closure, we might still ask how adequately are these matters addressed by the theoretical terms which Foulkes offers. On one hand, the whole thrust of Foulkes' thinking on groups runs counter to these 'Cartesian' ideas of the mind. He states, for example, that the 'old theory' of 'individual minds enclosed in each skull, interacting in the most complicated fashion with the others, acted as a great barrier to my understanding' (Foulkes 1973: 214). Again, he states that he 'does not share the psychoanalytic juxtaposi-tion of an "internal" psychological reality and an "external" physical or social reality' (Foulkes 1973: 214). This is all very well, but the roots of this problem lie very deep indeed, and in some respect we are mere-ly led out of the frying pan into the fire. For Foulkes finds himself in precisely the same psychologism from which he is trying to lead us.

Where Foulkes sees the most compelling evidence for his own 'interactive process' theory of mind is in the intercommunications of a group, seen as a 'psychic system' of mental processes. But insofar as our mental life is predicated upon the interaction of these mental processes (as Foulkes maintains is the case) we are no less caught up in psychologism than in 'the old theory'. The difference is, rather than being starkly monadic, minds are now linked by (purely hypothetical) mental processes—or, finally—are reducible to these processes.

This is illustrated in many of the remarks which Foulkes makes concerning the group matrix. With this concept, which he regards as quite central to all his thinking about communication in groups,[14] he elaborates the idea of a transpersonal network or common shared ground of conscious and unconscious processes. Of this matrix, he says:

> Its lines of force may be conceived as passing right through the individual members and may therefore be called a transperson-al network, comparable to a magnetic field. (Foulkes & Anthony 1984 : 258)

> We can imagine mental processes as penetrating the individuals which compose the group—going through them, transgressing them, and linking up with each other. (Foulkes 1975: 18)

These processes pass right through the individual, though each individual elaborates them and contributes to them and modifies them in his own way. Nevertheless they go through all the individuals—similar to X-rays in the physical sphere. (Foulkes 1990: 229)

No one, I suspect, reads these lines, with their ectoplasmic implications, without a feeling of considerable unease. Foulkes, aware of the awkwardness, points out that one cannot 'except in theory' abstract these processes or forces. However, this seems to be precisely the point at stake: that what Foulkes calls 'theoretical abstractions' carry so large a part of the burden of his argument, despite his recognition that 'it is ultimately always whole persons who interact with whole persons'. (Foulkes 1990: 228).

It is quite misleading to propose that persons are linked by mental processes. And it is deeply erroneous to propose that it is through the interpenetration of mental processes that we arrive at a shared world. It is worth noting that these conceptual pitfalls might have been negotiated more effectively had Foulkes taken his own advice, and paid more attention to the question of embodiment. We know that this was of interest to Foulkes because of his powerful endorsement of Paul Schilder's *Image and Appearance of the Human Body*, a work he regarded as being of 'fundamental importance'. A group-analyst without this 'as part of his equipment', says Foulkes, in a surprisingly forceful simile, 'would be comparable to a Psycho-Analyst without knowledge of the interpretation of dreams' (Foulkes 1983: 135). Some of the themes of Schilder's work are developed much more substantially—and with very far-reaching implications—in Merleau-Ponty's analysis of the lived body and intersubjectivity, but Foulkes does not follow this through.[15]

'It is possible', argues Foulkes, 'to claim a firm, pre-existing community or communion between the members, founded eventually on the fact that they are *human*'. (Foulkes 1990: 212) This common ground of humanity he refers to as the 'foundation matrix'. It is 'on top of this' that the 'dynamic' matrix processes which he observes in groups take place.

An attempt to grasp what Foulkes is struggling towards with this notion of a 'foundation matrix' leads us, I think, to nothing other than a concept of 'world'—a concept of world in which the other always already dwells. If we give full attention to the concept of 'world',[16] then we shall find that Foulkes' concept of 'foundation matrix' has much less work to do. We do not require it to be 'foundational' in the way that Foulkes wishes. Similarly, Foulkes' 'matrical processes' are not required to fulfil so many of the tasks for which he employs them. The usefulness of speaking of a 'group matrix' will depend upon how well it draws our attention to subtle aspects of group interaction and group interrelatedness which we otherwise might not have seen. This idea might help us understand how group members can be regarded as woven together in a fabric, or in a narrative, in very complex patterns, providing a rich and inexhaustible source of meanings. But the concept will not have to carry any metapsychological or metaphysical weight at all.

Conclusion

Whatever the shortcomings of Foulkes as a theorist, group analysis, along the lines explored and inspired by him, increasingly continues to be practiced. Although the more extravagant claims which Foulkes makes for group analysis have not met with general acceptance—it is, he claimed, 'far superior as a form of psychotherapy and the best method to study the theory of psychotherapy' (Foulkes 1990: 272)—group analysis has come to occupy an important place in the contemporary psychoanalytic field.

Foulkes, by his own admission—'because of the demands of group-analysis' (Foulkes 1990: 13)—did not keep up with psychoanalytic developments. His own idea of psychoanalysis will seem to many contemporary readers uncomfortably inflexible and restrictive. He himself clearly found it so. He comments, for example, on the way group analysis introduces 'features of an action method, so foreign to psychoanalysis' (Foulkes 1984: 129), as though the *authentic* psychoanalytic dialogue is purified of 'action'. No wonder he asserts that group analysis 'makes analysts shudder'(Foulkes 1984: 125).

'I think, on the whole,' suggested Foulkes, 'that the group analyst can be freer than the psychoanalyst' (Foulkes 1990: 295). 'The analyst in the group can be more natural and personal than in the psychoanalytical situation' (Foulkes 1990: 172). However, what is at stake here is not merely a 'personal' liberation from the constraints of a particular orthodoxy. By insisting upon recognition of 'the group'—for the most part, paradoxically, conspicuously neglected within the highly tribalised field of psychoanalysis—Foulkes draws our attention to that which, now that we see it, is obvious. More than this, he brings an openness of mind into a field where rigidity and dogmatism is all too often the rule. In doing so, he broadens our conception of the psycho-analytic dialogue.

Foulkes, referring to the notion of *citizenship*, speaks of 'the spirit in which these [analytic] groups are conducted' (Foulkes 1984: 64). The spirit we perceive in Foulkes' writings, is one of unswerving respect for the unique possibilities which the therapeutic group offers, to cultivate the *common ground* of human life. In the cultivation of this common ground—which is not, I would wish to emphasise, a *psychological* ground—and the fleshing out of its therapeutic possibilities, Foulkes brings us back to first things. These include a concept—implicit throughout all of Foulkes' work—which we rather take for granted, because so much depends upon it. It is the rather unfashionable, insufficiently appreciated, and highly subtle notion—a kind of bedrock in human affairs—which we call *common sense*. 'One could say', declares Foulkes, 'that group treatment means applying "common sense"—the sense of the community' (Foulkes 1984: 88). His work helps us appreciate some of the conditions under which the sense of the community may be drawn out.

We should leave the last word to Foulkes. Tucked away among the pages of his work are to be found these three short sentences. They might easily be dismissed as a mere—if somewhat uncharacteristic—rhetorical flourish. But perhaps they address the issue at the very heart of his work:

> Whose liberation? His or theirs? His *and* theirs is the answer, they are the same thing. (Foulkes 1984: 157)

Notes

[1] In fact, Foulkes' writings are generously sprinkled with what one might call 'handy tips' for the group therapist.

[2] See also Foulkes 1990: 215.

[3] On this, see Baron 1987.

[4] Whilst we can agree with Foulkes that the group analytic situation, being without 'occupation', favours the emergence of what he calls 'a more primary type of communication', his statement elsewhere (Foulkes & Anthony 1984) that 'group occupations, like the activities of passengers on a boat, serve as a protective screen, a defence against intimate personal interaction', is quite misleading.

[5] See also Foulkes 1984: 289.

6 See Foulkes 1983: 133; 1984: 163; 1990: 292..

7 See Foulkes 1984: 55-65. See also 'The Leader in the Group', in Foulkes 1990: 285ff.

8 Specifically, Freud's *Group Psychology and the Analysis of the Ego* (1921).

9 Foulkes is specifically concerned with the *ego ideal* at this point but, presumably, also has in mind *identification*. See Foulkes 1984: 15; 1990: 289.

10 For a discussion of this see Borch-Jacobsen 1988.

11 See Foulkes 1984: 60.

12 This is, I think, a misleading term for Foulkes to have chosen. Whatever nuances he tries to draw out by prefacing the word 'unconscious' in this way, we would be perfectly in accord with the whole thrust of Foulkes' thinking to ask: 'what other kinds of Unconscious could there possibly be?' See, for example, Foulkes 1990: 227.

13 See Foulkes 1990: 273; Foulkes & Anthony 1984: 41.

14 See Foulkes 1984: 110, 118; 1986: 132.

15 We can indicate something of the importance of Paul Schilder's work for Foulkes by noting how close are Schilder's ideas to those of the Gestalt school. Schilder's 'gestalt' concept of the body schema, or body image, is highly instructive, particularly with regard to those many ambiguous areas of human life which are reducible neither to the domains of physiology nor psychology—the phantom limb experience, for example. Foulkes clearly recognises something of the relevance of Schilder's body schema (which has little to do with the objectifications of 'body language') to questions of how we perceive ourselves—and, accordingly, others—in everyday life.

Merleau-Ponty's detailed critique of Gestalt psychology applies equally to the work of Schilder—that it does not go far enough in examining its own assumptions, and remains empirical/psychologistic. He also asserts that Gestalt psychology fails to recognise, for example, the significance of *intentionality*, as this concept is developed by the phenomenologists. Merleau-Ponty's work is resoundingly relevant to the work of Foulkes in its extensive discussion of the 'lived body', whose pre-reflective grasp of the world, and pre-reflective gestural coupling with the other, constitute a source of which our conscious knowledge is an elaboration. See Schilder 1935; Merleau-Ponty 1962, 1964.

16 Heidegger's lengthy analysis of 'world' in *Being and Time* comes to mind here. Heidegger's analysis of the indivisible unity of 'Being-in-the-world' as a minimal basis upon which man's being can be understood, and his subsequent analysis of 'Being-with', is of the utmost relevance to Foulkes' concerns. But Heidegger's idiom, for all Foulkes' favourable disposition towards 'the existentialists', would be quite alien to him. See Heidegger 1967: 78-145.

BION, FOULKES AND THE OEDIPAL SITUATION

Michael Halton

The continuation of mental growth in adulthood depends to a large extent on the capacities and resources which the individual has acquired over the course of their previous life experience. Mental structures which have developed in the course of life exert a major influence on whether new experiences can be utilised for further growth. However, there are a variety of pathological processes which render new experiences unserviceable for this purpose. In addition to this, the way in which an individual's internal objects are structured will radically influence the individual's attempts to organise his or her relationships with external objects. The most satisfying outcome of this is to achieve a correspondence between internal and external reality.

For each of us, then, the internal world is a dynamic thing. It is a product and process of continuous interaction between—on the one hand—our unconscious phantasies and defences, and—on the other—our external reality, both past and present. The way in which success or failure in relationships is determined by the nature of our internal objects is part of everyday life. We are all familiar with people who have grown up amidst difficult and straitened circumstances, yet manage to retain a capacity for lively and loving relationships, and show a fulsome engagement with life. At the other extreme are those for whom advantage and privilege leave a sense of depression, dissatisfaction or grievance. It seems that no external success or satisfaction can remedy the internal sense of poverty or deprivation.

What the individual adult patient brings to life and to therapy, therefore, both constitutionally and developmentally, will powerfully affect how further experiences are processed. The personality organisation of the individual plays a major role in determining the degree and extent of psychic development that is attainable—and not simply the type or quality of therapy undertaken. From this point of view, a psychoanalytic understanding of groups depends heavily upon on an understanding of how internal object relations are organised, and upon how the structure of subjective experience influences perception and behaviour in the external world.

Melanie Klein has shown that at the start of life, in the course of normal development, the infant's initial contact with the breast is followed rapidly by extension of rudimentary awareness to contact with other part-objects. This forms the basis of a primitive oedipal situation.[1] These very early experiences shape—and are shaped by—the infant's progression to *whole* object relations and the later, classical Oedipus complex, as described by Freud.[2] At the whole object level, the first 'group' is our family—or some variant thereof.

Psychoanalysis has progressed considerably since Freud's pioneering beginnings. We now have a better—if still incomplete—understanding of unconscious processes and the therapeutic factors that can optimise potential for mental growth. I shall return to these matters in connection with emotional experience and psychic change, but firstly I shall introduce the founding figures of group psychotherapy in Britain.

Bion and Foulkes

The two foremost proponents of group psychotherapy are W.R. Bion and S.H. Foulkes, each of whom fathered a distinct tradition. In Bion's case, it was the so-called 'Tavistock Model', which spawned the Group Relations conferences and study groups. In the case of Foulkes, meanwhile, it was 'Group Analysis', out of which grew a specific theory, training, and organisation for the development of group psychotherapy.[3]

It is widely believed that Bion's central contribution to the study of groups was his influential collection of papers, first published in the sociological journal *Human Relations* between 1948 and 1951. In these papers he seems interested in identifying primitive features of the human personality which impel us to be social animals. Bion states:

> The individual is a group animal at war, not simply with the group but with himself for being a group animal and with those aspects of his personality that constitute his groupishness. (Bion 1961)

Bion's observations revealed subtle, unconscious assumptions affecting group life, which had hitherto remained unnoticed. His startlingly novel style of thinking had a tremendous impact. He set out to develop a set of concepts and terms for group phenomena that were intentionally non-psychoanalytic, although insights from analysis inform his method of observation.

From this work he produced his well-known theory of the three basic assumptions.[4] Bion's analysis with Melanie Klein (1945-1953) was roughly coterminous with these writings, and this may have produced an undue avoidance of psychoanalytic formulations in his theorising. However, Bion's stated aim was to avoid a debased usage of psychoanalysis, and to develop ideas and terms that were appropriate to his new subject matter. Only later—in 1952—did he publish 'Group Dynamics: a Review' in a psychoanalytic journal, the *International Journal of Psycho-Analysis*. This paper was an attempt to bring his ideas and findings within a psychoanalytic—specifically Kleinian—framework.

The earlier group papers—together with the 'Review'—were published as *Experiences in Groups* in 1960. This volume had a profound impact on therapists, as well as non-clinicians such as social scientists, who were interested in the study of groups and organisations. However, with a few notable exceptions,[5] Bion's work did not give rise to a clinical technique, and no tradition of group psychotherapy has evolved from it.

In my view, the most important reason why clinicians have failed to develop Bion's theories on groups is that they were not originally tailored for use in the consulting room. Bion's opening chapter, entitled 'Intra-Group Tensions in Therapy', was written with John Rickman during World War Two. In it, their views and aims are stated quite clearly:

> The term group therapy can have two meanings. It can refer to the treatment of a number of individuals assembled for special therapeutic sessions, or it can refer to a planned endeavour to develop in a group the forces that lead to smoothly running cooperative activity. (Bion 1961)

They continue:

> In the treatment of the individual, neurosis is displayed as a problem of the individual. In the treatment of a group it must be displayed as a problem of the group. (Bion 1961)

Unlike Foulkes, Bion was not principally concerned with using groups as a medium to treat individuals. Insofar as treatment had a place in his later psychotherapy groups at the Tavistock Clinic, it was a by-product of his interpretative work on the preconscious and unconscious shared assumptions of the group members. His 'therapeutic' aim, then, was to liberate constructive reality-based forces in the group, by helping members gain insight into the regressive part they played in group life.

Bion emerged from the First World War a decorated and traumatised tank-commander. At the age of 40 he found himself a widower with a young child, and was thrown again into another world war.[6] He was profoundly concerned with making sense of the primitive levels of experience and behaviour that he had witnessed, and to elucidate the primitive qualities of the human mind which arose in individuals and bound them to their fellows in thinking and unthinking action.

One assumes that even before his analysis with Melanie Klein, Bion had a taste for seeing life unadorned. His powerful mind and deep curiosity drew him to essentials, and his achievements bear the hallmark of a towering intellect driven by an uncompromising search after truth. After his pioneering work with groups, Bion trained as a psychoanalyst and devoted the rest of his professional life to individual psychoanalytic work. His most creative and important discoveries came from this later period. After his death in 1979 some of his letters were published, which indicate that despite the popularity of *Experiences in Groups*, Bion regarded this book less highly than his other published work.[7] His move from groups to individual analysis is consistent, if one keeps in mind that his avowed interest was in studying the most primitive elements of the mind. He came to believe this would be best served by psychoanalytic work with individuals, particularly with those diagnosed as psychotic or borderline.

Foulkes was, in contrast, an entirely different kind of man. He came from a different psychoanalytic tradition, and moved in the opposite direction to Bion.

He first trained as a psychoanalyst in Vienna, and became Clinical Director of the Frankfurt Psychoanalytic Institute. His contemporaries included Frieda Fromm-Reichman and Erich Fromm. They were all deeply influenced by the prevailing ideas of modern sociology, known as the 'Frankfurt school'. He settled in England in 1936.

It was after training as a psychoanalyst that Foulkes developed an interest in groups. He came to believe that the patient on the couch was denied the range of therapeutic interactions which a group could offer. During the formative period of Foulkes' psychoanalytic apprenticeship, the dominant tradition was the classical Freudian one. This laid stress on active listening, but placed less emphasis upon the interaction between patient and analyst. This bias may have contributed to Foulkes' experience of a feeling of constriction and stiltedness in his one-to-one work.

Though Foulkes did not escape his own personal struggles, his view of the world has an altogether more rosy hue than Bion's. His emphasis is upon the group as a good object, to be trusted and valued for its creative potential. He made repeated claims for the positive and curative power of group therapy. For instance, he stated that the

> disruptive, anti-social destructive aspect to neurotic behaviour is forced to come out into the open and does not receive the sanction of the group... the individual in his neurotic aspects is set upon by the others, a process in which he participates actively in his turn... (Foulkes 1964)

Foulkes saw the individual as a nodal point in a web of relationships. In reading his work one often receives the impression of a deeply compassionate man, for whom the social often took precedence over the psychological, and for whom the group seemed more important than the individual.

Psychic change and defences

As group therapists, neither Bion nor Foulkes regarded their role in the transference as central to their technique. Indeed, both were wary of colluding in defensive situations, in which individual group members might attempt to form a parasitic relationship to the therapist and queue for individual attention, whilst ignoring their fellows.

However, most clinicians working within the British Object Relations tradition today broadly agree that the central plank in *any* therapeutic endeavour is a rigorous and detailed exploration of the transference/countertransference interaction.[8] There are significant differences of opinion concerning how much stress should be placed upon transference interpretations (not to mention differences over what a transference interpretation *is*, and differing views of narcissistic states and their ontogeny), but all agree that the aim is to make emotional contact—in the here-and-now—with what is most immediate and pressing in the patient's communications.[9]

For contemporary clinicians, therefore, the therapeutic endeavour is not so much to alleviate symptoms and produce cognitive understanding (important as these are), but to enable the patient to experience their inner and outer worlds more fully and deeply. Bion's later work on container/contained, and transformations of emotional experience into mental elements suitable for thinking, made a central contribution to this shift in therapeutic aims.[10] Knowing about oneself is of secondary importance to the inner freedom that comes from the *experience* and *felt* integration of previously split-off unconscious anxieties and parts of the self. In Bion's language, the aim is to produce an enhanced capacity to experience pain and pleasure, rather than the patient continuing to suffer these emotions in a blind, unconscious manner.

Clearly, psychic development can occur in settings other than therapy. Life itself—given sufficient impact and meaning—can provoke deep internal change. However, it is almost always the case that deep change comes from learning through painful experience. This is a disruptive affair, and is sometimes felt to be catastrophic.

The early pioneers of analysis underestimated the mental pain and upheaval that analysis evokes. Freud's reading of Sophocles casts Oedipus as a courageous seeker after truth. However, Steiner has suggested another side to this which, combined with Freud's account, gives a fuller and more recognisably human picture.[11] Steiner's Oedipus is someone who—as well as having heroic qualities in his search for truth and honesty—is also concerned with covering up his crimes. He turns a blind eye to the fact of his guilt, rather than fully facing up to it. Steiner's picture of Oedipus, then, has a more truthful resemblance to the patients of non-fiction. We, and those we see in our consulting rooms, despite many good conscious intentions to seek the truth, are at the same time struggling unconsciously to preserve the mental status quo.

Recent psychoanalytic thinking is increasingly concerned with the internal obstacles to psychic change. The emphasis has shifted towards the recognition of interlocking systems of anxiety and defence. The oedipal situation is viewed not only as a sexual drama of rivalry, possession and guilt (as outlined by Freud) but also—on a deeper and broader front—as the central conflict, determining how the inner world is structured, and how reality (both internal and external) will be apprehended and felt.

The role of the therapist and the role of the group

I will now proceed to discuss what I believe are the two central issues in group therapy. These are, firstly, the role of the therapist and, secondly, the role of the group and the oedipal situation. In individual treatment the therapist has the opportunity to study and intervene, to work with anxieties and defences in detail and over time. In comparison, the group therapist has considerably fewer opportunities. I think the full impact of this limitation on the group therapist's sense of potency and worth, together with conscious and unconscious feelings of guilt and hopelessness, has led to a defensive denial of the difficulties of group therapy and a compensatory idealisation of group processes as therapeutic. As a corollary to this, there has also been a tendency to de-emphasise the psychoanalytic responsibilities of the therapist.

For instance, Bion makes group-centred interpretations about shared phantasies, often in relation to himself, but avoids working with the transference of each individual. In practice, each person is expected to work out for themselves how they consciously and unconsciously play a part in the collective group phantasy.

In effect, whether intentionally or not, Bion's focus on group-centred interpretation renders himself unavailable for more intimate relations. In my view, Foulkes' method creates the same no-go area, prohibiting intimacy between group member and therapist. In both cases few interpretations are offered which enable individuals to observe and deepen emotional contact with 'their' unconscious relationship to 'their' therapist. This is not to devalue or deny the way in which group members will often challenge each other's disturbed views, or support them, or give feedback, and so on, but these interventions are predominantly at a conscious level and are related mostly to interpersonal conflicts and perceptions.

There is certainly creative potential to be found and mobilised in groups. However, for Foulkes, this is taken as given and is assumed to be readily available. In what appears an act of blind faith, it is assumed that destructive forces will be consumed in the mutual analysis between members. If this state of affairs is transported to a parallel situation—say, the family—then parental authority is being abnegated in favour of governance by the children. The siblings are left to raise themselves, and the essential asymmetry of the parent-child relationship is side-stepped, along with all the problematic emotions of dependency, rivalry, envy and jealously. Put simply: the reality of generational differences and the oedipal situation is evaded.

The Foulkesian tradition advocates that the interpretations should come from the group itself. The group should be allowed to function—

unimpeded by the therapist—and, wherever possible, the therapist's activity should be directed to liberating the group from passivity and dependence. The therapist's responsibility is, therefore, to empower and facilitate communication, rather than to make lunging interpretations which lead to fear and idealisation of the therapist.[12] The assumption of an omniscient and omnipotent stance by the therapist is obviously unhelpful. However, this overall view of the group is, to my mind, simply an idealisation of another kind. I think the technique of minimalist intervention may derive partly from an early and outmoded model of psychoanalysis, in which the analyst gives interpretations only when a block has occurred in the patient's associations. According to this model, the analyst waits unobtrusively until the patient's unconscious conflicts and symptoms have fully emerged in the transference neurosis, and then they are dealt with interpretively, almost as a matter of intellectual deconstruction.

My experience of running groups is that one cannot assume that people who come together from a sense of distress and a conscious desire for help are, *ipso facto*, able to reach the necessary depth of experience and insight with the minimal help that is offered by Bion and Foulkes. Experience suggests that one has to be interpretively active, particularly in relation to persecutory anxieties which often arise at the beginnings of a group, but also sometimes for long periods, in which more aggressive and psychotic anxieties become excessive and barely tolerable. Often, the object that can best contain these anxieties is the therapist. Hopefully, as a result of his or her training and position in the group, the therapist will not need to deny or re-project these anxieties in a desperate way. If the therapist cannot be relied upon to receive these projections, members will arrange themselves defensively—as they have done in other areas of their lives. I believe this is the case even with relatively well-balanced patients, as well as with disturbed neurotics and the psychiatrically ill.

A clinical example at this point will illustrate what I mean. The following concerns a group of trainee psychotherapists who had been meeting weekly for about one year at the period in question. Although they were not 'patients', the problems and dynamics which arise in an experiential group like this are not significantly different from a therapy group. Consequently, the technical problems are pretty much the same. Usually, I take responsibility for ensuring that the physical setting is comfortable and secure from external intrusions. However in this group, for a number of practical reasons, I did not organise the seating arrangements, but allowed the members to arrange themselves as they pleased.

For some time the members had been struggling with their mistrust and fear of exposure amongst themselves. A recurrent complaint was that I refused efforts to be befriended, although I sensed I was trusted at some level, otherwise they would not have felt safe to complain so much! The evidence for my distant, uncaring manner was that I did not arrange the chairs before each group and make the place cosy.

On the occasion I wish to discuss, someone who used the room prior to my group had left it in perfect condition. Each chair was positioned at an exact orientation to the other, all in a neat circle. The first member to speak said how she felt stronger this week; she was getting to know the other members more, and felt far less threatened by the facilitator than hitherto. There was a chorus of agreement with the idea of things getting easier, and one member looked at me and said how warmer and more human I seemed. I was perceived as being more cheerful and less severe (although I was not feeling any more cheerful, or otherwise, than usual). Another person pointed out how kind I had been to arrange all the chairs. This idea was then taken up with great gusto by everyone. I cannot convey the urgency and power of the discovery of my goodness, and it quite took over even the most observant and steady members of the group, so much so that the atmosphere became ever more unreal and saccharine. My countertransference reaction was very different. I felt I was being constructed as something quite false, with no substance, and being drawn into a sticky and cloying relationship, which—if I refused it—would confirm my harshness and monstrous inhumanity.

Now, there are many ways we can view this material. We could view it as a basic assumption of dependency, constructed from a pseudo good object, in order to defend against an underlying terror of being in the presence of a persecutor or an unavailable or inadequate object. We could regard it as an attempt by the group members to find a softer, more nurturing element in an otherwise aloof or brittle object—or even, perhaps, to bring together a good parental couple in the person of the therapist. We could understand the preoccupation with me as a defence against the imperfect setting, in which less than perfect relationships might be exposed between the members themselves, and so on... However, what I find striking about this example, is that it illustrates how a group of perfectly able, intelligent, and not terribly disturbed people can collectively lose parts of their minds in the face of anxiety. Instead, they construct a defensive system based not upon a perception of current reality or previous experience, but upon wishful thinking.

The interpretation I gave was that against all the evidence—that is, all the other weeks when I had not been seen to put the chairs out—there was an unquestioned assumption that I had arranged the chairs. I spoke about how the desperation to find a 'good me' was so great that they were prepared to sacrifice their sense of doubt and reality to achieve it.

At first my comments were rejected and a sense of confusion took over. Eventually one person said that she now realised she had felt increasingly odd and confused as the session progressed. Another said he felt amazed and embarrassed that he had been drawn into something unreal, just as he had as a child, when he and his sister believed in their parents' version of love. He spoke movingly about how it was only as an adult that he recognised his parents as selfish and cruel. They had put their careers first, and had sent the two children away to boarding school at a rather early age.

My contention, then, is that unless the therapist is active interpretively, and recognises the need to work in the transference with underlying paranoid anxieties, the result will be that false and collusive cultures will develop, inhibiting real emotional progress.

Here is an example from another group—this time, a group of patients. It had been characteristic of the individuals in this group to intellectualise and scrutinise their thoughts very carefully before speaking, so there was little spontaneous, lively talk. I had approached this problem from a number of angles, according to what I perceived as the leading, shared anxieties at any given moment, as well as what I thought particular, individual anxieties might be.

One man who was doing his best to get involved—but in a compliant way—brought a dream. I thought that underneath his compliance he was projecting a great deal of aggression, which left him frightened and anxious. In the dream he was climbing a mountain. Half way up he found a small hut, inside which were members of the group. Everyone was shoving and pushing, and there was hardly any room to breathe. He was trying to put on some elbow and knee-pads. He managed to escape the hut and found himself hang-gliding around the mountain range, gently spiralling, supported by air-thermals. There was no claustrophobic, potentially damaging scramble; everything was serene and beautiful. Tranquil glances were exchanged between him and the other gliders in their mutual, heavenly state.

When the dreamer and the other group members started to discuss the dream, they showed no awareness of the possible dangers of hang-gliding, nor of the manic state which—to me—it seemed to represent. They responded to the scrambling inside the hut, and this was linked to a common feeling of competition and rivalry—particularly for my attention—which had been the subject of an earlier discussion. The dreamer associated the gliding to a remark I was supposed to have made the previous week: about letting go of conscious control of thoughts. No-one except myself seemed to find the dream worrying; they concluded that if they could all trust one another a little more, and open up together, then perhaps the group could take off.

Once again, there are many ways in which one could interpret this dream. To my mind, the most urgent issue involved the scene inside the hut, which symbolised the real, bruising hard work to be done. However, the manic flight *away* from this work was instead idealised, becoming linked to a distorted version of my purported comment from the previous week. I suspect that in the unconscious mind of the dreamer both the group and myself were idealised as a defensive measure. It seemed that I was experienced as offering false, unsafe solutions to the problem of rivalry and hate within the group. In the imagery of the dreamer, the therapist was felt to be saying 'follow my advice and I will give you air for support!' Free association to the dream raised a real, psychic danger, in the shape of *actual contact* between the dreamer and his own mind, and the minds of the other participants. The sibling rivalry of the scene in the hut was a frightening reality. It resonated at an oedipal level for everyone in the group, and resulted in their eager readiness to idealise the experience.

This is a very common occurence. Often, a group cannot find its way through its defensive manoeuvres unless someone—usually, but not always, the therapist—actively helps it to break through to deeper, unconscious fears. The therapist—hopefully—possesses the legitimate and functional authority to do this. However, if members of the group *persistently* take on the therapist's role, one begins to wonder where the members' own disturbed parts are being projected and why.

It is my view that the therapist's interpretative work is essential to the evolution of the group; it creates the opportunity for each member to risk experiencing their more primitive fears. The therapist differs from the other members by dint of his or her specialised knowledge, and his or her privileged position as a *participant observer*. The therapist's task is to experience and contain projections; to subject them to thought, yet not to react or return them—as other group members might. At the same time, the therapist must strive not to become an 'honorary member' of the group, simply in order to propitiate hostile feelings directed at their unique position and authority. The therapist's interpretations to the group will—hopefully, over time—demonstrate a tolerance for psychic reality, in all its most painful and unwelcome aspects, and thus lead to a greater willingness on the part of its members for a similar acceptance.

However, the therapist's interpretations will inevitably be experienced by the group as destabilising. The case above is an instance in which the establishment of defensive, rigid systems was undermined by interpretation. This result of this is chaos, as mental states oscillate between fragmentation and integration. Bion represented this state with the symbol: Ps↔D (Bion 1991b). In time, however, an equilibrium is restored, minds settle, and each member finds his or her role and place—that is, until the balance is disturbed afresh.

If all goes well the 'growing pains' embodied by this process occur again and again, and—imperceptibly—are met with acceptance, trust and warmth. Idealisation is no longer so necessary, and a truer, deeper confidence emerges. This confidence is based on a shared struggle with chaos and paranoid anxieties, which allows depression, sadness, guilt, regret and—sometimes—love, with a sense of discovery and survival, to come to the fore. Members separately and collectively gain more awareness of the psychotic and neurotic processes in and between themselves, which otherwise constrain and cripple their interactions.

This task of providing an object, which can receive and contain projections experienced as incomprehensible and transform them into something knowable, is no different from the task of individual therapy. Bion described this in terms of a commensurable relationship between container and contained. In his account, the infant's primitive emotional/sensory experience (composed of what Bion called 'beta elements'), undergoes a transformation, via the receptive willingness of the mother to share her infant's experience (which Bion described as her 'alpha function'), into something ('alpha elements'), that can be stored in the mind and used at a later stage for thought.[13]

It should be emphasised, however, that by 'containment' Bion did not intend a passive, bland acceptance of projections, but rather an active experiencing and engagement. Sometimes it is the therapist who has to feel mad, violent, depressed, helpless, and so on, as the members of the group cannot bear to contain such experiences and forcibly project them. If one is fortunate, there are sane and loving parts of the individual and group with which the therapist can link. However, there are often times when the therapist cannot look to the group, and must depend instead upon a sense of coupling with his or her own internal good objects. Underestimating the severity of psychic disturbance generated by group therapy places a burden on the group members which they are often ill-equipped to carry.

The group and the Oedipal situation

In 1952 Melanie Klein wrote:

> The infant's capacity to enjoy at the same time the relation to *both* parents which is an important feature of his mental life and conflicts with his desires prompted by jealousy and anxiety to separate them depends on his feelings that they are separate individuals. This... implies the greater understanding of their relation to one another and is a precondition for the infant's hope that he can bring them together and unite them in a happy way. (Klein 1997b[1952b]: 79)

As I mentioned at the beginning of this chapter, participation in a group very concretely presents the patient with a tantalising dilemma. The primary object or part-object which is perceived to possess that which is most desired and needed for survival and growth—be it the breast or the penis—is projected into the therapist, or another group member, or the group as a whole. Yet, if reality is to win out, the desired object must be shared. The idea of omnipotent possession can never be realised, except through the perpetuation of archaic oedipal fixations. These defensive phantasies allow the individual to sustain the idea of a special relationship with the desired object, and to deny feelings of exclusion, jealously, envy and loss.

I shall present some clinical material which, I think, illustrates this very well.

A psychotherapy group met weekly in a psychiatric out-patient clinic. One particular woman, somewhat envied because of her work and social position, became pregnant. When the pregnancy became known to the other patients she was treated with a marked reverence, in contrast to previous hints of dislike over her aloofness and air of superiority.

The patient seemed intermittently aware of her superior manner, and anxiously deflected envious attacks by playing herself down. However, on this occasion she risked bringing a dream, prompted by a growing sense of courage, a pressing need to be understood, and a competitive wish for attention (as there had been a spate of dreams brought by other members in the previous two sessions).

In the dream she was in a plane. Two seats were vacant, marked 'For Couples'. After much indecision she allowed herself to take one of these seats, but was overwhelmed with anxiety. She felt she did not have a proper right to the seat, yet was simultaneously aware she was an adult and heavily pregnant. She remarked in the group that the dream was still with her, and that she could not understand why it troubled her so. After all, she was pleased to be pregnant and her husband was also pleased.

Various members said how jealous they felt, yet without showing signs of real jealousy. There was a wide discussion of each person's circumstances: some had children, others not, some expressed regrets concerning this, but pointed to the compensations. There was some bland talk about ambivalent feelings, memories of brothers and sisters being born—and so on—but all in very pleasant, reasonable tones. The patient, meanwhile, sheepishly demurred. One woman eventually referred to the dream and remarked how she had also felt uncertain when she first became pregnant, and then everyone agreed that you never felt ready to be a parent irrespective of age and experience.

The material in this session pointed strongly towards considerable anxiety regarding a primal scene: a fear of curiosity, and of real emotional contact with events was very much in evidence. However, as the therapist, I felt what was most crucial was the transference to myself and the group, demonstrated by the dreamer through the way in which the dream enacted her fear of taking her seat as part of a couple.

I was perceived by her as the father/partner with whom she was coupled, but it was feared that if this belief became public then the group would unleash terrible retribution against her. The group was thus experienced by her internally as a third object—an envious or jealous maternal figure. The other members of the group colluded with this, however, by being ever-so sensible and ignoring the multitude of subtle and—indeed—not-so-subtle clues which they could observe in the patient's unspoken behaviour towards me. I interpreted that nobody must openly acknowledge what was a common belief amongst the group—that the pregnant patient had a special relationship with me. This had to be denied and ignored by her, by me, and the rest of the group. At this point, the pregnant patient blushed bright red, and so did two or three others. After a long and difficult silence a few people acknowledged, with some anger and shame, that they could not compete with her pre-eminence in the group, and that if they did then they would feel humiliated to be caught doing so. The atmosphere changed. Although a number of people were still pained and embarrassed, there was deeper contact and more sensitivity.

The pregnant patient who had been in quiet turmoil all this time said there was another part to the dream which she had kept back. She was white-water canoeing with a man in a smart suit. It was dangerous, but exciting. The man was in charge, and she felt safe and good to be seated next to him. Suddenly two huge boulders appeared in the middle of the river, with lots of people standing on top. She thought she recognised her mother and sister, and two members of the group. They seemed to be signalling danger, but they could also have been Indians doing some kind of war-dance. The canoe was drawn by the current, and was about to crash into the boulders when she woke up.

I cannot detail all the associations which now emerged. Suffice it to say that the dreamer recalled I had been wearing a suit the week before. Another person remarked that I probably had an important meeting, or was going out to the theatre with someone. I remembered on a previous occasion the pregnant patient had described how her mother, when angered, would become as hard and unmovable as a brick wall.

This further material seemed to confirm how the woman's oedipal anxieties were stirred up by being a patient and pregnant, and were enacted in the group. I believe the war-dance stood for the group/mother's harsh reaction against her oedipal relationship with an over-exciting and possibly over-sexualising therapist/father. Was mother 'impenetrable' like the boulders—a pair of breasts made from stone? Did this encourage a premature turning towards father for love? Did her sister and her mother form an exclusive pair, or did her possession of father make mother and sister turn against her? Is there a suggestion in the dream of the mother as a helpful object—trying to warn her daughter of the dangers of the oedipal rapids—or is it a global warning against men? How much is the patient's perception of her objects a function of her projections?

These are complex issues which—perhaps—can never be answered in a group, given that there are usually seven or eight other people with similarly complex internal worlds, all interacting and pressing for attention. What I wish to underline here, however, is the deeply moving therapeutic moment in which omnipotent longing for exclusive possession of the object can be faced and made real in the transference. The other members of the group also underwent a moving experience, through confronting—in a very real way—their jealousy and envy, and their sense of exclusion from the primal scene.

Omnipotent oedipal phantasies depend psychically upon a denial of the sexual relationship between the parents, and a denial of the difference between the parent's relationship with each other and their relationship with the child. The former is genital and procreative; the latter is not. If split-off or maintained in the mind in a semi-conscious or unconscious state, these phantasies impede maturation and contact with reality. Britton points out that the capacity to comprehend and relate to reality is contingent upon working through the depressive position. This involves relinquishing the idea of sole possession of the object, and leads ultimately to a profound sense of loss and—later—envy. He goes on to say that if the pain of this recognition is not tolerated, it is replaced by a sense of persecution, grievance or self-denigration.[14]

I did actually like the pregnant patient, and thought she had many admirable qualities. However I did not like her greatly more than I liked the others. Her omnipotent desires and fears prevented her from finding her place in the group, from having a more open and intimate relationship with me and the others, and from being able to tolerate envy and jealousy in herself and in others without absolute panic and terror.

The central conflict which emerges in group therapy, using the psychoanalytic method, is between the desire for (or the fear of) an exclusive one-to-one relation with the therapist, and the maintenance of a link with the other group members. This is my impression after years of working with groups aimed at treating patients who are roughly diagnosed as 'neurotic'. By this term I mean those patients whose early relationship to the breast was, in Winnicott's terms, 'good enough' (Winnicott 1954). They have managed to internalise a sufficiently stable primary object, but may have encountered problems in weaning, or the birth of a sibling, or some other later difficulty. My impression of Foulkes and Bion on group technique is that both of them bypass the patient's developmental need, and the patient's desire to have the therapist actively available as a transferential object. Contemporary psychoanalytic technique and theory is hugely indebted to Bion and Winnicott's work on the maternal function. In particular, Bion's later discoveries concerning the function of maternal reverie in the establishment of the infant's capacity to develop thoughts, and to tolerate emotions, is a major conceptual innovation (Bion 1991a). If Bion had continued to explore groups in his later work, then I am certain that he would have revised his earlier approach along these lines.

Doubtless, there are times when the group evokes an internal constellation which resembles a loving family group. Sometimes this entails the added containment of figures such as grandparents, aunts, uncles, and so on. These may make it possible to contain conflicts experienced as overwhelming within the oedipal group (composed solely of parents and siblings). However, containment—in the sense of 'managing'—is not enough if deep conflicts are to be worked out at the level of primary objects.

Where the anxieties involved are more at the level of the depressive position, one observes groups functioning in very impressive and moving ways—much as a good family can provide a loving setting— in which individual sorrow can be incorporated by a sense of belonging to something larger. When this is the case, the family is not only a unit that contains conflict and regulates emotional distance; it also allows for the possibility of reparation and making amends. In contrast, where the conflicts involved entail disturbances in the early relationship to the breast, a loving and accepting setting is simply not enough. Enabling group members to explore and resolve differences may be helpful at one level but, at another, this may collude with the evasion of underlying difficulties. These most often concern the unconscious rivalry over the therapist. These anxieties may turn out to be very uncomfortable—not only for the group members, but also for the therapist.

One of the primary aims of any therapeutic venture, then, is to deal with persecutory anxieties. If these are tackled adequately, then they release and harness reparative processes. Clearly, the therapist has to process much more complex material in a group setting than in individual therapy—although only rarely do patients in a group free associate all at once!

Working with groups, the therapist inevitably gives each patient less attention than the maximum from which they could benefit. Ask most mothers what they feel about the care of their second child; very few will fail to report a sense of guilt and strain at being pulled in more than one direction, and at not giving more to both children. There are, of course, negative effects of over-involved parenting, which can impede stage-appropriate separateness and healthy independence, but it is undeniable that some issues can only be worked through at suffi-cient depth in a one-to-one setting. 'Best' for all of us was that time—mythical or real—when mother was attentive to us and us alone. At the risk of repetition, our normal developmental steps are from 1 to 1, and thence to 1 to 2. The repeated nightmare of the group therapist is con-frontation with a host of panicky, needy patients, all expecting to be nourished. However, this nightmare has to be endured if unconscious anxieties over sharing and shortage are to be worked through.

Suitability for group treatment

I shall conclude with a consideration of the appropriateness of differ-ent types of group technique for different types of patient.

The type of group therapy I have described in this paper would not prove suitable for those patients whose primary relationship to the breast was of a catastrophic nature. In these cases, attempts to work transferentially and to facilitate a regression would probably precipi-tate a psychotic breakdown. Patients of this type have almost no toler-ance of exclusion from the parental couple. The primal scene simply provokes great violence towards the self or others, or else a massive emotional withdrawal. In these cases a more appropriate form of treat-ment would be intensive, five sessions per week analysis, with hospi-tal back-up, or, perhaps, much less intensive and more supportive ther-apy.

In my opinion, psychoanalytic group therapy is better suited to those people who have some capacity to bear the rage and envy aroused by exclusion. Patients most likely to benefit are those who are able to protest and fight against exclusion, yet—with help and time—gain insight into their omnipotent desires, mourn their unachievable wishes, and move on along the path of the depressive position. Britton has described such patients as people for whom an awareness of the primal scene, and of the link between the parents, produces a 'psychic trauma' rather than a 'psychic catastrophe' (Britton 1989).

Additionally, group therapy—in which the aim is to facilitate treat-ment of the group by the group—may prove the technique of choice in two other cases. Firstly, in the case of patients for whom a facilitated self-help model is appropriate. Secondly, for those whose difficulties are much more severe, for whom one-to-one relationships threaten to evoke terrors of engulfment, dismemberment, and profound loss of ego-identity.

Patients who fall into the second category often find a group setting more tolerable, because it approximates to a less threatening and impersonal grouping of—for instance—siblings, uncles, aunts, grand-parents, neighbours, and friends. This acts as a mediating factor against the terrors of a mad internal primal object, or horrifying com-bined objects.[15] In these cases the early, normal defence mechanism of splitting has been employed to an extreme, and consequently there is a lack of differentiation between part-objects (such as the breast and the penis). Patients of this type often present as severely phobic, schizoid, or borderline. However, their condition can improve greatly through affiliation into a stable group of people. They may also obtain consid-erable benefit from a facilitating and receptive therapist, who refrains from making penetrative transference interpretations. Interpretations of this type often serve to traumatise and strengthen primitive defences in these cases. Steiner describes such patients as existing in a borderline position between desperation and despair, in which the need to be understood is urgent, but knowledge and the desire for understanding is felt to threaten a total collapse.[16]

Bion's group technique has proved itself, over time, to be a useful educative procedure for helping people become acquainted with unconscious processes in groups. As a result, many who have experi-enced a group relations conference may have emerged better equipped to become constructive members of a team, organisation, or family. However, this process cannot produce the kind of psychoanalytic expe-rience which could be thought of as 'therapeutic' in the stricter sense. As we have already noted, there is little evidence to suggest that Bion's technique has attracted much support from practising clinicians work-ing with distressed and ill patients. Foulkes' model has undergone a number of developments, and has enjoyed a greater following amongst clinicians. Some of the criticisms discussed above have been addressed by Foulkes' followers.[17] However, there still seems a reluc-tance to give the transferential role of the therapist a prominent place in technique, theorising and training.

In the psychoanalytic model of group therapy which I am propos-ing, the group should be conceptualised *developmentally*, as existing in the mind on a number of different levels and in a variety of modalities.

Firstly, the group might exist as a *part-object* (such as the breast) or sub-element (such as the nipple). As such, it can be variously desired, feared, experienced as gratifying or frustrating, as giving or taking away. Typically in this case 'the group' is felt to be regulating the amount of contact and intimacy that the individual has with the therapist or other members, in the same way that the nipple is felt to prevent unrestricted access to the contents of the breast, or that the penis/father intrudes between baby and breast/mother.

Secondly, the group, including the therapist, is perceived to form a variety of concealed *dyadic bonds*. Through projective identification, these bonds take on the characteristics of the internal primal couple. These pairings can take the form of: (1) the therapist and the rest of the group; (2) the therapist and one or more members of the group; (3) the member, and one or more members of the group; (4) one sub-group and another sub-group, and so on...

Thirdly, if the anxieties and unconscious ideas belonging to these two preceding stages are tolerated, then a differentiated relationship to the therapist, to individual members, and to the group as an *internal family*, can come into being. Comfort and pleasure can be found through a sense of belonging, which includes at times being an observer and not a participant in every intimate interaction. Britton suggests:

> If the link between the parents perceived in love and hate can be tolerated in the child's mind, it provides him with a prototype for an object relationship of a third kind in which he is a witness and not a participant. A third position then comes into existence from which object relationships can be observed. Given this we can also envisage being observed. (Britton 1989)

In the group context, this can be seen when a patient demonstrates that he or she can feel either more or less part of the group, and can maintain separate and differentiated relationships with other people, without undue fear of envious attack. It is also in evidence when, in turn, a patient can tolerate relationships between members, or between members and the therapist, without a sense of overwhelming threat to their own internal security, or their place in the mind of others.

Notes

[1] See Klein 1997a[1928], 1997b[1945].

[2] See Freud 1900, 1924.

[3] There have been many valuable reviews of these two figures. For Bion see, Grinberg et al. 1975, 1985; Pines 1985; Trist 1985; Sutherland 1985. For Foulkes see Pines 1983; Anthony 1983;

Brown 1994. For comparisons of their different theoretical approaches, see Brown 1985. In what follows, I shall not aim to pursue their points of difference in detail, except where these touch upon my concern with psychoanalytic group aims and technique.

[4] See Grinberg et al. 1975 for a summary.

[5] Such as Ezriel 1950 and Sutherland 1985.

[6] See Bion 1982.

[7] See Bion 1985.

[8] See Joseph 1989, Stewart 1992, and Sandler 1984. These writers—representing the Kleinian, Independent, and Contemporary Freudian traditions, respectively—all agree that what is projected and enacted in the analytic dyad are *internal object relations*—often very early, sometimes pre-verbal, and which the analyst tries to make conscious and explicit through interpretative work.

[9] Betty Joseph (see Joseph 1989) has particularly emphasised the therapeutic value of focusing in great detail on the moment to moment interactions in the transference and countertransference between analyst and patient. This might include how contact is made, developed, avoided, lost, perverted or destroyed. She stresses that it is the accumulated sum of these momentary experiences of contact with hitherto split off or repressed mental states which leads to a greater capacity to tolerate and integrate parts of the mind.

[10] Bion 1991a.

[11] Steiner 1985, 1990.

[12] See Pines 1983.

[13] See Bion 1991a.

[14] See Britton 1985, Britton et al. 1989.

[15] See Klein 1997a[1932].

[16] See Steiner 1993.

[17] See Brown & Zinkin 1994.

MASS PSYCHOLOGY THROUGH THE ANALYTIC LENS[1]

Otto F. Kernberg

Freud's 1921 work *Group Psychology and the Analysis of the Ego* is a bold outline of the contribution of psychoanalysis to mass psychology. The very title of the book, *Massenpsychologie und Ich-Analyse*, includes the term *mass psychology*, changed to the term *group* in the *Standard Edition* for a questionable and never explained 'sake of uniformity' (editor's footnote, Freud 1921: 69). Sixty-eight years after its original publication, a reader interested in the psychoanalytic theory of organisational and group dynamics finds it an impressive, extremely rich contribution, full of penetrating observations.

Mass psychology, although foreshadowed in some of Freud's earlier works, *Totem and Taboo* (1913b), *On Narcissism* (1914a), and *Beyond the Pleasure Principle* (1920), is developed fully only in this 1921 essay. He returns to issues of mass psychology briefly in 1927, 1930, and 1939, but without adding or modifying the central concepts contained in this essay.

Reaching beyond the psychoanalytic community in a restricted sense, *Group Psychology and the Analysis of the Ego* has had an impressive, one might say fundamental, impact on philosophers, particularly of the Frankfurt school, on sociologists, particularly Alexander Mitscherlich (1963) in Germany, Serge Moscovici (1981) in France, and Christopher Lasch (1977, 1978) in the United States, and finally, on another of the great twentieth century humanists, Elias Canetti, whose book *Crowds and Power* (1960), which led to his receiving the Nobel prize in literature in 1980, was conceived under the direct challenge and stimulation of Freud's essay.

Freud's *Totem and Taboo* and *Group Psychology and the Analysis of the Ego* provided a theoretical underpinning for generations of neo-Marxist philosophers from Wilhelm Reich (1962) to Althusser (1976). The patriarchal family was seen as the locus of the repressive ideology of capitalism, linked with the sexual prohibitions of the oedipal father. Where Freud thought that the repression of sexuality was the price paid for civilization, Reich thought that the repression of sexuality represented the effects of a pathological superego determined by the social structure of capitalism. Soviet Russia's sexual repressiveness, he proposed, reflected the Soviet authoritarian power structure. Marcuse

(1955) agreed with Reich that the repression of sexuality created the danger of aggression taking over in human affairs. He differed from Reich, however, in thinking that it was not genital sexuality, but pre-genital polymorphous infantile sexuality, that the capitalist system repressed. Marcuse believed that the system wanted to restrict sexual functions to the genital zone so it could use man's unsatisfied, pent-up eroticism in the service of social production.

More recently, Foucault (1978), in contrast to earlier neo-Marxist thinkers, suggested that bourgeois society had evinced a keen interest in studying sexual phenomena and in viewing them in scientific and medical, instead of moral terms. He proposed that this keen interest had been accompanied by an interest in controlling sexual behaviour, thereby controlling the family structure, and in manipulating sexual behaviour to assure state requirements. Althusser (1976) used Freud's concepts of the unconscious to construct a new theory of ideology, which he saw as a system of unconsciously determined illusory repre-sentations of reality. Specifically, the ideological system derived from the internalisation of the dominant illusion that a social class harbours about the conditions of its own existence. This dominant illusion stems from the internalisation of the paternal law, which in turn is part of the internalisation of the superego.

The analysis of ideologies, particularly regarding their level of humanistic universalism as opposed to totalitarian sectarianism and cultism, from the viewpoint of regression in mass psychology and leadership is a new development of this approach that leaves behind the narrow Marxist application of Freud's thinking. Mitscherlich (1963) pointed to the cultural consequences of the absence of the father at the social and familial level. He described the rejection of the father in con-temporary society as part of the rejection of traditional cultural values, and pointed to the intoxicating effects of mass production. Mass pro-duction promises immediate gratification and consequently fosters a psychology of demand for immediate gratification, and it contributes to the lack of a sense of individual responsibility. Mitscherlich described the new 'mass person' as classless, stressed the real absence of the father in the contemporary family due to the industrial revolu-tion, and pointed out that the individualised functions of the father were lost in the large contemporary institution.

Writing under the pseudonym André Stephane, Janine Chasseguet-Smirgel and Bela Grunberger in *L'Univers Contestationnaire* (The Contested Universe) (1969) analysed the social psychology of both

French fascism and the New Left in the context of the 1968 student rebellion. They interpreted several characteristics that the left and right movements had in common as a symbolic rejection of both paternal and maternal authority. The group, left or right, symbolises a preoedipal mother who provides love and diffuse sexual gratifications without demands for either individual differentiation or commitment within couples.

Christopher Lasch (1977, 1978) also suggested that the family no longer serves as a source of moral guidance. As a consequence of parents trying to avoid conflict by compromising and offering instinctual gratification, the development of the child's superego is undermined. When the child's superego development is faulty, the child depends internally on sadistic and primitive superego precursors and overindulges in impulse gratification. This dynamic leads to a secondary overdependence on external sources for the gratification of self-esteem, and the corrosion of authority within the family is amplified by a general societal shift from a traditional mode of social leadership that derived from ethical principles and intellectual consistency to a mode of leadership that has abandoned its moral justification and basis of control.

Perhaps the most comprehensive utilisation of Freud's 1921 essay and its update to the present was achieved in Serge Moscovici's book *L'Age des Foules* (The Age of the Crowds) (1981). Moscovici critically retraces the background to Freud's book as well as Freud's contribution to mass psychology, and presents dramatic illustrations of Freud's theory of the historical origin of the primal horde in the analysis of the cult of the hero established in Soviet Russia after Lenin's death, and its development into Stalin's totalitarian regime. Moscovici enriches Freud's perspective with his phrase 'communication as the Valium of the people.' He describes the combined effect of the activation of a pseudocommunity by mass communication that affects masses simultaneously, a process that goes hand in hand with the actual expansion of concentrated areas with large populations, thus creating conditions that foster the development of mass psychology. Moscovici agrees with Freud in that mass psychology is as fundamental as individual psychology in determining cultural phenomena, and considers Freud's contribution a crucial step in the future development of mass psychology as a rigorous science.

I believe that the richest yield from Freud's contribution to mass psychology may be gained by juxtaposing his work with that of two other major contributors mentioned: Canetti's *Crowds and Power* (1960) and Moscovici's 1981 (*The Age of the Crowds*) work. Freud looks at mass psychology as a concerned outsider who has not only recognised the dangerous, irrational, and violent power of mobs and mass movements, but also has found the intrapsychic dynamics that foster the individual's participation in and creation of mass psychology. Canetti explores mass psychology from the intoxicating experience of being a participant of the mob—from the seductive, exciting, destructive inside. Moscovici adds the sociological perspective, the social and cultural factors contributing to the condensation of real and imaginary masses by means of the effects of modern communications systems and the population explosion. He thus takes up, at a deeper level, what Ortega y Gasset intuitively had observed in his book *La Rebelion de las Masas* (The Rebellion of the Masses) (1976). In fact, I believe that, looking again at Freud's work with a combined perspective of those two 'outsiders', the depth and scope of Freud's discoveries emerge in sharper focus.

In what follows, I shall critically review Freud's themes under a number of different headings, pointing to new developments in these areas, but also to some of Freud's observations that acquire new significance in the light of these developments. It must remain an open question to what extent this 'new reading' is faithful to Freud's original intention and/or to what extent it reflects new perspectives from our own time.

Freud's central thesis

Freud (1921), in defining mass psychology, proposed:

> [T]o isolate as the subject of inquiry the influencing of an individual by a large number of people simultaneously, people with whom he is connected by something, though otherwise they may in many respects be strangers to him. Mass psychology is therefore concerned with the individual man as a member of a race, of a nation, of a caste, of a profession, of an institution, or as a component part of a crowd of people who have been organised into a mass at some particular time for some definite purpose. (Freud 1921: 70)

In this quotation, I have changed 'group' back into the original 'mass' in order to keep it close to Freud's original thinking. It is puzzling that, while Freud himself clearly recognised McDougall's (1920) pivotal distinction between crowds and more organised types of group formation, the *Standard Edition* homogenises all these concepts under the term *group*. A crowd is a large collection of people without any formal organisation; a horde or mob is a crowd that has a certain rudimentary but clearly visible organisation of direction, purpose, or motivation, usually characterised by a high emotional intensity. One might say that mobs are temporary hordes and that certain social and political conditions may transform a crowd into a mob.

Insofar as Freud was referring to the psychology of large collections of people characterised by some organised but highly emotional and irrational behaviour, he was describing hordes or mobs. The term *mob*, however, has deprecatory connotations that are absent in the German *Masse*: it should be stressed that this connotation is inappropriate and irrelevant and should not be implied in the discussion that follows. Finally, Freud uses the term *artificial masses* in referring to the church and the army, corresponding to what would now be designated specialised social organisations. Freud's essay, therefore, deals with a vast spectrum of mass psychology, including that of crowds, mobs, social and political movements, and stable institutions or social organisations that are characterised by organisational structure and leadership, as well as by manifestations of mass psychology.

Freud described the primitive, emotionally driven, unreflective behaviour of hordes or mobs, and explained the sense of immediate closeness or intimacy of individuals with each other in mobs as derived from the projection of their ego ideal onto the leader, and the identification of the members of the horde with him as well as with each other. The projection of the ego ideal onto the idealised leader eliminates individual constraints as well as the higher functions of self-criticism and responsibility that are so importantly mediated by the superego. Throughout his essay, Freud uses the term *ego ideal* rather than *superego*, which had not yet become part of his theoretical vocabulary. The mutual identifications of the members of the mob bring about a sense of unity and belonging (which protects them, we might say from today's perspective, from losing their sense of identity) but is accompanied by a severe reduction in ego functioning. As a result, primitive, ordinarily unconscious needs take over, and the mob functions under the sway of emotions stimulated and directed by the leader. For Freud, the influence of the leader on the members of the mob is primary in leading to the latter's consolidation. By projecting their individual ego ideal onto the leader, the members of the mob create the precondition for their mutual identifications.

Freud linked these concepts with the ideas contained in *Totem and Taboo* (1913b), suggesting that the leader of the primal horde was the original father, killed by the alliance of the sons. The leader of a horde represents the idealised, mythical hero; but, by the same token, the idealisation of the leader also includes the original idealisation of the oedipal father. This, in the briefest terms, is the central thesis of Freud's essay.

Critical review and update of major themes

The following themes reflect an exploration, from the viewpoint of contemporary developments of psychoanalytic theory of group processes and mass psychology, of Freud's ideas contained in his 1921 essay.

Libido as a binding force and the role of aggression

At first (1921: 94-95), Freud is explicit in stressing that the ties of all mass formations are libidinal. He goes to great lengths to point out that the projection of the ego ideal onto the leader and the attachment to the leader that replaces the attachment to the individual's own ego ideal, clearly imply libidinal ties, while the mutual ties with the others reflect an identification, that is, the earliest form of object tie is a libidinal relationship.

But, in the second part of his essay (Freud 1921: 120-121) Freud argues against the origin of mass formation in the absence of a leader by pointing to the rivalry and envy among the siblings, and secondary, reactive nature of mutual identification of group formation in early childhood. Here, the earliest ties of the potential group formation of childhood (which, in Freud's view, are the basis of group and mass formation later on) are based upon the reaction formation against aggression: the earliest ties, then, are aggressive and not libidinal ones. Also, as Freud describes the relationship between the primal horde and the primal father as its leader, he points to the uncanny nature of the relationship of the members of the horde to that primal father, in parallel to the uncanny aspect of the relationship that occurs in hypnosis. Freud describes the individuals' fear of looking into the eyes of the leader, reflecting the representation of an all-powerful and dangerous, deified personality with regard to whom the individual has to react passively and masochistically. The horde wants to be dominated by a personality with unlimited power, to bend to his will, to submit masochistically to him. In the postscript, Freud re-examines the myth of the father of the primal horde stressing that he was the ideal for each member, simultaneously feared and admired, thus giving rise to a community of brothers dealing with guilt over the murder of the primal father.

It was only one year earlier, in 1920, that Freud published *Beyond the Pleasure Principle*, where he formulated, for the first time, the dual drive theory of libido and aggression; and yet he does not apply the ideas contained there to his theory of mass psychology. In his description of the dynamics of mass formation he points to the importance of both aggression and libido, but in his theoretical formulation he confines himself to the libido theory alone. Even when describing the decomposition of the mob under conditions of panic, he refers to the fear of outbreak of hostility, as well as to the dissolution of libidinal ties.

From the perspective of the contemporary psychoanalytic theory of the entire spectrum of group formation—from the small and large groups to the transitory and stable organisations—one would stress the enormous importance of both libido and aggression, the functions of splitting processes that give rise to idealisation as well as to persecutory fears, and other primitive defensive mechanisms dealing with this dialectic at every level of complexity of group formation.

The dynamic characteristics of various group formations

The intervening years since 1921 have seen actual observations and experiments with groups of various types and sizes. These investigations have yielded ideas that partly support, partly refute, and partly extend Freud's ideas. In what follows I describe the works on which my own conclusions are based and then present those conclusions.

In works written in the 1940s and early 1950s, Bion (1961) described the regressive processes that occur in small groups of seven to twelve members. Bion described these regressive processes in terms of three 'basic assumptions', emotional states motivating the group which potentially exist in groups at all times, but which are particularly activated when the glue holding the group together, the task structure or 'work group' breaks down.

The first 'basic-assumptions group' operates under a 'dependency' assumption. Members perceive the leader as omnipotent and omniscient and themselves as inadequate, immature, and incompetent. They match their idealisation of the leader with desperate efforts to extract from him the qualities they attribute to him—knowledge, power, and goodness. The group members are thus both greedy and forever dissatisfied. When the leader fails to live up to their ideal, they react first with denial and then by devaluing the leader and searching for a substitute. Thus, primitive idealisation, projected omnipotence, denial, envy , and greed, together with their accompanying defences, characterise the dependency group.

The second group operates under a fight-flight assumption. The group unites against what it vaguely perceives to be external enemies. This group expects the leader to direct the fight against such enemies and also to protect the group from infighting. Since this group cannot tolerate opposition to the ideology shared by the majority of its members, it easily splits into subgroups which fight with each other or flee. Here, prevalent features include the group's tendencies to control or to experience itself as being controlled by the leader, to experience closeness through shared denial of intragroup hostility, and to project aggression onto an out-group. In short, splitting, projection of aggression, and projective identification prevail. In the fight-flight group, the search for nurture and dependency that characterises the dependency group is replaced by conflicts around aggressive control, along with suspiciousness, fighting, and dread of annihilation.

The third group operates under what Bion called a 'pairing' assumption. Members tend to focus on a couple within the group, usually but not necessarily heterosexual, which symbolises the group's hopeful (conscious or unconscious) expectation that the couple, and with it, the group will in effect reproduce itself and thus preserve the group's threatened identity and survival. The pairing group experiences general intimacy and sexual developments as potential protections against the dangerous conflicts around dependency and aggression that characterise the dependency and the fight-flight groups. While the latter two groups have a pregenital character, the pairing group has a genital character.

Both Le Bon (1920) and Freud (1921) referred to the direct manifestations of violent aggression in mobs. In contrast, the potential for violence is still generally under control in small groups. Not only do small groups make use of the mechanisms just described, but the existence of eye-to-eye contact and mutual acquaintance helps small groups to maintain a certain civilised attitude. Occasionally, however, the external enemy is absent, and this raises the small group's tensions to a high pitch. An external enemy serves to absorb the aggression generated with the group, and this aggression threatens the basic-assumptions group of fight-flight which cannot define or locate an enemy on the outside.

Rice (1965) and Turquet (1975) studied the behaviour of large unstructured groups of 40 to 120 persons, using methods similar to those Bion had used in his study of small groups. The group leader only observed and commented upon the developments within the large group, whose members were sitting in concentric circles; he refrained from any structuring or organising behaviour. Turquet described how, under these conditions, the individual member of a large group experienced a temporal but total loss of personal identity. Concomitantly, there was a dramatic decrease in any individual's capacity for realistically evaluating the effects of his or her words and actions. In the large group, the ordinary social feedback to the individual member's verbal communications disappears. Nobody seems to be able to listen to anybody else, all dialogue is drowned by the discontinuity of communication that evolves, and efforts to establish small subgroups usually fail. The individual is thrown into a void. Even projective mechanisms fail, because the ability to evaluate realistically the behaviour of anyone else disappears. In this context, projections become multiple and unstable, and the individual has to find some kind of 'skin' that will differentiate him or her from the others.

Turquet described fears of aggression, of loss of control, and of the violent behaviour that could emerge at any time in the large group. Fear is the counterpart to provocative behaviours among the group's members, behaviours that they partly express at random but which are for the most part directed at the leader. Gradually, it becomes evident that those individuals who try to stand up to this atmosphere and maintain some semblance of individuality are the ones who are attacked most ferociously. At the same time, any simplistic generalisation or ideology that permeates the group may be easily picked up and transformed into an experience of absolute truth. In contrast to the simple rationalisation of the violence that permeates the mob, however, the large group resorts to a simplistic philosophy that functions as a calming, reassuring doctrine and reduces all thinking to obvious clichés. Turquet believed that aggression in the large group for the most part takes the form of envy of thinking, individuality, and rationality.

Anzieu (1971) proposed that under conditions of regression in the unstructured group, individual instinctual needs are fused with a fantastic conception of the group as a primitive ego ideal, equated with an all-gratifying primary object, the mother of the earliest stages of development. The psychology of the group, then, reflects three sets of shared illusions: (1) The group is constituted of individuals who are all equal, thus denying sexual differences and castration anxiety. (2) The group is self-engendered, that is, a powerful mother of itself. (3) The group itself might then repair all narcissistic lesions, since it becomes an idealised 'breast-mother'.

Chasseguet-Smirgel (1984) expanded on Anzieu's observation, suggesting that under such conditions any group, small or large, tends to select leadership that represents not the paternal aspects of the prohibitive superego, but a pseudopaternal 'promoter of illusions'. Such a leader provides the group with an ideology—a shared system of ideas that serves to unify the group. The ideology is an illusion that confirms the individual's narcissistic aspirations of fusing with the group as a primitive ego ideal—the all-powerful and all-gratifying preoedipal mother. Basically, the small- or large-group members' identification with each other permits them to experience a primitive narcissistic gratification of greatness and power. When groups are violent and are operating under the influence of ideologies that have been adopted under such psychological conditions, their violence reflects their need to destroy any external reality that interferes with that ideology. The losses of personal identity, of cognitive discrimination, and of any differentiating individuality within the group are compensated for by the sense of omnipotence that all its members share. According to Chasseguet-Smirgel, the regressed ego, the id, and the primitive (preoedipal) ego ideal of each individual are fused in the group illusion.

In earlier work (Kernberg 1980: chapter 11), I suggested that some of the strikingly regressive features of small groups, large groups, and mobs may be better understood in the light of our present knowledge of the internalised object relations that predate object constancy and the consolidation of the ego, superego, and id. Based on the preceding psychoanalytic observations of mobs, large groups, and small groups, I suggested that owing to the nature of the regression that occurs in groups, group processes pose a basic threat to the member's personal identity, linked to a proclivity in group situations for the activation of primitive object relations, primitive defensive operations, and primitive aggression with predominantly pregenital features. These processes, particularly the activation of primitive aggression, are dangerous to the survival of the individual in the group, as well as to any task the group needs to perform.

I proposed that Turquet's (1975) description of what happens in large groups constitutes the basic situation against which both the idealisation of the leader in the horde described by Freud, and the small-group processes described by Bion, are defending. To blindly follow the idealised leader of the mob, as described by Freud, reconstitutes a sort of identity by identification with the leader, permits protection from intragroup aggression by this common identity and the shared projection of aggression to external enemies, and gratifies dependency needs by submission to the leader. The sense of power experienced by the individual identified with the mob of which he forms part also gratifies primitive narcissistic needs. Paradoxically, the essentially irrational quality of mobs (i.e., of crowds temporarily organised into group formation by a shared idealisation of a leader and a corresponding ideology) provides better protection against painful awareness of aggression than what obtains in large-group situations with undefined external enemies, and in small groups where it is hard to avoid being aware that the 'enemy' is right in the midst of the group itself.

The study of large-group processes highlights the threat to individual identity under social conditions in which ordinary role functions are suspended and various projective mechanisms are no longer effective (because of the loss of face-to-face contact and personal feedback). Obviously, large-group processes can be obscured or controlled by firm or rigid social structuring. Bureaucratisation, ritualisation, as well as well-organised task performance are different methods with similar immediate effects.

Large-group processes also highlight the intimate connection between threats to retaining one's identity and fear that primitive aggression and aggressively infiltrated sexuality will emerge. My observations from the study of individual patients, of small groups, and of group processes in organisational and institutional life confirm the overwhelming nature of human aggression in unstructured group situations.

The point is that an important part of nonintegrated and nonsublimated aggression is expressed in vicarious ways throughout group and organisational processes. When relatively well-structured group processes evolve in a task-oriented organisation, aggression is channelled toward the decision-making process, particularly by evoking primitive leadership characteristics in people in positions of authority. Similarly, the exercise of power in organisational and institutional life constitutes an important channel for the expression of aggression in group processes that would ordinarily be under control in a dyadic or triadic relation. Aggression emerges more directly and much more intensely when group processes are relatively unstructured.

A multiplicity of primitive self and object representations predominate as intrapsychic structures of the individual before the consolidation of ego, superego, and id—and, therefore, before the consolidation of ego identity. The regressive features of part-object relations that evolve when normal ego identity disintegrates are remarkably parallel to the relationships that exist among all individuals within a large-group situation.

There is a striking tendency in large groups to project superego functions on the group as a whole, as part of an effort to prevent violence and protect ego identity by means of a shared ideology. The concomitant need of all groups to project and externalise superego functions onto the leader reflects not only sadistic and/or idealised aspects of primitive superego precursors, but also the realistic and protective aspects of more mature superego functioning. The indissoluble union of primitive and advanced aspects of the superego makes this a tragic externalisation: the morality of groups and institutions influenced by projection of primitive superego features comes closer to the primitive morality of the unconscious superego than to the conscious morality of the mature individual.

More recently (Kernberg, 1984, 1986, 1989a, 1989b, 1991), I have examined the nature of the defensive activation of idealisation processes under various group conditions in relation to the activation of paranoid developments in them. I believe that, in contrast to the dominant group characteristics of the unstable, threatening, potentially violent, and identity-diffusion fostering quality of the large group, small-group formation deals with the idealisation-persecution dichotomy in the respective activation of Bion's dependency and fight-flight groups. The activation of the pairing assumption may be considered an ambivalent effort to escape from primitive conflicts around aggression, primitive object relations, and primitive defences by ambivalent idealisation of a selected sexual pair. The large group does not usually split up into small groups but rather, undergoes a transformation into a static large group that has the quality of what Canetti (1960) described as the typical 'feasting crowd', engaged, we might say, in dependent and narcissistic behaviour, and a corresponding search for a calming, narcissistic reassuring mediocrity in their leader.

I have described this level of regression as characteristic of the mass psychology of conventionality (Kernberg 1989a), reflecting the type of ideology characteristic of a latency child superego, and represented typically by mass entertainment. As an alternative, the large group evolves into a dynamic mob characterised by predominantly paranoid features, selection of paranoid leadership, and typically represented by the mass psychology of revolutionary mass formations. Conventional culture, on the one hand, and violent revolutionary movements with totalitarian ideology, on the other, may be considered the corresponding mass psychological outcomes of idealisation and persecution as basic group phenomena.

At a more advanced level of organisation that involves more mature forms of mass psychology as described by McDougall and Freud, Bion has characterised the army as the institutional structuralisation of the fight-flight group, and the church as the institutional structuralisation of the dependency group. Functional social organisations in such areas as government, industry, education, and health care would represent maximum control, reduction, and sublimation of mass psychology as part of organisational task systems. Here, the interesting issue is that, regardless of the protective and corrective measures instituted by social organisations, such as functional leadership and appropriate bureaucratic organisational systems (with means for redress of grievances and other measures geared to reduce 'paranoiagenesis') (Kernberg 1989b), it is unavoidable that spontaneous emergence of aggression in the form of sadistic behaviours develops in institutions and infiltrates at various points the institutional process, including the very mechanisms that usually protect the institution from excessive paranoiagenesis.

In summary, then, the unavoidable activation of primitive aggression in the individual's functioning within social groups reflects a universal latent disposition for regression to preoedipal levels of intrapsychic organisation. Within this regression, the projection of aggression onto parental figures, the reintrojection of such parental figures under the distorted consequences of projected aggression, and consequent vicious circles involving projection and introjection of aggression are dealt with by massive splitting mechanisms, leading to idealisation processes, on the one hand, and to paranoid, persecutory processes, on the other. These primitive psychic operations, derived in the last resort from the dyadic relationship with the mother, resonate with later triangular problems reflecting the oedipal situation, and transform the disposition to multiple pre-oedipal transferences into the typical triangular oedipal ones that become dominant in the relationship with authority. The distortion of rational authority resulting from these projective processes, in turn, leads to defensive activation of narcissistic affirmation, regressive relationships to feared and/or idealised parental leadership, and this process is completed by a generalised tendency to reproject the more advanced aspects of superego functioning on the total institution.

The projection of superego functions on the institution *in toto* increases the subjective dependency of the individual on the institution's evaluation of him, decreases the individual's capacity to rely on internalised value systems, and provides the direct trigger for the individual's contamination by ideological crosscurrents, rumours, and regression into primitive depressive and persecutory anxieties when objective feedback and reassurance in the organisation fails. Under these conditions, not only is there a threat of emotional and characterological regression in the personality, but also regression in the moral dimension of individual functioning. Here the 'paranoid urge to betray' (Jacobson, 1971) is only a logical consequence.

Re-examining Freud's essay in the light of all these more recent contributions, his description of mass psychology corresponds mostly to the characteristics of large groups and mob and/or horde formation. Freud's emphasis on libidinal links among the members as a defence against envious rivalry corresponds precisely to the condensation of and defence against preoedipal, particularly oral envy and oedipal rivalry that characterises the activation of primitive object relations under conditions of large-group process. Freud's description of the ambivalent relation to leadership, the combination of idealisation and what might be called paranoid fears of the leader and submission and subservience to him, reflect the expression of the struggle between idealising and persecutory processes characteristic of large groups and mobs.

Freud (1921: 129-133) points to the remarkable lack of differentiation between the ego and the ego ideal under many circumstances, and to the consequent implication that the relationship to the leader, under these circumstances, becomes in essence an identification of the individual's ego with the leader. In doing so, Freud points to the narcissistic gratification of the exercise of power as part of mass psychology, the sense of freedom from moral constraints and omnipotence given by what Elias Canetti (1960) described as the 'density' of the dynamic mob. The mob, by means of libidinal gratification in the form of primitive narcissism, and of aggressive gratification in the infiltration of the leader's and the mob's grandiosity and omnipotence with aggression, acquires characteristics analogous to the patient with the syndrome of malignant narcissism (Kernberg 1989c). In my view, Freud comes close to pointing to the aggressive as well as libidinal sources of mutual identification of the mob as a profound motivation for the way mobs behave.

I question Freud's assertion that it is the personality of the leader that brings about the consolidation of mass formation. Rice's (1965) and Turquet's (1975) experiences with large groups illustrate the immediate regression into a most primitive type of mass psychology of the unstructured large group. Anzieu's (1971) and Chasseguet-Smirgel's (1984) findings suggest that there is always an implicit primitive leadership in the fantasy of small as well as large group formation, a leadership closer to the primitive maternal ego ideal than to the father of the primal horde. But even granting this fantasy structure, it already would seem to defend against the basic threats to identity and threats of violence in the large group. In short, I think that mass psychology predates the crystallisation of the identification with the leader.

Identification processes and the nature of leadership

Throughout his discussion of identification and the ego ideal, Freud focuses almost exclusively on the father as object, mentioning the mother only in connection with male homosexuality, as he does in his paper on narcissism (1914a). He proposes that identification is the first type of an object relationship, and that to become like the object will continue as a potential regression from the wish to have an object. He does not, however, explore the male and the female infant identifying themselves with mother as the earliest object. Today, thanks to his subsequent fully fledged conceptualisation of the superego (1923), we are aware of the various developmental levels of identification processes, so that earliest introjections, later partial identifications, and complex identity formation may be differentiated from each other.

Above all, the dyadic nature of all identification processes, that is, that identification occurs not with an object but with a relationship between self and object is a concept that emerged years after Freud's death, as a result of the contributions of Melanie Klein (1997b[1946]), Ronald Fairbairn (1994), Erik Erikson (1959), Edith Jacobson (1964), and Margaret Mahler (Mahler & Furer 1968).

The very nature of primitive, part-object relationships related to splitting processes and expressed by primitive projective and introjective mechanisms in the group situation can be differentiated from more advanced types of internalised total or integrated object relations that reproduce more clearly the dyadic and triangular relations of early family life. I have proposed that one might consider two levels of internalised object relations. A basic level would be characterised by multiple self and object representations that correspond to primitive fantasy formations linked with primitive impulse derivatives. Each unit of self and object representation carries a particular affect state, and is split off from other corresponding units with diametrically opposed affect states. The second and higher level of internalised object relations would be characterised by sophisticated, integrated self and object representations linked with higher levels of affect dispositions. These higher level object relations reflect more accurately than the basic level object relations of infancy and early childhood the experiences and conflicts between the individual and his or her real parental figures and siblings. At the higher level, the integrated self concept, together with integrated, related, realistically invested object representations constitute ego identity.

Regardless of the individual's maturity and psychological integration, unstructured small and large groups that lack an operational leadership and lack or lose clearly defined tasks to relate them to their environment tend to bring about an immediate regression in the individual. This regression consists in the activation of defensive operations and interpersonal processes that reflect primitive object relations. The potential for such regression exists within all of us. When we lose our ordinary social structure, when our ordinary social roles are suspended, and when multiple objects are present simultaneously in an unstructured relationship, reproducing in the interpersonal field the multiplicity of primitive intrapsychic object relations, then primitive levels of psychological functioning tend to be reactivated. It is this propensity to regress which determines the threat to personal identity and the fear that primitive aggression will be activated in unstructured group situations, and motivates the typical defensive operations in groups that have been described. I believe this is the basic dynamic that promotes group psychology and underlies mass psychology at all levels.

Another proposed modification of Freud's views refers to the nature of the symbolic meaning of the leadership of small and large groups. Here I draw on the work of Jacobson (1964) and Chasseguet-Smirgel (1984). In summary, the projection of superego constituents on group leadership depends on both the level of organisation of any individual's superego structure and on the nature and degree of regression under which a group operates. Under conditions of advanced types of large-group regressions, typically, the static large group with benign narcissistic leadership, or a leadership that fosters an ambivalent narcissistic dependency and an only moderately moralistic ideology, the individual's regression is to the latency period, and the projection is of the latency period superego with its typical infantile value systems. These values include the characteristics of a simplistic, conventional, black-or-white morality, oedipal prohibitions are in place, and so is the corresponding dissociation of affective engagement from genital erotism. Mass culture also corresponds to this ideology, and its dominant artistic expression, kitsch; the corresponding leadership is perceived as that of the oedipal father of the advanced oedipal stage of childhood.

When regression develops further, from the narcissistic-dependent to the predominantly persecutory-paranoid type of leadership, the activation is of the early, prohibitive oedipal superego, the father who potentially threatens with castration the child's untamed oedipal rivalry and violence. Here the leader is seen as the prohibitive—in contrast to the generous—father. Even further regression in the group situation brings us to the pseudopaternal promoter of illusions described by Chasseguet-Smirgel (1984), characteristic of the primitive ego ideal that depends mostly on the introjection of the preoedipal, all-giving, all-gratifying maternal image. This ego ideal, in turn, protects the individual and the group against archaic aggression toward mother and the distorted maternal image (resulting from projection) as extremely threatening. This is an archaic level of aggression typically expressed as the violence against an external world that threatens the utopia of the gratifying group-breast described by Anzieu (1971). Finally, we may point to the mature superego derived from the postoedipal parental couple—the rational, protective, moral functions of the parents—as the symbolic meaning of the rational leadership of functional organisations, the polarity opposite to the large-group regression.

In contrast to Freud's description of the prototypical leader of the mob as the symbolic father of the primal horde, we may now formulate a spectrum of different types of symbolic leadership reflecting the degree of regression in the group. It was Bion who first pointed to the 'role suction' of small groups, where the dependency group tends to promote infantile narcissistic (and even psychopathic) leaders, in contrast to the fight-flight group that seeks a leader with paranoid characteristics. Freud described some qualities that are required of the leader of the mob that are highly relevant here. He pointed out (Freud 1921: 123) that the leader needs to be free from needing the love of others, able to love himself and thus to crystallise, in his narcissistic self-love, the crowd's aspirations for a jointly projected ego ideal. The leader must be self-confident, independent, and self-assured; he may be dominant and absolutely narcissistic. And Freud states elsewhere (Freud 1921: 127) that he also must be able to evoke fear and convey an unlimited power to control the group.

In the light of contemporary contributions to the analysis of leadership functions, including those stemming from a psychoanalytic background, and in the light of the nature of regressive group processes that we have examined, I have proposed (Kernberg 1991) five major, desirable personality characteristics for rational leadership: (1) high intelligence; (2) personal honesty and noncorruptibility by the political process; (3) capacity for establishing and maintaining object relations in depth; (4) a healthy narcissism; and (5) a healthy, justifiable anticipatory paranoid attitude in contrast to naiveté. The last two characteristics, namely, a certain amount of narcissism and paranoia, are perhaps the most surprising and yet the most important aspects of task leadership, already pointed to in Freud's 1921 essay. A healthy narcissism protects the leader from overdependency on approval from others, and provides strength to his capacity for autonomous functioning. A healthy paranoid attitude alerts the leader to the dangers of corruption and paranoiagenic regression—the acting out of diffuse aggression unconsciously activated in all organisational processes. He is also thereby protected from a naiveté that would prevent him from analysing the motivational aspects of institutional conflicts.

The danger, of course, is that organisational regression will accentuate narcissistic and paranoid features of leadership and will constitute powerful regressive forces that mobilise further regression along narcissistic-dependent and/or paranoid-sadistic lines. This regressive development, however, is precisely what characterises mass psychology at all levels: the always present danger that the aggressive drive derivatives that infiltrate social and institutional life will corrupt the very mechanisms established to control them. I would suggest a modified formulation of mass psychology: in essence, both leaders and people in groups regress along two axes. The first is of dependency, narcissism, primitive hedonism, and psychopathy. The second is of moralism, paranoid-persecutory control, sadism and violence.

The couple and the group

In the postscript to *Group Psychology and the Analysis of the Ego*, Freud wrote: 'Two people coming together for the purpose of sexual satisfaction, in so far as they seek for solitude, are making a demonstration against the herd instinct, the group feeling. The more they are in love, the more completely they suffice for each other' (Freud 1921: 140). Freud also stressed the intolerance of crowds to sexuality, citing the church and the army as institutions that did not tolerate sexual relations between men and women. He saw this intolerance as a derivative of the original danger facing the primitive horde, namely, the rivalry among the sons in their competition for their mothers and sisters. Freud proposed that the totemic incest taboo protected the social structure at the cost of repressing sexual urges within it.

The activation of sexuality that is infantile in nature is a striking characteristic of regression at all levels of group formation. As Bion (1961) pointed out, in the small group, sexuality emerges when the basic assumption of pairing serves as a defence against primitive aggression. In the large group, sexuality is either denied or is expressed in sadistically infiltrated sexual allusions. Usually it goes underground in the large group, and couples form secretly as a direct reaction to and defence against large-group processes. In the horde, the unchallenged idealisation of the leader has a counterpart in the horde's intolerance of any couple that attempts to preserve its privacy and its identity as such. Freud (1913b) saw intolerance of sexuality as a derivative of the original danger that faces the primitive horde, namely, the sons' rivalry and competition for their mothers and sisters. Anzieu (1971) and Chasseguet-Smirgel (1984) both stressed the denial or oedipal sexuality in unstructured group processes.

The projection of superego functions onto the group and its leader and the related submission to authoritarian leadership does protect against both violence and the destruction of couples within the group.

It is condensed, however, with a prohibition against incest and the most infantile aspects of sexuality. Thus, group morality veers toward a conventionalised de-erotisation of heterosexual relations, toward the suppression of erotic fantasy insofar as it involves infantile polymorphous trends, and toward acknowledging and sanctioning only the more permissible love relations. In large groups, the alternative to these defensive efforts—and to their miscarriage in repressive ideologies—is the eruption of a crude and particularly anally tinged sexuality which is very reminiscent of the sexualised group formations of latency and early adolescence.

In earlier work (Kernberg 1980: chapter 15), I suggested that there is a built-in, complex, and fateful relationship between the couple and the group. Because the couple's stability depends on the successful establishment of its autonomy within the group setting, it cannot escape from its relation to the group. Because the couple enacts and maintains the group's hope for sexual union and love in the face of the potential destructiveness activated by ever-available large-group processes, the group needs the couple. The group cannot, however, escape from the internal sources of hostility and envy toward the couple that derive from envy of the happy and secret union of the parents and from the deep unconscious guilt over forbidden oedipal strivings.

Given the ever-present danger of group regression in contemporary mass society and mass culture, the dangerous effects of such regression on the control of aggression, particularly violence, under such regressive conditions, and the dramatic deterioration in ethical functioning that group regression and mass psychology carry with them, the study of mass psychology so crucially influenced by Freud's contribution is an urgent task in our time.

Notes

[1] This paper was presented at the symposium 'Through the Looking Glass: Freud's Impact on Contemporary Culture', sponsored by the University Museum of Archaeology-Anthropology, University of Pennsylvania, the Philadelphia Association for Psychoanalysis and the Philadelphia Psychoanalytic Society, Philadelphia, September 23, 1989.

THE SOCIAL UNCONSCIOUS IN CLINICAL WORK[1]

Earl Hopper

The central theme of this chapter concerns the constraints of social systems on individuals and their internal worlds, and, at the same time, the effects that unconscious fantasies, actions, thoughts and feelings have on social systems. This field of knowledge is usually known as 'The Individual and the Group', and group-analysis or psychoanalytical group therapy is a particular application of it. An analyst who is unaware of the effect of social facts and social forces cannot be sensitive to the unconscious re-creation of them within the therapeutic situation. He will not be able to provide a space for patients to imagine how their identities have been formed at particular historical and political junctures, and how this continues to affect them throughout their lives.[2]

The unconscious constraints of social facts and social forces

The study of groups is always contextual, as is the study of individuals, which is why it is virtually impossible to consider the one without the other. Contexts are infinite in number and variety, as for example, we have the ecological, the social, the cultural, the psychological, and the physiological, amongst others. Groups are exceedingly 'open' systems, and, therefore, highly dependent on the provision of 'goods and services' from beyond their own boundaries. Usually, group analysts focus on the psychological context, but here I am concerned with the social context and how a group and its members are affected by it. Many features of the social context are involved: for example, the culturally supported models and analogies that might be used for descriptions of a group, for descriptions of the healing process and the role of the therapist, as well as the structure of referral networks, the education and training systems for therapists, the social welfare institutions, and so on...

The effects of social facts and forces are as likely to be unconscious as conscious. The social unconscious is not merely a matter of the preconscious, and cannot be reduced to questions of awareness. The social unconscious is *lawful* in the same sense that the dynamic unconscious operates according to *primary process*. Structural dilemmas and contradictions abound, and some arrangements and cultural patterns preclude others. The concept of the social unconscious refers to the existence and constraints of social, cultural and communicational arrangements of which people are unaware. Unaware, in so far as these arrangements are not perceived (not 'known'), and if perceived not acknowledged ('denied'), and if acknowledged, not taken as problematic ('given'), and if taken as problematic, not considered with an optimal degree of detachment and objectivity. Although social constraints are sometimes understood in terms of myth, ritual and custom, such constraints are in the realm of the 'unknown' to the same extent as the constraints of instincts and fantasies, especially in societies with high status rigidity (Hopper 1981). However, 'constraint' is not meant to imply only 'restraint', 'inhibition', or 'limitation', but also 'facilitation', 'development' and even the transformation of sensations into feelings.

The concept of the social unconscious may be used to refer to the social and cultural elements and processes that exist within three categories of unconscious phenomena: that of which people are unaware but of which they were formerly aware, for example, the thoughts and feelings denoted by the 'Oedipus complex'; that of which they are unaware but of which they were partly aware, for example, fantasy life that occurred prior to language acquisition; and that of which they are unaware, and of which they were never aware. Information that was and is barely accessible to knowing, and that could not and cannot really be known directly, is called 'archaic', or more helpfully 'the unthought known' (Bollas 1987), although I prefer to think in terms of the 'dynamic non-conscious'.

It is misleading to assume that people have unconscious minds in the same sense that they have complex brains; it is more appropriate to assume that people are unconscious, pre-conscious and non-conscious of much thought, feeling, fantasy and even sensation. Similarly, social systems do not have 'unconscious minds' or any kind of mind, and the use of the concept of the social unconscious should not be taken to imply otherwise. After all, social systems are not organisms, and the notion 'group mind' is rather misleading. Nonetheless, whereas we have come to accept the validity and utility of the concept 'unconscious' for phenomena originating in the body, we need a concept like the 'social unconscious' in order to discuss social, cultural and communicational constraints.

It is virtually impossible to learn about some aspects of such constraints, because inevitably we are caught up within them and formed by them. Also, attempts to understand the social unconscious are met with a mixture of personal and social resistance, because feelings of personal and social powerlessness follow from increased insight into social facts and social forces. The appreciation of 'social causation' and the limits it sets on the fundamental notion of 'free will' is a blow to our narcissism and confuses our sense of ourselves as moral beings.

One type of social resistance with which group analysts are especially familiar is 'normative reticence', manifest in socially governed blank stares and silence, the very root of social secrecy, which 'core' groups may use to peripheralise and marginalise the newcomer and the outsider. Ideology is the most common form of social resistance. 'Messengers' and 'truth-sayers' about the social unconscious are usually regarded as 'difficult', 'adolescent', 'rebellious', 'bad-mannered', 'paranoid' even, which reflects a 'labelling' process by those in power which is the first line of social defence and control.

Although Karen Horney (1937) was the first psychoanalyst to apply the 'social unconscious' to clinical work in a creative and systematic way, the concept was introduced by Fromm (1984). It has never gained popular usage, perhaps because it has an oxymoronic quality: although suggesting radical intentions, it is based on an organismic analogy that has conservative implications. The ideas that underpin the concept have a long history in the social sciences, and include the work of Durkheim, Weber and especially Marx.[3]

The concept of the social unconscious differs from the traditional Jungian concept of the collective unconscious, with its emphasis on the inheritance of acquired characteristics. However, it is similar to more contemporary Jungian views of the 'shared unconscious', which emphasise the interpersonal, the inter-subjective and socialisation in general (Zinkin 1979). It is also similar to the 'cultural unconscious' introduced by the American psychoanalyst Ethel Spector-Person (1992) in her recent article 'Romantic Love: at the Intersection of the Psyche and the Cultural Unconscious'.[4]

Within the tradition of group analysis, Foulkes awarded special importance to the recognition and analysis of social forces at both interpersonal and trans-personal 'levels', and it is assumed that from the beginning of life the psyche is both organic and social. He wrote:

> ...the group-analytic situation, while dealing with the unconscious in the Freudian sense, brings into operation and perspective a totally different area of which the individual is equally

unaware. Moreover, the individual is as much compelled by these colossal forces as by his own id and defends himself against their recognition without being aware of it, but in quite different ways and modes. One might speak of a social or inter-personal unconscious. (Foulkes 1964)

Foulkes' (1957) concept of matrix was intended to convey both inhibition and facilitation, as well as 'mould', and his 'foundation matrix' meant that people and groups are rooted within species, societies, cultures and systems of communications (De Mare 1972). The seminal work of Moreno (1934) suggests that psychodrama and group analysis have common origins. This perspective is far more specific than the weak, residual theories of the 'social' suggested by either Bion's (1967) concepts of the container and the contained or Winnicott's (1967) theories of 'holding', which are 'interpersonal' in terms of the secondary response of the primal object to the infant's primary expression of feeling and impulse.

It may be helpful to present here two examples of the unconscious effects of social and cultural facts and forces from non-clinical settings. I will confine my examples to the unconscious effects of stratification systems on ambition, which is usually considered only in terms of the Oedipus complex. I will present further examples as I develop my argument, and I have discussed such phenomena at length in *Social Mobility: A Study of Social Control and Insatiability* (1982) *and Adult Students: Education, Selection and Social Control* (1975).

In an unpublished study of the social class background of mothers who used child guidance clinics in the National Health Service, I found that although the expectation was that the mothers should have been 'working class', that is, married to men in manual work and be in manual work themselves, in fact they came from lower middle class backgrounds, and were very capable of utilising the system. The problems of the children could then be understood in terms of family patterns within the lower middle class, involving mothers and fathers who had themselves experienced inconsistent definitions of their class and status by the system of education and stratification, partly because they were socially mobile. The mothers were often employed as secretaries for men who were in more powerful positions than their husbands. They put enormous pressure on their children to achieve more and more. The Oedipus complex of their sons included the male employers of the mothers, and collusion between mothers and sons to denigrate the authority of the father was commonplace, and frequently associated with latent homosexuality and difficulty in making a satisfactory identification with fathers.

There are many other sources of the normative limitations to ambition. I remember putting one of my daughters to bed when she was about five years old. In a very seductive and manipulative way she began to cry a little, and said, 'You know, Daddy, I am very sad, because I have just realised that I will never be Queen'. In the United States I would have understood this communication in terms of a fairy tale, and realised that she was communicating her struggle to renounce her oedipal wishes. However, how should I have understood such a communication in England, where there is a Queen, where the renunciation of oedipal wishes involves acquiescence in a particular system of social stratification, based on ascribed rather than achieved characteristics, and on the inheritance of privilege in an especially rigid and particular way? In England little girls who want to be Queens must wait for a Prince, who may actually come. My daughter had to realise that not only would she never be my wife, but also that she would never be a Queen, and all that this involved, unless she married a Prince. What would she have to give up in order to marry a Prince? Whatever the comparative strengths and weaknesses of American society and culture, people are brought up with the conviction that there is nothing they cannot be, provided they want it badly enough and are prepared to achieve it, which carries its own problems of culturally supported omnipotence, grandiosity and insatiability.

Another example of the constraints of social facts on intrapsychic life and interpersonal processes are the effects of normative orientations to authority with regard to how frustrated people become under conditions of close and punitive supervision at work, and the effects of normative orientations with respect to the expression of feelings on how aggressive they become when they have been frustrated (Hopper 1965). In a study of frustration and aggression and its effects on productivity among female workers in machine tool factories in England, I found that middle class women were less receptive than their working class counterparts to the exercise of close and punitive supervision, and, therefore, were more likely to become frustrated and to feel aggressive in response to this style of supervision. However, they were also more likely than their working class counterparts to suppress their aggressive feelings, and, therefore, more likely to displace their aggressive feelings into lowered productivity, even when this resulted in lower income for their work. In other words, social and cultural facts must be taken into account in attempts to understand the nature of aggressive feelings and of aggression.

The unconscious repetition of social situations and processes of equivalence

In various kinds of social systems, people tend unconsciously to recreate situations (in terms of actions, fantasies, object relations and affects) that have occurred at another time and space, such that the new or later situation may be taken as 'equivalent' to the old or previous one (Hopper 1980). Although 'equivalence' is based on the social unconscious, it is analogous to a person's creation of symptoms or dreams in terms of unconscious fantasies emanating from the biologically based unconscious mind or id, at least from the point of view of traditional psychoanalysis. Equivalence occurs through forms of externalisation and internalisation, including projective and introjective identification, in the service of expulsion and attack, mastery and control, but, above all, as a result of attempts to communicate non-verbal and ineffable experience, all of which may be considered as elements of the repetition compulsion. In fact, equivalence can be seen as a kind of group-transference of an unconsciously perceived situation from its social context to its present situation.[5]

An example of 'equivalence' follows. In the 1970s I began to work with survivors of concentration camps. Although there had been some work on the Survivor Syndrome, partly in connection with Reparations by the German government, generally, after the initial shock had worn off, no one talked about this entire issue: not the survivors themselves, nor their General Practitioners or Family Doctors, nor the religious leaders in the community. In my view, the renewed interest in the Survivor Syndrome and the willingness to discuss concentration camp experience were caused by the outbreak of conscious and unconscious anti-Semitic sentiments and actions in conjunction with the economic crisis of the mid 70s, the oil crisis associated with Israeli-Arab difficulties, and the consequent terrors for many members of the Jewish community.

In September 1979, Caroline Garland, Celia Read, myself and others (1980) organised a conference about the Survivor Syndrome. We arranged for much of the work to be attempted in a Large Group, because this allowed us to bring together all elements of the

Conference, and because we felt that the kind of regressions that occur in large groups might teach us something about the crowd and large group phenomena associated with war and the Shoah experience in particular. However, we all became so miserable and despairing within the Large Group that we could barely work within it. Eventually we realised that we had recreated what we had imagined unconsciously to be the concentration camp experience, including psychic numbing and identification with the aggressors. Many of us who participate in Conferences are familiar with such phenomena. In fact, equivalence in smaller groups of larger and more complex units within a Conference offers an important opportunity for learning about the dynamics of the Conference as a whole, and for monitoring its success.

The concepts of the social unconscious and of equivalence emphasise the importance of the experience of personal and social helplessness and powerlessness. They are, therefore, especially useful for understanding how and why groups recreate various aspects of social trauma which have occurred at another time and place. The anxieties connected with the trauma as well as the perceptions of the trauma itself are usually subjected to 'denial' and other forms of primal protections (Kinston & Cohen 1986) and, therefore, it is only to be expected that they will be enacted within situations in which people have regressed, as they are most likely to do in groups, and especially in large groups. Such traumas are likely to be enacted before they are re-experienced, which is why the provision of a space safe for acting-in is so important in all forms of psychotherapy.

'Social unconscious' and 'equivalence' are part of my more general view that envy develops as a defence against feelings of personal and social helplessness and powerlessness rather than as an expression of the anxiety inherent in the putative 'death instinct' (Hopper 1987, 1991b, 1993; Joffe 1969), which is an extension of Fairbairn's (1994[1952]) discussion of the 'moral defence'. This hypothesis connects the theoretical traditions of the British Object Relations School associated with the Group of Independent Psychoanalysts of the British Psycho-Analytical Society (Rayner 1990; Kohon 1988) to those of Group Analysis associated with the Institute of Group Analysis.

In sum, people are affected profoundly by social and cultural facts and forces, and such constraints are largely unconscious at all phases of 'life trajectories' (Hopper 1981). Situations characterised by extreme helplessness tend to be repeated, precisely because people remain unconscious of their fears and the dynamics of the situations in which their fears first arose. Especially in connection with trauma, but also in general, psychoanalysts and psychoanalytical psychotherapists, both in dyads and in groups, tend to ignore the social unconscious and processes of equivalence, and, therefore, are liable to engage in collusive defensive manoeuvres under the guise of 'going deeper'. This constitutes a problem within our profession, which itself warrants analysis of the unconscious social and cultural constraints upon it.

Before illustrating the clinical application of these concepts and hypotheses, I will locate them within a more general frame of reference for clinical work, using two paradigms each of which indicates the scope of my own version of a 'complete interpretation'.

Paradigm I: realms of clinical work in terms of time and space for patient and therapist

Although my clinical work and theoretical approach to psychoanalytical group therapy owe more to Foulkes and his colleagues than to Bion and his, especially in connection with the importance that I attach to the sociality of human nature, I always begin with Bion's (1961) remark in *Experience in Groups,* that the basic assumption group knows no time and knows no space,[6] which is as relevant to the boundaries of the psychoanalytical dyad as it is to therapeutic groups and to social systems of any kind. On the basis of this utterance, I would construct a paradigm of the realms of clinical work in terms of time and space for patient and therapist.

The dimension of time can be dichotomised into 'Now' and 'Then', and the dimension of space into 'Here' and 'There'. Thus, this paradigm consists of four cells : 'Here and Now', 'Here and Then', 'There and Now', and 'There and Then'.

		SPACE	
		HERE	THERE
TIME	NOW	1	2
	THEN	3	4

Paradigm One. Realms of Clinical Work. Time against Space, in terms of the preoccupations of patients and therapist

Communications between the analyst and the patient can be considered in terms of each of these four cells: Here and Now, Here and Then, There and Now and There and Then.

Cell One: Here and Now

The 'Here and Now' is denoted by a communication such as the patient saying, 'I do not want to lie on the couch, because I want to see your face', and the analyst responding 'You are frightened that if we take our eyes off each other, we will not exist for each other, and you will be alone and unprotected, and I will turn my mind elsewhere'. We have been taught to give special emphasis to the communications between analyst and patient within the 'Here and Now'. From the point of view of the ascendant paradigm in psychoanalysis, at least in London, we are taught that although traditionally the prudent analyst worked from surface to depth, that is, he went from where it is coolest to where it is hottest, it would be better to proceed as quickly as possible to where it is hottest; and it is asserted that it is hottest in the 'Here and Now', in the sense that affect is strongest within this particular juncture of time and space.

Although traditionally the transference was understood in terms of defence and resistance to insight, and as a source of interference with helpful reconstructive work, currently the 'transference' refers to the total relationship between analyst and patient, and not to an inappropriate repetition of past experience as a specific strand within this total relationship (Joseph, B. 1989). By definition, therefore, work within the transference is work within the 'Here and Now', and it is asserted that this should take precedence over all other elements of therapeutic work—and some would argue that this constitutes the entire scope of therapeutic work. In any case, the very nature of unconscious fantasy distorts the perception and introjection of objects in their 'true' state, and, therefore, personal history cannot be told with any degree of 'objectivity'. From the point of view of 'existential psychotherapy', we are taught that there is nothing available but the 'Here and Now', and it is inevitable that reconstruction will be based on retrospective projection. In other words, whether the relationship between patient and analyst should be understood entirely in terms of the transference, or whether entirely in terms of its existential reality, it is essential to work within the 'Here and Now'.

These points are both truisms and unnecessarily restrictive. They are as defensive in their own way as the original view to the effect that reconstruction is not only possible but curative in itself, based on the 'catharsis' and the 'Eureka!' theories of the value of discovering buried, historical, personal truths. Apart from the fact that it not always hotter in the 'Here and Now', the basic concept of the 'Here and Now' should not be confused with the idea of the 'a-historical present', which is based on the entirely untenable assumption that it is possible to have an a-historical situation comprised of individuals. It may be possible to have an a-historical situation comprised of 'organisms' in a limited biological sense of the term, but individuals and their situations are always in the 'historical present' by definition. In my view, the analysis of the transference is the primary task of therapeutic work; however, whereas the transference consists of much less than the total relationship between analyst and patient, the analysis of the transference must include a great deal more than merely the 'Here and Now'.

Cell Two: There and Now

The 'There and Now' is denoted by a communication such as the patient saying, 'My wife does not understand me, and is not really interested in my point of view', and the analyst responding, 'Perhaps she would understand more and be more interested in your point of view if you spoke to her as a wife and not as your business partner, who she seems to feel, you would prefer to spend your evenings with'. 'There and Now' refers to what is happening between the patient and his 'significant others', a wife or a partner, peers, or people who are at the social nodules in his interpersonal network. In many ways, this is the stuff of conscious material, but this is also where we meet the social unconscious.

Cell Three: Here and Then

The 'Here and Then' is denoted by a communication such as the exchange that I have quoted above, 'I do not want to lie on the couch...' followed by the response '...I will turn my mind elsewhere' but extended by the analyst's adding the sentence, '...as you felt when your mother read her book while she fed you'. The 'Here and Then' includes the work of reconstruction, in that traditionally we try to connect what is taking place in the 'Here and Now' with what has happened in the person's early life. We can go back and back and back, to the then and then and then. Therefore, the 'Here and Then' refers to the trajectory of the patient's interpersonal world, starting in the womb, if not before. From the point of view of the patient and the analyst, however, the treatment relationship, the entry of the analyst into the patient's life, is a recent event. Thus, I would include the treatment relationship within the 'Here and Then', because it refers to what happened between analyst and patient a 'moment before', and then the 'moment before that', and the 'moment before that' within the history of the treatment relationship. 'Yesterday' or even 'earlier in the session' is part of the 'Here and Then'.

Cell Four: There and Then

We all work in the 'Here and Now', and we try to connect these phenomena with the 'Here and Then' and the 'There and Now', and vice versa. For example, we try to help a patient understand that he is relating to us in the same way that he related to a parent at an earlier phase of life, and this is how, for example, he seems to relate to his wife or partner. These three cells constitute the three angles of the classical therapeutic triangle. However, I would like us now to consider a 'fourth angle', in effect to try to square the therapeutic triangle.

The 'There and Then' is denoted by a communication such as the patient saying, 'I feel that my mother could not concentrate on me', within the context of repeating his complaints that when he was a little boy during the War, his mother was always preoccupied with other matters and other people, always listening to the radio and making telephone calls to her mother, and the analyst responding, 'She may have been preoccupied with the news that her cousins were caught in the Warsaw Ghetto, and felt that she was lucky to be alive and to have you, as well as that she was very helpless and guilty about them'. The 'There and Then' refers to the patient's earlier experience of social facts within his broader social context, especially but not exclusively as mediated through his relationships within the 'Here and Then', such as his family and other early primary groups.

Let us consider another example. Members of that 'generation' born between 1945 and 1949 in countries involved in World War II are often helped by realising that they have in common a particular pattern of experience over which they had virtually no control. After the war there was an atmosphere of hope and optimism based on the conviction that the world had been made safe for democracy by husbands, fathers and men in general who were returning from battle. Yet, millions of children were then born into the new 'working class suburbs' in which they went from birth to 'latency' without having seen their fathers more than occasionally, perhaps on weekends. The decision to build so much marvellous housing did not take account of the fact that the lives of those who moved into these White suburbs of detached homes with gardens would be utterly and irrevocably changed, if not destroyed, because Father's work remained many miles away. Moreover, one part of the extended family moved, but other parts stayed put, thereby creating millions of isolated housewives without support from their mothers, sisters and friends, and without traditional shops and services. The changes in the society and culture that were brought about by the fulfilment of the necessary requirements for new cars and roads were of a magnitude comparable only to the introduction of the horse into the lives of the Plains Indians a few thousand years ago. Many members of the 60's generation of post-war baby boomers whose fathers were experienced as intrusive part-objects, because that is really what they tended to be, continue to experience males in authority in more or less the same way. At present it seems to be exceedingly difficult in many countries involved in World War II to maintain a connection between power and authority, clear boundaries of gender roles and a consensus about the nature of perversion and its normative status.

Although we are taught that in good clinical work we should avoid discussions of material that could be categorised as 'There and Then', because it is an attempt to escape from more pressing, immediate anxieties—a collusive defensive manoeuvre—I have come to disagree. The interpretation of the transference within the 'Here and Now' is not complete without reference to the 'There and Then'. Malan's (1979) notion of the 'therapeutic triangle' must be changed to the 'therapeutic square'. We must be able to help a patient put together the pieces of both his social and psychic communities. Of course, we should not try to make a complete interpretation all at once, but build it over a period of months, if not years.

Paradigm 2: Realms of clinical work in terms of patient's preoccupations with political and social phenomena, and of therapist's emphasis on internal or external reality.

How do we think about material located in the 'Now and There' and 'Then and There', in cells two and four of paradigm one? To be more precise : How do we think about this material in ways that are useful clinically, in ways that are likely to foster maturation on the part of our patients? In order to begin to answer these questions I would propose a second paradigm of realms of clinical work in terms of two dichotomies. The first is whether the patient is consciously preoccupied with political and social topics (for example, discourse about the conflict in what used to be called Yugoslavia or in the EU), or with apolitical and asocial topics (for example, discourse about what happened in the family, what the patient is feeling, the nature of his sexuality and so on). The second dichotomy is whether the therapist's interventions are derived from those theories, hypotheses, concepts and data that emphasise external social facts (for example, the structure of authority and power relationships within which the patient works and is unconsciously constrained) or internal psychic facts (such as the unconscious Oedipus complex). It is important to remember that in terms of the social unconscious a person may be as unaware of external social facts as he is of internal psychic facts.

This paradigm has four cells, in terms of whether the content of the patient's material is consciously political and social or apolitical and asocial, and whether the therapist's concerns emphasise the constraints of the patient's internal psychic world or those of his external social world.

		INTERNAL REALITIES	EXTERNAL REALITIES
		Therapist's intervention emphasize the constraints of:	
Patient's Preoccupations	ASOCIAL & APOLITICAL	1	2
	SOCIAL & POLITICAL	3	4

Paradigm Two. Realms of Clinical Work: preoccupations of the patient in terms of social and political phenomena against intervention by the therapist in terms of internal and external realities.

Communications between analyst and patient can be considered in terms of each of these four cells:

Cell One: The patient's material is consciously apolitical and asocial, and the analyst emphasises the patient's internal world.

This cell is denoted by a communication such as a patient's reporting a dream about being lost in a large house containing many rooms, wandering from room to room and becoming increasingly more frantically as he searches for his analyst. The analyst interprets in terms of the patient's search for a part of his father that will help him negotiate his independence from the influence of his mother's mind, if not from her very body, and, therefore, help him with his identification as an adult male. The analyst also interprets in terms of how these unconscious fantasies and infantile relationships are repeated within the transference. However, the analyst does not draw attention to such connotations of 'large house' as 'wealth', 'privilege' and 'social location'.

Cell Two: The patient's material is apolitical and asocial, and the analyst emphasises the patient's external world.

This cell is denoted by a communication such as a patient's talking about his relationship with his father when he was a boy, and how this is related to what he thinks and feels about his analyst in that very session, and the analyst's interpreting how the patient's relationship to the analyst is unconsciously affected by the structure of authority in the patient's work situation. Or, a patient's discussing her desirous cravings for a male child, and the analyst's helping her to understand that this is based not only on envy and its vicissitudes in connection with aspects of her very early relationship to her mother's body and subsequently to her relationship to her father and, perhaps, her brothers and their bodies, but also, and perhaps even primarily, on the social fact that in her society there has been limited opportunity for the experience of the expression of her power and mastery and creativity except through the use of her body and its products, and, therefore, that it is hardly surprising that she should wish to have control over a male child.

To help a patient understand that during the first few months of life the difficulties he had at the breast can be traced to difficulties that his mother had in feeding him, because she and her husband were constrained by a terrible recession, her husband was unemployed and felt humiliated and jealous of the new baby, and needed her attention and help almost as much as the patient did, is as liberating as, that his mother withdrew from him, because he was hateful towards her due to a surfeit of innate malign envy. In other words, the examination of envy and greed and the impulses to eat and to bite and to chew must be contextualised not only in terms of the body, which is obvious, but also in terms of the family, class and status groups of the society at a certain point in time.

Cell Three: The patient's material is consciously political and social, and the analyst emphasises the patient's internal world.

This cell is denoted by a communication such as a patient's referring to the systematic dismantling of the institutions of the Welfare State, and the analyst's interpreting in terms of the patient's anxiety about losing his mother's attentions when his brother was born, and about how this is repeated within the transference in connection with a forthcoming long weekend when his analyst will have to cancel Friday and Monday sessions.

Cell Four: The patient material is consciously political and social, and the analyst emphasises the patient's external world.

This cell is denoted by a communication such as an upwardly mobile patient's bemoaning his own greed and insatiability for status, and the analyst's interpreting his chronic dissatisfaction with the analysis in terms of: the unconscious effects of his multiple comparative reference groups on the nature of his ambition; the connection between his ambition and his personal, sexual and professional identities; the effects of his serial friendship groups on his inability to form and to anchor his normative expectations for stratification goals (Hopper 1981). This does not prevent the analyst from drawing attention to his patient's conflicting intrapsychic loyalties to his father and mother, and to his attempts to free himself from his collusive engulfment by his mother in the service of denigrating his father who was regarded as merely an uneducated manual worker.

From the point of view of traditional psychoanalysis, the interpretative work in Cells Two and Four is really very problematic, defensive and collusive. However, I believe that it is essential to include this perspective. It is equally defensive and collusive not to discuss social and political facts, and to avoid anxiety about them by turning to more familiar concerns and concepts. I believe that there are ways of creating space for the discussion of social reality and political issues without taking sides, and without advocating particular solutions. An important case in point is that many Shoah survivors had very long analyses in which their Shoah experiences were neglected (Simon 1992).

Clinical illustrations of the unconscious constraints of social and cultural facts in group analysis.

I will now illustrate work in the second and fourth cells of the two paradigms presented above—that is, in the 'There and Now' and 'There and Then', the interpretation of intra-psychic processes and conflicts in terms of inter-personal processes that reflect the constraints of past and present social and cultural facts. The concepts of the social unconscious and of equivalence inform my approach. Again, I usually work within the first and third cells of these two paradigms, that is, in the 'Here and Now' and in the 'Here and Then'. These different sources of explanation of the transference and counter-transference are not mutually exclusive. On the contrary.

Clinical illustration (i)

The following clinical vignette is based on several sessions from one of my twice-weekly Groups.

A forty year old woman, who was in the group for about fifteen years, and who I know got a lot from it, eventually made a good relationship with a man, had a baby and left the Group. As one of the first patients in the Group, she had become central to it. None of the women could find a way to take her place. They were so competitive with one another as to who might take her place that they were immobilised. For a while after she left, we were all bereft, but also pleased for her. Slowly the Group mourned the loss. However, they insisted that I continued to be bereft. I felt that this was not really true. I was under some pressure to introduce a 'replacement' patient, who was referred to me by a senior psychoanalyst colleague who had taken ill and to whom I felt loyal and indebted. The patient needed help, and I wanted to be of help, and to demonstrate how helpful my Group could be. Therefore, about three months after she left, but before I was convinced that the Group was ready for her, I introduced a new female member. She was an extremely talented, distinguished neurologist. She was also tall, slender and blonde with very big eyes. She was a great threat to the women in the Group, although they expressed their shame at having such feelings, especially given their own achievements as well as their ideology concerning such competition.

One evening an equally distinguished male director of clinical work at a Teaching Hospital in London, who was lean and handsome but youthful in appearance, told the Group that he had a problem. Thanks to the help he had received from the Group, he could no longer engage in certain sadistic and humiliating sexual behaviour with his wife, with whom he worked, and found that instead he was compelled to go to prostitutes. On the way home from the Group he had to pick up a street prostitute, return to her room, almost always in a run-down hotel, and after attempting to have a discussion with her about politics and her own personal life history, make her take off her clothes, which he would denigrate as 'common' and 'vulgar', and then spank her. He traced this change as occurring a few weeks after the new woman had come into the Group.

While he was speaking, I began to think about how 'split' the new female member seemed to be, and how unresponsive she was to the men in the Group, yet how involved she was with me, and, necessarily, I with her, although no words were spoken between us. While my mind was moving towards the obvious connection between the prostitute and the new female member, I also began to think about myself and the prostitute from the point of view of a type of narcissistic identification, and how this might be the basis for certain kinds of perverse behaviour. I then began to connect perversions and perverse impulses with an inability and refusal to mourn and with the fear of annihilation, and to think about competition among the women and the difficulty men have in competing with 'sisters' for parental attention, because this requires an acceptance of their own femininity and vulnerability, and that—in effect—life is easier for women. The point was that I had introduced into the Group an 'object' rather than a person, in the sense that it must have felt that I regarded one person as the same as another, if the loss of a person could be managed by my simply bringing in another person, and that the loss of the breast could be managed by substituting a pacifier—or a 'dummy', as it is called in the UK, a word that not only rhymes with 'mummy' (meaning both 'mom' and a dead Egyptian), but also a mannequin or a ventriloquist's puppet.

My thoughts were interrupted when one woman began to talk with a sense of urgency about her father who seemed to be having what might be described as a depressive breakdown as he approached 70 years of age. However, she wondered if he had Alzheimers Disease (a diagnosis that she, as an accountant, was, perhaps, not qualified to make). She was very sad about this, and wondered what she could do to be of help. A member of the Group who was a psychiatrist said rather abruptly, 'He needs a psychiatrist.' She ignored him completely, and went on to say something like, 'Oh! I wish Earl would see him. He needs somebody like Earl, somebody who is very nice, not like my mother, sisters, cousins and me who never let him finish a sentence. He needs somebody who will listen...' Suddenly the psychiatrist slammed his fist down on the chair, and said, 'He needs a psychiatrist.' He scared the hell out of us. She looked at him, looked at me and went on talking. A few minutes later she turned to him again and said, 'What did you say?' He said, 'It's too fucking late. It's too fucking late, you bitch. I spoke. I said "He needs a psychiatrist", but now I am not going to explain what I meant.' Although the psychiatrist was absolutely correct that her father needed a psychiatrist, a Black social worker said, 'Look, you see what I have to cope with. You see what I have to cope with. You see how these psychiatrists behave'. It went on like that. We did not have a chance to focus on this issue.

I found myself continuing to think about the 'scene' before this rather dramatic exchange took place. I was wondering about the need for a vulnerable, sad male to be rescued from an engulfing, manipulating female, and about how the unconscious themes of the Group had remained more or less constant despite the apparent variety of more conscious, secondary process themes of the manifest content of their communications. I shifted to wondering if the woman whose father had become ill might be expressing for the whole Group its feeling that in my silence and perhaps inappropriate introduction of the new member into the Group I had become ill. However, these thoughts remained private. The Group were talking so much and so furiously! I could not have got a word in edgeways unless I had wished to take over the Group. I was able to take a more silent and receptive role than usual— to lead from behind, so to say—while at the same time waiting to see where the Group would take me. As far as I know the Group did not experience my silence as a withdrawal but as 'active and attentive' listening.

Over a period of a couple of weeks the Group was a veritable Tower of Babel. Although an outsider might have thought that it was falling apart, I did not regard the Group as being in a state of 'disarray' (Turquet 1975), because there is a sense in which only a fairly cohesive social system can contain the expression of such conflicting opinions. This particular Group has a disproportionate number of members from the helping professions—as do most twice-weekly groups recognised as suitable for candidates at the Institute of Group Analysis. However, the four members of the Group who were not members of the helping professions, two women and two men, felt left out of the sub-group of professionals, and felt very envious of them. A man said, 'Who the fucking hell are all of you so-called "professionals", telling us how to live our lives? None of you works for a living. You don't actually make anything. You don't manufacture anything'. Two women agreed that having escaped from receiving so much formal education, they had lived more interesting lives, and they knew more about feelings and relationships than the female professionals ever would. The Group became preoccupied with questions such as: Who had I been fucking? Who was the mother of this new baby? This was the group's language, not mine, although for the most part I do use their vernacular. Also, over the years, various colleagues have been named as the mothers of my new patients, depending on the publicity such colleagues may be having at the time, and depending on their fields of interest—for example, trauma, female perversions, gender issues, and the like—and any new patient is assumed to have the problems associated with the colleague's special interest. There was complete 'chaos'. This was not a mere 'squabble'. The passions were very strong.

I could have intervened in various ways, and one way need not necessarily have excluded another. There is no such thing as a right or a wrong interpretation on the part of a Conductor of a Group who is experiencing such material. However, I was moving towards making an interpretation that I hoped, based on an understanding of the psychological context of the transference, would elucidate the situation. We had lost a soft, feminine woman, who also exemplified the best work that the Group could do. We were in mourning, but could not acknowledge it. I may have been more concerned with my very ill colleague than with the patient who left, and they may have been more concerned with their perceived loss of my involvement with them, perhaps with a degree of accuracy. While the members of the Group were projecting into me their own inability and refusal to mourn, they were themselves retreating into paranoid-schizoid modes of experience. In response to their experience of failed dependency as a consequence of my bringing a new woman into the Group before they were really ready, they were regressing further into a shared fear of annihilation. At the intrapsychic level this fear was experienced as fission and fragmentation and, at the level of group process, as aggregation, one of the bi-polar forms of incohesion, including sub-grouping. The members of the helping professions were fighting one another for who would be on top of the pile, and the non-professionals were wrestling for social dominance and for control over access to me and the 'objects' for whom I stood. However, both professionals and non-professionals were united in their hatred of the new, successful, professional woman, who was perceived as both an unyielding and intrusive foreign object, and as very needy and vulnerable. She 'carried' split-off parts of me and of themselves, and, therefore, she was regarded as interfering with their perfect 'communion' with the Group as a whole and with me. This process of scapegoating was a consequence of projecting unwanted parts of the whole Group into one particular member, and was based on shared experiences of encapsulated trauma, which involved similar experiences in the early lives of several of the members of the Group. Various members of the Group were leading the processes of aggregation—for example, the man who expressed his perverse impulses and crustacean defences.[7]

In fact, I did not intervene. Instead, the Group itself began to try very hard to understand the meanings of all this in terms of what I have called the 'Here and Now' and the 'Here and Then', more or less in a traditional manner. They demonstrated considerable maturity in their ability to contain their psychotic anxieties and in their willingness and ability to understand how they had been engaging in defensive and protective manoeuvrings in order to avoid the experience of the pain associated with such states of mind. However, I felt that their insights were not authentic, that is, they were correct but without appropriate affect. They were too 'intellectual'. They were based on an 'imitative identification' (Gaddini 1992) with me, involving imitation without internalisation, suggesting an underlying rage and anxiety about loss and separation from me.

While I was contemplating all this, a woman, who is not a member of the helping professions, intervened quietly and tentatively with a kind of interpretative question. She wondered aloud if the Group was worried about what had been happening in the National Health Service, and about the social unrest that we had been reading about all over Europe in connection with the 'Maastricht Treaty'. The Group became silent and thoughtful. I thought to myself that the only thing wrong with this interpretation was that I had not formulated it myself, which was, of course, one of its best features! Various members of the Group acknowledged the validity and pertinence of this interpretation. They expressed their concerns about being helpless and powerless in response to various social and political problems in Britain and in Europe generally, problems that have been expressed in conflict once again between Blacks and Whites, Jews and non-Jews, and the native born and immigrants. Within the National Health Service and other institutions of the withering Welfare State, such problems have been expressed between medical and non-medical hospital staff generally, especially between psychiatrists and non-medical managers in hospitals, I suppose because nowadays the demarcations in their skills are less clear-cut, and their respective positions are characterised by status incongruence (Hopper 1981). So many non-medical managers are upwardly mobile and Black, and so many psychiatrists are neither. For several weeks the Group was pre-occupied with these issues and their anxiety about them. They attempted to become more aware of the unconscious constraints of current social and political developments. The Group even talked about football hooliganism, and had some very interesting things to say about it!

To summarise: The Group shared a fear of annihilation, and evinced processes of aggregation, including sub-grouping. However, their collective and individual transference material in the 'Here and Now' was connected to social constraints in the 'There and Now'. The effects of 'Maastricht' were as unconscious as the effects of various aspects of their experience as infants and children. This was not a matter of the social 'pre-conscious', a simple matter of a lack of awareness of social turmoil in their current society and region of the world. I would argue that the Group recreated a situation that was 'equivalent' to what was happening within their wider social context, precisely because they were unconscious of their feelings of helplessness and powerlessness, and of their feeling confused by social and cultural changes, which they did not understand. Slowly, the Group made connections between the material of the 'Here and Now' and 'There and Now' to what had happened in Europe when most of them were either children or not yet born, or, in other words, to social facts and forces in the 'There and Then'. This was not a defensive respite from the powerful feelings of anxiety about the aggression that had occurred. Nor was it an attempt by the woman whose father had become ill to be helpful to me, at least not primarily. Nor was it an attempt by the Group to avoid mourning the lost female member—at least not primarily. It was an attempt to mourn losses associated with World War II and the subsequent demise of the United Kingdom politically, socially and economically, and to work through anxieties associated with the loss of social order and a sense that the nation could sustain an attitude of hopeful optimism. The Group may even have been working with the unconscious anxieties and preoccupations of their parents. Such issues cannot be reduced to more personal idiosyncratic concerns, which is not to suggest that they are not completely intertwined with more contextual concerns. In fact, I was reminded of Weber's (1947) concepts of group-charisma and group-disgrace, and their association with pride and shame. I emphasised the unconscious constraints of social facts and forces in the 'There and Then' and 'There and Now', because to have interpreted their anxieties and perceptions of my failures and inadequacies primarily as a repetition of their more personal experiences of failed dependency during infancy and childhood within the 'Here and Then', would have been collusive with and defensive against the anxieties of their current social and political situations. However, never to concentrate on the 'Here and Then', or even to give too little emphasis to it, would be equally collusive with and defensive against other anxieties. In fact, many months later, when another female patient left the Group and the Group began to evince processes that were similar to the ones that I have described, the interpretative work was directed almost entirely to the 'Here and Then'.

Clinical illustration (ii)

The following clinical vignette is based on several sessions from another of my twice-weekly Groups. It also illustrates the constraints of social facts and social forces within the 'There and Now', closely connected with events within the 'There and Then'.

The sessions occurred in July 1982, a few weeks before the summer break, when my Groups were meeting in the Group Analytic Practice, near Baker Street Tube Station, not far from Regent's Park, in Central London. Seven or eight Groups were meeting at the same time, from 6 p.m. -7.30 p.m. Before my Groups began I usually had coffee with colleagues in a small room across the corridor from the room in which my Group met. I noticed that people were a bit early, which usually indicates some anxiety. As far as I knew the Group was not going through a difficult period, yet I sensed that they had come early because they wanted the safety of the Group room and the Group situation.

I entered the room promptly at 6 p.m. The Group began with an inordinately long silence. This is not common in my Groups, although when it does happen it is never without meaning, although not always the same meaning. In any case, this silence felt inconsistent with what I had experienced in the previous few sessions. When the silence was broken, there was a great deal of space between words and sentences. People would speak, lapse into silence and start again. It was hard for me to understand their communication, because the sentences were split up and fragmented, the clauses of sentences were not connected in a meaningful way—what Britton (1994) calls the 'language of either/and'—people spoke slowly, using non-sequiturs. There was an absence of eye contact. The members of the Group might have been attempting to imitate or caricature a type of group analyst who does not say very much, keeps his body very still, his arms close to his body or folded, his legs crossed at the ankles, looking down at the table.

Suddenly we became aware of a symphony of tummy rumbles (borygmie). One person's stomach began to rumble, another's made a similar but louder noise, a third's replied in a higher pitch. My own stomach began to thunder. Amidst laughter, this continued for what seemed to be ages, but must have been at most a couple of minutes. These noises continued from time to time during the rest of the Group.

This was a mature Group in which the current members had a lot of experience of one another. They began to say that they were hungry and angry. Someone suggested the Group was anticipating being separated from me and from one another during the forthcoming holiday. Another said, 'Clearly, we are beginning to take in too much air as Mummy pushes us away, and we have a little indigestion'. There is nothing wrong with this type of interpretation, of course, apposite as it is for separation anxiety before holidays. Moreover, we were aware that separation anxiety is very closely associated with fear of annihilation, and, therefore, when it is actually experienced it is very painful. However, I felt that the Group's own interpretation was an attempt to shelter us from something explosive, rather than an exploration of the nature of their hidden feelings. I felt that there was some anxiety about separation and the withdrawal of protection, some personal fission and fragmentation and a vague sense of protective alienation as a response to this kind of anxiety. And, therefore, there was low cohesion as manifest in aggregation, expressed primarily in non-verbal communications, such as gaze avoidance, and in massification, in which the search for safety is expressed in fusion and confusion within the Group, and in the wish, if not compulsion, to communicate in silence— in this case undermined by their interpersonal borygmie. I realised that although I could sense the anxiety and describe the interpersonal defences, I did not really know why they were so anxious. Therefore, in response to their 'interpretations', I said, 'This does not feel right to me'. After a moment's silence, I continued, 'I wonder if we feel safe enough to find out more about this, and if not, why not?'

The Group lapsed into a thoughtful silence which seemed to go on forever. Finally a woman said, 'Do you know ... there's just been an explosion. A bomb has just gone off at the bandstand in Regent's Park

where the Queen's Military Band (The Royal Green Jackets) was playing'. The bandstand was less than 1,000 yards from where we were sitting. In fact many of us in the flat had heard the explosion while we
were drinking coffee before the Groups started. It sounded like a big
lorry had backfired. None of us had said a word about it. We had continued to drink our coffee. It could be said that this was a denial, given
the number of explosions that had occurred in London during the preceding week. Of the nine members of the Group, four said that they
had come from Baker Street tube station and had heard the explosion;
three had come individually through the park, and each had seen
human limbs on the grass, many dead bodies, fire-engines and police-
cars speeding through the area, and a lot of blood. We were all
shocked, but especially those of us who had witnessed this terrible
event. Three of us who had not, including myself, felt rather left out.
We continued to discuss this horrifying experience, and to offer some
comfort to one another, until the Group stopped.

At the next session, forty-eight hours later, a woman of Irish and
Welsh background who was upwardly mobile from the 'working class'
and whose family, especially her father, were highly politicised, started by talking about her social origins. Not once during her previous
four and a half years in the Group had she been able to do this. ('Class'
remains so important, but is rarely discussed. England still has a high
degree of status rigidity, and people are ashamed of having lowly
social origins. It is easier to learn about a patient's most secret, bizarre
masturbation fantasies than about what his father did for a living.) She
went on to talk about her violent feelings against the middle class
women in the Group, who she felt did not accept her despite the fact
that she had gone to university, had done very well and was a qualified social-worker.

She was interrupted by a homosexual psychiatrist from abroad. He
expressed his strong desire to bomb the Institute of Group Analysis,
because he believed that homosexuals were not accepted for training.
The patient assumed that he would not be accepted, and he quoted an
early book by Foulkes to the effect that homosexuality should be a criterion for exclusion from training. He cried, and he talked about his
sadistic impulses, not only towards me, but also towards the entire
establishment in which the Group was embedded. This was very much
to his benefit, because we were able to shift the issue and his feelings
about it from the realm of secrecy to one of privacy, and he was able to
begin to test the reality of his concern.

I would suggest that this development in the Group would not have occurred if we had concentrated on separation anxiety in terms of psychotic anxieties originating within the first few months of life, and in terms of a repetition of these anxieties in response to the impending holiday break. In fact, it would have produced 'false self' protections supporting the encapsulation of traumatic experience, as seen in the Group's secrecy and attacks on the coherency of their mother tongue. Perhaps the experience would have been discussed eventually, after we had read the newspapers and watched TV reports, but by then the scarring would have begun. We would never have been able to share the feelings of being right in the middle of such explosive material, and to help one another make sense of this experience.

It does not take a great deal of intelligence and theoretical acumen for analysts to say, 'This does not feel right to me'. It does take a sense of authenticity and a willingness to think 'laterally' or 'horizontally' without feeling that interest in the social context is defensive or superficial. In fact, it may be worth thinking about 'horizontal depth'.

I discussed the effects of this terrible, calamitous event with my colleagues who were conducting Groups in the other rooms in the Practice. I learned that my Group was the only one who brought up this material. All the other groups concentrated on anxieties about the impending holiday, with the exception of one in which there had been a great deal of laughter, and the particular therapist felt that such laughter expressed relief and happy anticipation at having a few weeks without the obligations of therapy, and that this was not a manic defence against depressive anxiety. One of my colleagues assured me that his Group were able to stay 'right with their despairing feelings' about the summer break, and that they had not needed to escape into a discussion of 'distant' events.

Clinical illustrations of the maturation of individuals in group analysis

In group analysis and in all forms of group psychotherapy it is necessary to keep in mind the welfare and development of each individual member of the Group. I would like to focus on certain individuals in the two Groups presented. This requires a model of maturity. A model of maturity is implied in my theory of the unconscious effects of social and cultural constraints. This model is based on modifications to the model of 'genital maturity' in traditional psychoanalysis. Genital maturity emphasises the capacity to procreate, to love and to relate to other people within the context of a biologically based phase of development denoted by a 'balanced' super-ego, indicating a satisfactory resolution of the Oedipus complex (Pollack & Ross 1988). This rather simplified version of the classical model has many precursors within Western and other traditions of thought and therapy (Rustomjee 1993), and many modifications to it have been suggested by both psychoanalysts and others in the field of human development. For example, many (Brown 1961) have argued that social relationships require more emphasis, because they are the basis of the development of intrapsychic object relations, rather than the other way around. The idea that social and cultural patterns of love and love relationships establish situations that people must negotiate in order to mature, is not central to psychoanalytical thought. Nor is the idea that the Oedipus complex is resolved in terms of socially structured domestic authority and power, and also in terms of the normative basis of passivity and activity, within the context of the total system of stratification of the wider society (Malinowski 1937). For example, the normal Oedipus complex in the Southern Italian rural family is not normal for a Northern Italian industrial family (Parsons 1957); what is normal in Tel Aviv is not normal for certain kibbutzim (Bettleheim 1969); and, to flog a dead horse, what is normal in Rye, New York, is not normal in University City, Missouri, in Taiwan or Hampstead or Hampstead Garden Suburb. The 'Oedipus complex' is an 'ideal type' for purposes of illustration and theory building. Clinical work requires specific contextualisation, because abnormality can only be understood in terms of normality, which is always defined in terms of the social and cultural context (Joseph, E. 1982).

Another modification of the classical model of maturity is that maturity involves the willingness and ability to work. Of course, to 'work' has many meanings: eating and doing what is necessary in order to eat; defecating in order to avoid indigestion as well as to repay Mother and to give her presents, which may be based on a bargain that has been struck unconsciously in terms of the exchange value of milk and faeces, which itself may be based on the value that Mother has placed on her feeding and that Baby has put on the work involved in good sucking. However, male and female parental power and influence are based on being able to fulfil an occupational role and to derive both primary and secondary pleasures from it. In fact, the identity of an adult is governed by his location within the 'world of work', as is the anticipatory identity of a child, and certainly, an adolescent. Work occurs in occupational roles that are part of a specific system of economic, status and political stratification that implies *specific* authority and power structures and a *status quo*, which says more than that occupational roles exist in complex organisations with authority structures (Richards 1948).

It is necessary to mention – at least—the work of Maslow (1954) and many others on the stages of life from birth (if not conception) to death, with particular emphasis on maturation throughout the life cycle. Erikson (1959) gave special emphasis to the importance of social and cultural constraints for the continuing development of the ego. Lacan (1977) stressed that maturation is never complete, in that, virtually by definition, it is impossible to fulfil the aphorism that where id was, there shall ego be. Many of these ideas have been discussed in connection with the issue of termination in psychoanalysis (Pedder 1988). The 'Kleinian development' (Spillius 1988) implies that 'maturation' and 'termination' be reconsidered more fundamentally in terms of the stability of depressive position functioning, the security of the internal good object and the capacity to feel gratitude. In emphasising the constraints of parental character rather than instincts, the interpersonalists have taken up similar themes in their polemic against both classical Freudian and classical Kleinian schools, but are wary of going beyond the confines of the bi-personal field (Mitchell 1994).

There is, however, yet another theme in the critique of the traditional model of psychological maturity. It was first raised by Erich Fromm (1963) in a little known paper called 'The Revolutionary Character'. I rather like the title, but I can see that some people might be bothered by the connotations of 'revolution', and by the even more disturbing fact that the book in which it was published was entitled *The Dogma of Christ*. Fromm writes:

> 'The Revolutionary Character' is someone who is identified with humanity, and therefore transcends the narrow limits of his own society and who is able therefore to criticise his or any other society. He is not caught in the parochial culture in which he happens to be born, which is nothing but an accident of time and geography. He is able to look at his environment with the open eyes of a man who is awake and who finds the criteria of judging the accidental and that which is not accidental according to the norms which are in and for the human race. (Fromm 1963: 111)

By 'revolutionary character' Fromm really means 'the mature person', rather than a character type or character disorder. He is suggesting a stage of development in which a person can be sufficiently detached to be able to take his social circumstances as problematic, but sufficiently involved to be able to identify with them and to be affected by them and, in turn, to be willing to affect them. To reach a point whereby one can be compassionate, sympathetic and empathetic, yet sufficiently detached to take a situation as problematic, is really a great psychological achievement. An infant cannot do this. Human beings must *strive* to achieve a sense of balance between involvement and detachment, and such 'balance' indicates that a certain kind of maturity has been reached. Fromm would say: that which is not accidental is that which is 'rational', or at least which can be explained rationally, according to the laws of science or even of social science. The mature person is one who has been able to transcend the limits of his own particular background, and, therefore, to reflect upon his circumstances, to take them as problematic and to locate them within their historical and contemporary social context. He is able and willing to think about his own psychic life and that of others, his own inter-personal community and that of others, and about his own identity and that of others (Fonagy 1989). He will be aware of the relativity of social and personal ethics, even if ignorant of the language needed to discuss it; and he will have considered the traditional free-will/determinism problem, even if he has never learned that the idea that we must try not only to understand reality but also to change it, was a Marxist, revolutionary idea. The revolutionary character will be able and willing to take the risks involved in attempting to change the very social circumstances within which he has come to be able to think, to make judgements, to act and to be creative.

An essential feature of increased 'psychic muscle' is the ability to withstand and even to make creative use of social resistance to 'revolutionary' action. The revolutionary character must be able to make the social unconscious conscious, which compliments the traditional idea that maturity requires the substitution of ego for id. Obviously, attacks on authority are not always an expression of unresolved oedipal struggles, just as attempts by those in authority to maintain the *status quo* are not always an expression of their sense of responsibility and probity.

We could include this idea of the revolutionary character within 'genital maturity', but it seems to me that the concept of a revolutionary character subsumes the concept of genital maturity. This is the essence of de Mare's (1991) concept of citizenship: 'maturity' implies the willingness and the ability to take the roles associated with the status of 'citizen'. Of course, this is also a group phenomenon in that people cannot take such roles if they have not also ensured that citizenship is available, which is a political process.[8] The willingness and ability to take the roles of citizenship and to ensure that such roles exist within a democratic society can be facilitated through what Foulkes (1957) termed 'ego training in action'.

I will now illustrate the clinical relevance of these ideas by describing certain aspects of the behaviour and feelings of three members of the Groups presented above. In the first Group, the man who expressed so poignantly his frustrations arising from his work with colleagues who were members of the medical profession, became more active in the politics of his profession and in his hospital. He initiated a new committee consisting of both medical and non-medical personnel, and it seemed that this committee would do some good work in alleviating the anxious concerns that were interfering with the clinical work in his particular Department. This man was an immigrant. He became more proficient in understanding other sub-cultures as well as his own, because he recognised that his own 'world view' (Serrano 1990) was problematic, that is, based on a number of dimensions of his life experience which were not shared by others. It was then possible for him to adopt the folk ways and styles of his colleagues and the new culture within which his work roles and life in general were embedded. In his political activities within his hospital he conducted himself with determination and resolve, but also with dignity and self control, despite the usual pressures put upon him by his opponents, especially those in authority.

Another personal development can be seen in the self-image and actions of the woman who was so concerned about the welfare of her father. She was able to take the necessary and appropriate steps to arrange proper care for him, which included both medical and non-medical intervention, and in general was able to help her entire family respond constructively to this domestic catastrophe. She acknowledged that when she thought about her vulnerable father, she thought about him as her 'Jewish father', and connected this image with her inability to make relationships with Jewish men, whom she felt were 'weak' and 'feminine'. This caused her some sense of confusion because she wanted to please herself as well as her parents who wanted her to marry a Jew. She also acknowledged that she thought of herself as a Jewish boy or specifically as a Jewish son who could feel herself to be a woman only in relationship to Christian men. Eventually she may recognise her desire to be mothered by the women whom she perceives to be behind the men in her life, but in the meantime she is in the process of discovering that it is possible to negotiate her own gender identity, although for reasons of both biology and of sociology, not entirely as she pleases.

A third personal development, or lack of it, is manifest, as discussed in the second vignette, in the case of the homosexual psychiatrist from abroad who wished to become a group analyst. He became convinced that homosexuality was a counter-indication for acceptance for training by the Institute despite assurances and evidence to the contrary. Rather than confront the relevant committees and their perceived policies, he renounced his aspirations. He was unable to make use of the views offered by the other members of the Group and myself that not only was he frightened to be judged and assessed by authorities whom he respected, but he was also terrified to learn more about how he used his homosexuality to defend against psychotic anxieties, and to express his sado-masochistic desires. Following a prolonged period of hatred of another male candidate, he left the Group at short notice. I was unable to communicate to him in a meaningful way that he was repeating his hatred of his 'chosen' little brother, and his conviction that I preferred his brother to him, as would the Institute. I would regard this as an example of a therapeutic 'failure'—mine, and his.

These data illustrate how, by making it possible for Groups to work in the second and fourth cells of the two paradigms that I have described, people were able to take some steps towards becoming what Fromm called a 'revolutionary character'. They became more ready to participate as citizens, and they developed their sense that they could make history as well as be made by it.

Afterthoughts

Rather than draw conclusions in the usual sense, I would emphasise two of the sub-texts of my thesis. The open and honest discussion of traumatic events and their consequences should not be confined to situations that have been defined as 'therapy'. In democratic societies this always presents a dilemma: if space is not provided for working through traumatic events, they will never be worked through; and if space is provided, those in power will have to deal with threats to their authority. Unresolved, this dilemma usually stops those in authority from providing the space for full discussion, and gives rise to situations that require the exercise of managerial power over and over again, because traumatic events tend to be repeated over and over again, not only in societies but also in organisations of various kinds ranging from large industrial firms to child guidance clinics. I am reminded of Winnicott's statement that people in psychoanalytical treatment often get worse before they get better, the clinical observation that very depressed patients often commit suicide just after their depression starts to lift, and the sociological insight that revolutions occur just after there have been dramatic improvements in the standards of living of deprived sections of the population, especially in the lower middle classes. I would prefer to work with such possibilities than to suffer the repetition of catastrophes.

It may not be possible for psychotherapy to help break these vicious circles. I do not suggest that if we could just talk in therapy groups about, for example, the situation in Northern Ireland, terrorism would stop and peace would erupt. However, it must be acknowledged that the study of the social unconscious is neglected in the training of group analysts, and is utterly ignored in the training of psychoanalysts (Hopper 1985). Unless candidates are encouraged to think in these terms, and at least to reflect upon the key debates in the development of psychoanalysis and all forms of group psychotherapy, they can hardly be expected to be sensitive to the questions and problems that I have described. Our training programmes reflect the unconscious constraints of social, cultural and political aspects of our profession and of the societies in which it functions. In societies with a high degree of status rigidity and with education systems characterised by premature specialisation in either the natural sciences or the 'Arts', the social sciences are defined as peripheral to 'knowledge', in parallel with categories of people whose qualifications are defined as 'inferior' and 'marginal'. Selection processes in these societies are based on theories of intelligence and mobility that emphasise the importance of the innate as opposed to the 'environmental', and such processes are repeated in later professional training. However, in all societies physicians are especially at risk. Immigrants and refugees, who may include the socially and geographically mobile, find it easier to learn about social facts and social forces, and to do the intellectual and emotional work that is required in order to explore the trans-cultural aspects of personal identity. Nonetheless, marginality can generate a search for a professional identity that overrides social and cultural diversity and dislocation (Budd & Hopper 1992). Perhaps this is one of the reasons why professional training in psychotherapy is characterised by an unacceptable degree of religiosity.

It is time to consider the prevailing and ascendant definitions of the boundaries of psychoanalysis and group analysis, with their implications for the structure of training programmes and patterns of professional identities and affiliations. It is possible to improve our system of professional training, but not if we continue to deny the importance of the social unconscious in both our theories and our clinical work. The Kleinian aphorism may be correct that when it comes to helping patients understand how they are constrained by external social and political events, analysts are no better than any other Tom, Dick or Harriet, but I would argue that they should be, and that some of the social sciences should be an obligatory part of their training, at least as much — if not more — than the study of biology and physiology. The irony in Freud's aside to Jones 'Out of this world we will not fall', was misplaced. He might just as well have said 'Out of our bodies we will not fall'. Actually, both points of view are essential.

Notes

[1] This is an edited version of a paper with the same title, published in *Group* (Hopper 1996a). A previous and less developed version was published as 'Il tempo del cambiamento', in F. di Maria and G. Lavanco (eds.), *Nel Nome Del Gruppo* (Hopper 1994). Two versions have also appeared in German (Hopper 1995, 1996b). This work has benefited from discussions with A. Aguirregabiria, D. Brown, B. Elliot, H. Reijzer, and D. & J. Scharff.

[2] A deeper view of groups is inseparable from a wider view of groups, and a psychoanalytical view of persons is inseparable from a sociological one, which is why I am both a psychoanalyst and group analyst, whether I am working with one person, a couch and a chair, or with several people, a table and a collection of chairs. In making this point I am emphasizing my view that in the beginning there is no such thing as an infant but only an infant/mother couple within a social context: two bodies, one mind. The mind is not the same as the brain; although the mind cannot be touched, it is 'real'. An ego of adaptation precedes an ego of agency, which is emergent, and based on social interactions mediated through communications. As a complement to 'body-ego' we need 'society-ego' or 'other-ego', which is more than merely 'self-object', a notion that is not free from its origins in the classical theory of primary narcissism. The infant starts life in a state of 'unintegration', which implies that individuation occurs out of the infant/mother couple as the society, often through the voice of the father, impinges upon it; 'disintegration' follows trauma, especially a break in the early infant/mother couple. Social impinge-

ment is not only a matter of external constraint, but also one of creative facilitation and enablement. Psychic facts are preceded by both social and organic facts. The first psychic act is not a projection of the anxiety inherent in the putative 'death instinct', and the first emotion is not innate, malign envy; psychic life begins with processes of internalization.

3 The tradition of Marxist thought is now so politicized that we forget how much we are indebted to it for our understanding of such topics as alienation and the sociality of human nature, and for attempts to integrate 'system' and 'action' perspectives. My own appreciation of the concept has been influenced by the work of American sociologists such as Merton, Reisman, Gerth and Mills, and of those American anthropologists who developed the field of 'culture and personality' (Le Vine 1973). Of special interest is 'A Memoir of my Father' by Bendix (1966), an entirely overlooked study of the personification of social forces within the traditions of Frankfurt Sociology. Winnicott (1965) was searching for the concept when he introduced the notion of 'environmental mother', as was Kernberg (1993) in his recent studies of shared super-ego functions within the couple. Puget (1989), Kaes (1979) and Rouchy (1987) are each attempting to elucidate the concept of the social unconscious, as illustrated most recently by Le Roy (1994). A number of novelists and dramatists have demonstrated their understanding of the social unconscious, as exemplified by *Sense and Sensibility* by Jane Austen (1995), *Portnoy's Complaint* by Phillip Roth (1995) and *Miss Julie* by Strindberg (1992), not to mention Shakespeare in virtually every play he wrote.

4 'Social unconscious', 'shared unconscious' and 'cultural unconscious' are reminiscent of the past debates between American and British anthropologists about the differences between what used to be called American 'cultural' anthropology and British 'social' anthropology. It was said that American social scientists were somehow unable to work with problems of social constraints and power structures, were more interested in problems of personal adjustment and adaptation of individuals to their circumstances, and were unable to recognize that culture develops both within and in response to social and political arrangements, which are themselves not made in heaven. Of course, British anthropologists were only able to make these claims because they focused their attention on tribal societies rather than on Britain itself.

5 In one way or another equivalence has been studied by many in our own and in adjacent fields. Especially pertinent are the studies of social dreaming by Lawrence (1991), and of the social concerns of groups by Khaleelee and Miller (1985). So, too, is the novel *Mr Sammler's Planet* by Bellow (1970). Moreno's (1959) discussions of synchronicitous events in terms of inter-subjectivity are helpful. Jung (1951) was attempting to discuss equivalence when he discussed 'synchronicity', but he became preoccupied with the mystical connections between co-incidental events. In this tradition, the 'alternative scientist' Sheldrake (1987) describes in terms of 'morphic resonance' what he postulates to be the increased rate at which certain events occur (or recur) following the incidence of a prototype event.

6 This aphorism implies that our interventions will always be political actions that give value to some phenomena and devalue others, and will always reflect our own location within an infinite field of time and space, of which it is impossible

ever to be fully conscious, although this is not to suggest that we are free from the obligation to try. It is disciplined self-reflection upon this matter by which the professional is distinguished from the amateur, no matter how talented and well-meaning the latter may be.

7 I have discussed elsewhere (Hopper 1989a, 1989b, 1991a, 1991b, 1993, 1997) my ideas about encapsulation in groups and its basis in processes of aggregation and massification as bi-polar forms of low social cohesion. This is a fourth basic assumption (Hopper 1997) in the unconscious life of groups and group-like social systems, as manifest in their interaction, normation and communication systems. The characteristics of people who are most likely to become the leaders and the followers of this particular basic assumption group are what Tustin (1981) called 'crustacean' and 'amoeboid' forms of autistic encapsulation as typical bio-psychological protective responses to severe trauma. They are linked to what Kohut and Wolf (1978) termed 'contact avoidance' and 'merger hunger', and to different aspects of what Blegler (1966) termed 'epiloid states' in response to 'ambiguity'. This is the foundation of my work in groups with people who have borderline and narcissistic disorders, and with those who have survived massive social trauma. Groups of victims of trauma of various kinds e.g., war in the Old Yugoslavia (Klein 1993), social collapse in the old USSR (Kroll 1992), earthquakes in Mexico (Burman & Roel 1986), the military dictatorship in Argentina (Puget 1989), concentration camps (Hopper 1993), child sexual abuse (Miles 1993), and the Vietnam war (Koller 1993, Koller et al. 1992), all evince very similar processes.

8 The idea of 'citizenship' may be contrasted with Turquet's (1975) notion that being an 'individual member' of a group is an indication of maturity. I have discussed this in the context of my theory of Incohesion as a Fourth Basic Assumption, and have suggested that 'singletons' are prevalent during states of aggregation, and 'membership individuals' during states of massification.

THE DILEMMAS OF IGNORANCE

Philip Boxer

We hear a lot about new ways of doing business. We hear about new forms of 'virtual' organisation, and about revolutions in the way we—as customers and clients—will be enabled to live our lives. We hear that this is to come about through the *strategies* pursued by businesses, which will produce 'revolutions' in the way industries are organised.

But in what sense can 'strategy' be 'revolution'? This cannot be 'strategy' as in 'long-range planning'. Instead, it is 'strategy' as *the management of ignorance*. Hamel[1]—for instance—encourages businesses to change what they ordinarily *ignore*, in order to create new possibilities for growth and development. A process such as this cannot be wholly rational, otherwise it would indeed boil down to yet another form of 'long-range planning'. So how are we to make sense of this idea of 'managing ignorance'? One way of approaching this question is to consider the relationship of the conscious ego to the Freudian unconscious. From this perspective, 'revolution' becomes an effect of 'listening' to unconscious processes.

The Tavistock paradigm

In the English-speaking world, it is difficult to think of listening in this way without considering the legacy of the Tavistock—whether this means the Tavistock Clinic or the Institute.[2] Although this work is rooted in the Tavistock Clinic, it represents a much broader approach to organisations, due to the way it rests on a *socio-technical systems approach* to organisations. Predominantly, however, it adopts a view of the individual's relationship to the organisation which is based ultimately upon a Kleinian theory of object relations. I shall refer to this broad approach as the *Tavistock paradigm*.[3]

My own experience of this paradigm reflects the view of Paul Hoggett, that

> [it is] frustratingly marginal to the concerns of those British practitioners to whom... [it] should have an enormous relevance—[such as:] change agents in organisational and social systems, managers and policy makers in the human services, etc. (Hoggett, 1997: 132)

The aim of this chapter, then, is to engage critically with the Tavistock paradigm, and to ask how exactly it could have become so 'frustratingly marginal'.[4] This is not to dismiss the paradigm, but to understand how we might build on its foundations, yet learn to undergo our own revolution as practitioners.

Criticism of the paradigm

Hoggett criticises the Tavistock paradigm on the basis that it employs a 'systems approach' more as a private metaphor than as a real link to the wider movement of systems thinking. This results in a fundamental failure of the paradigm to address the nature of *relations of power*.

As an example, Hoggett takes up the notion of *primary task*. This concept is defined as 'the task which an organisation must perform if it is to survive' (Miller & Rice 1967: 25). The problem with the notion of primary task is that it emphasises only questions of *viability*. By doing so, it obscures an alternative definition of the tasks within an organisation as being primarily a *development of the interests* of those involved.

Hoggett argues for the retention of both definitions—the one relating to the survival of the organisation, and the other to its development. He draws upon the work of Armstrong, whose notion of *primary process* offers a way beyond this impasse. Armstrong formulated the concept of primary process in the context of a Health Authority providing high security psychiatric services. He describes the function of this organisation as:

> the emotional task of 'managing vulnerability', or more exactly
> of managing the emotional experiences of being vulnerable and
> of making others vulnerable to oneself. (Armstrong 1995: 6)

In effect, then, Hoggett draws on the *psychoanalytic* notion of 'primary process' to define what the consultant is working with – that is, the emotional experience of the organisation *in* the people who work within it, rather than simply the emotional experience *of* the people. He invokes Bollas' notion of the 'unthought known' (Bollas 1987) as a way of understanding how this emotional experience *in* people relates to the organisation as a whole.

Hoggett's argument is that the future development of the Tavistock paradigm:

hinges upon the construction of a more sophisticated approach to 'the social' than existing models can provide. Power saturates all human relations, and consultants and researchers are part of these relations of power. Effective consultancy requires a double reflexivity, to one's own emotional experience of the collective organisational unconscious and to the nature of one's agency within the dynamic field of forces at play in any organisational setting. (Hoggett, 1997: 137)

Hoggett, then, argues for a much greater appreciation of the 'interpenetration of the realms of the emotions and unconscious and the realm of power and politics' (Hoggett, 1997: 138).

Michel Foucault's 'three dilemmas of governance'

We can turn to the work of Michel Foucault to consider—before continuing—a paradigm which *does* take account of the effects of power. Foucault approached language games as 'discursive practices', through which the subject was constituted as such, and also made the subject of the practices of power.[5]

Foucault's analysis of discursive practice concentrated on the particular ways in which it was possible to speak as a knowing subject, and—as such—to have the power to command others' obedience. Through this he implied that the effects of power were installed in the subject through the very practices of knowledge itself. Foucault suggested the 'power/knowledge' effects of a discursive practice were achieved according to the particular ways in which they negotiated three dilemmas.[6] These dilemmas can also be expressed in terms of the problems of governance which face organisations:[7]

- *The command dilemma* ('top-down' vs. 'bottom-up', or 'the transcendental' vs. 'the empirical'). The basis on which something can be said to be true.
- *The communications dilemma* ('espoused explanations' vs. 'explanations-in-use', or the 'cogito' vs. 'the unthought'). Whether or not it is possible to say what we 'know'.

- *The control dilemma* ('affiliation' vs. 'alliance', or 'the retreat into the past of the origin' vs. 'the return into the present of the origin'). Where (in time) the origin of author-ity is vested.

Foucault's analysis of the conditions for knowing subjectivity presented the very notion of the subject with a challenge. Foucault sought to answer this challenge in his later writings on sexuality.[8] Both Foucault and Lacan demonstrate a certain commitment to an ethics centred on the subject's relation to truth (Rajchman 1991). However, in contrast to Lacan, Foucault chose a *constitutive* ethics. For him, the displacement of the transcendental through the constitutive effects of discursive practice also entailed a refusal of the effects of the unconscious.[9] Not for him, then, Freud's subject of the unconscious—a *being* where *it* was.[10]

The origins of the Tavistock

It is likely that the genesis of the Tavistock Clinic had a significant influence on its subsequent work. It was formed in 1920 to work with the neurotic disorders, initially labelled as 'shell-shock', believed to be 'endemic and pervasive in modern society' (Trist & Murray 1990: 1). This work developed to include 'an understanding of and treatment of the stresses of military life in time of war' and, following World War II, took the form of 'a special relationship with the British Psycho-Analytical Society'. This reflected the role of the BP-AS in 'the widespread optimism and commitment to social change—"winning the peace"—that was already driving the formation of the reborn Tavistock, and that had swept a Labour government to power in 1945' (Mosse 1994: 3).

Miller and Rose use Foucault's notion of 'governmentality'[11] to characterise the part played by the Tavistock in this movement, and in terms of its contribution to three elements of the notion of government:

> [A] conception of government as a varying set of rationales and programmes which seek to align socio-political objectives with the activities and relations of individuals; the constitutive roles of psychological and managerial techniques and vocabularies; and a notion of subjectivity as a capacity promoted through specific regulatory techniques and forms of expertise. (Miller & Rose 1988: 171)

This standpoint is reflected also in the concepts to which the Tavistock paradigm awards central place: namely, that leadership is directly related to the aims and the primary task of the organisation, and that in the organisation there is congruence between authority and power.

The Tavistock paradigm thus entails that organisations are viewed as open systems, defined by 'input-conversion-output' processes. The effective management of these processes depends upon management of the boundaries which make the articulation of the processes possible. In addition to this, however, is the influence of 'symbolic expressions from the unconscious' (Halton 1994: 11), which arise from unconscious institutional anxieties and the defences against them. These are reflected in the 'basic assumption mentality' of people within the organisation. The basic assumption mentality is a way of dealing with institutional anxieties, by 'attempting to meet the unconscious needs of its members by reducing anxiety and internal conflicts' (Stokes 1994: 20). In extreme cases, this basic assumption mentality can become an end in itself, causing both leaders and members of groups to lose their ability to think and act effectively.

The Tavistock paradigm's view of the unconscious as the locus of anxiety, and as giving rise to symbolic expressions and defences against this anxiety—at individual, group and institutional levels—is well-defined. In terms of Foucault's three dilemmas, it problematises the first dilemma ('command': 'top-down' vs. 'bottom-up') in order to explore questions surrounding the second dilemma ('communications': 'espoused explanations' vs. 'explanations-in-use'). The second dilemma focuses on the extent to which it is possible to say what we 'know'. As such, the Tavistock paradigm is a crucial and important contribution to changing the level at which the organisation's processes can be brought into question, and thus shaping the consulting processes whereby this can be achieved.

The Tavistock paradigm in context

However, even though the Tavistock paradigm takes the unconscious into account, it has nevertheless ended up as being 'frustratingly marginal'. We might be forgiven for beginning to wonder—at this point—whether there is something simply incommensurable between questions of power and of the unconscious.

To understand how the Tavistock paradigm may have gone astray, it is necessary to situate it within the wider context of thought on organisations. I shall take Ed Schein's work, *Process Consultation*, as my starting-point, since this is regarded as a founding text in its field.

Schein regarded process consulting as 'anchored deeply in social psychology, sociology, and anthropology' (Schein 1969: 13). Here, then, a fundamental link was being made between thinking on organisations, and the realm of the social (sciences). Working within a humanistic theoretical framework, Schein's process consultation built on the group-dynamics training methods associated with the National Training Laboratories (Schein & Bennis 1965).[12]

Schein pointed out that it would be inadequate if the consultant intervened only on the *structure* of an organisation. Since people occupy a network of positions and roles, they introduce *processes* into the structure, which constitute an *informal* organisation and serve to *mediate* the effects of the formal organisation. It was on these mediating relationships between people and groups—that is, *processes*—that the process consultant, in Schein's view, should intervene. However, Schein himself never theorised the exact *nature* of these processes, despite the way in which they constitute the object of the process consultant's work.[13]

Whereas Schein's work may be taken as paradigmatic of the process consulting approach, Peter Checkland's work on 'soft systems methodology' exemplifies the *systems approach* to organisations.[14] From this point of view, the thought-models which structure both formal and informal processes must be made explicit, so that the combined effects of both kinds of process can be considered in relation to one another. In addition, a model is also constructed by the participant observer of the observer's *own* descriptive methodology. This creates a dualism between 'real world' and 'systems thinking world' models. It is within the latter that the observer makes his/her observations. More recently, Checkland has recognised that this dualism between the 'real world' and 'systems thinking world' is problematic.[15] This is because it seeks to install systems thinking as a kind of common language, which thus conceals the effects of the observer and the effects of power. Consequently, Checkland has come to see soft systems methodology as suffering from the limitations of any 'private metaphor'—in the same way that Hoggett regards the 'systems thinking' of the Tavistock paradigm. Perhaps, then, what is in evidence here is not simply a problem with the Tavistock paradigm, but a difficulty in the use of systems thinking itself.

Humberto Maturana's theory of 'languaging' sought to address this very difficulty. He proposed that language should be viewed not merely as a 'medium' in which metaphors were constructed, but as a means by which reality itself was constituted as such. However, although this view privileged language as uniquely characteristic of human beings, it also implied that languaging itself was *nothing but* that which arises in the co-ordinations between people.[16] This theory had the advantage of abolishing the dualism created by Checkland's approach, but—by abandoning the notion of an independently existing reality—it also abandoned the possibility of a radically 'Other' Freudian unconscious. Nevertheless, as an exemplar of second order cybernetics,[17] Maturana's use of this radical constructivism in systemic therapy was developed by the Milan Group, in order to understand the language 'games' of families and organisations.[18] This provided an effective approach to disentangling the different levels and contexts of communication within organisational life, yet within a paradigm of seeking to 'work together harmoniously', in which power was an effect of the relationship to language.[19]

Jaques and Foulkes

Also conspicuously absent from the Tavistock paradigm are some other key ideas from the immediate post-war period. I shall list two, and discuss each in turn:

- Jaques' elaboration of *accountable hierarchies* in terms of requisite organisation. He describes these hierarchies as composed of: 'those institutions whose articulated structure and functional arrangements provide solidly regulated conditions of trust in working relationships, and hence of authority with freedom and justice' (Jaques 1989: 132).

- Foulkes' problematisation of the relation between the individual and the group.

Jaques's absence is particularly notable here. His stratified systems theory provides an elegant unification of the implications of Foucault's dilemma concerning the basis of transcendental vs. empirical truths (See page 149, above). Thus, consideration of the organisation as a stratified structure of processes of symbolisation – an *architecture* in its own right—is absent, despite the usefulness of this theory as a means of addressing the problem of *inter-group* relations. This point of view brings together definitions of organisation based on 'developmental aims', and those based on the viability of 'primary task'.

Jaques later repudiated the Kleinian notion that 'bad' or 'dysfunctional' organisations were a reflection of pathological psychological forces, to be understood and resolved by the application of psychoanalytical concepts and methods. Nevertheless he continued to maintain that 'the managerial hierarchy is a direct reflection of the hierarchical structuring of human mental complexity in working' (Jaques 1995: 348). For our purposes, however, it is the absence of this notion of architecture which is most noteworthy.

Foulkes' ideas are also absent from the Tavistock paradigm. Considering the emphasis this paradigm places upon boundary management in the control of organisations, this is quite puzzling. Foulkes problematises the very formation of the individual and group in relation to 'the matrix':

> In the group-analytic group, the manifest content of communication, broadly speaking, relates to the latent meaning of this communication in a similar way as the manifest dream relates to the latent dream thoughts. This matter is so important and so bound up with our concept of a *group matrix* that I shall once more take occasion to stress the group matrix as the operational basis of all relationships and communications. Inside this network the individual is conceived as a nodal point. The individual in other words is not conceived as closed but as an open system. An analogy can be made with the neuron in anatomy and physiology, the neuron being the nodal point in the total network of the nervous system which always reacts and responds as a whole (Goldstein). As in the case of the neuron in the nervous system, so is the individual suspended in the group matrix. (Foulkes 1964: 118)

This is a point of view that closely parallels Foucault's notion of discursive formation as formative of subjectivity. Foulkes uses the group like an externalised model of the mental apparatus—ego, id, and superego—the dynamics of which are personified and dramatised.

It is not only the individual which is viewed as a node in a network of relationships and communications; the group itself is also a node. Thus Foulkes—like the Tavistock paradigm—is concerned with the way in which symbolisation, in a wider context, constitutes the group itself.[20] This time, it is Foucault's second dilemma which is approached through the articulation of a form of 'unthought known', formulated as a matrix, in relation to which the individual's and group's languaging is constituted.

Reasons for the failure of the paradigm

Why, then, are these ideas absent from the Tavistock paradigm? Two 'explanations' suggest themselves. The first is that there was simply no wish to include these ideas, given that the Clinic had no wish to open up controversies between the 'old' consensus of hierarchical forms of organisation—born out of the post-war institutional reforms of which it was an essential part—and other forms of organisation, other architectures, capable of enabling Human Service Organisations to function effectively. This is the explanation which Miller and Rose propose. Clearly, to take up Jaques' project would make this 'old' consensus all too visible. A debate about architecture would lead to a debate about the very forms of (command) hierarchy which brought the post-war Tavistock into existence, within the context of the NHS.[21] Yet it is this very NHS context, with its 'internal market' and 'fund-holding' reforms, which is currently having to face questions concerning its own architecture, at the same time as the Tavistock paradigm appears to have become 'frustratingly marginal'.

The second explanation concerns the nature and primacy of unconscious phantasy as formulated by the Kleinians. Symbol formations which arise to contain/defend against these anxieties are awarded a secondary/derivative nature. Klein wrote:

> I believe that phantasies operate from the outset, as do the instincts, and are the mental expression of the activity of both life and death instincts. Phantasy activity underlies the mechanisms of introjection and projection, which enable the ego to perform one of the basic functions mentioned above, namely to establish object relations. (Klein 1997b[1952a]: 58)

The Tavistock paradigm is founded upon the primary place given to phantasy by the Kleinians, and also upon the associated notions of the paranoid-schizoid and depressive positions and their symbol formations. These fundamental axioms themselves rest upon a particular reading of Freud's death drive in relation to phantasy. Foulkes—for one—did not wholly agree with this reading:

> [N]otwithstanding the great dynamic power of phantasies, are
> we to regard them as [the] primary motor directing instinctual
> energy and reality, or are instincts (*drives*) and their reality-
> objects the primary agents, leading to the formation of phan-
> tasies under conditions of conflict, frustration, etc.? (King &
> Steiner 1991: 430)

Foulkes is arguing that it is the *drives* which are primary, and that
phantasies are a response to them. When it comes to the interpretation
of these phantasies, he writes,

> we are always given to understand that the elucidation of the
> patient's unconscious phantasies, inner objects, etc., is the result
> of painstaking labour on the part of the analyst, belonging as
> they do to the deepest unconscious levels. Surely, what Dr
> Heimann describes is the outcome of her own interpretative
> work with the patient and not comparable to the spontaneous
> conscious statements, reactions, etc., with which the psychiatrist
> is concerned... (King & Steiner 1991: 431)

The point at stake here is not simply the primacy of unconscious
phantasy, but also the mediating effects of the analyst's own interpretative processes. If symbol formations are secondary to phantasy, then
the analyst's interpretations also remain secondary. But, if the reverse
is the case, if phantasies *are* symbol formations, then it raises the question of what is authoritative in the work of the analyst. The analyst's
interpretations become as much *elaborations* of his or her own phantasy (*qua* symbol formation) as of those of the analysand. This is what
makes the work of the analyst such a labour: to be effective, he or she
must be working explicitly within the third dilemma.

This question is indeed at the root of Foucault's third dilemma, concerning the point of origin in relation to which knowledge is constructed—the retreat and return of the origin. Rendering the *drive* primary, rather than phantasy, renders problematic the processes by
which the 'counter-transference' can be regarded as a reliable guide to
the interpretation of phantasies. This, in turn, calls into question the
whole basis of the authority of the psychoanalyst's interpretations.
This problem will be illustrated dramatically in the case studies which
follow.

Our first 'explanation' of the deficiencies of the Tavistock paradigm concerns the wish of the Tavistock not to call into question its hierarchical place within the referral networks. Similarly, our second 'explanation' concerns the wish of the Tavistock to avoid re-opening professional controversies surrounding the origins of the Kleinian movement. This would run the risk of either re-discovering or displacing those origins. No wonder then that Foucault's third dilemma is avoided altogether, because it was precisely upon this issue that the Controversial Discussions raged—namely, the basis of authority of the psychoanalyst.

Is this the 'incommensurability' between relations to the unconscious and to power, which I mentioned earlier? This would entail that Foucault's third dilemma—'affiliation' vs. 'alliance'—is also the dilemma of 'power' vs. 'the relation to the unconscious'. If so, then this indicates that the wish of the Tavistock paradigm to avoid a re-examination of its origins is predicated more upon relations to power than upon relations to the unconscious.

This is not to imply, however, that the 'wishes' of the Tavistock were part of the conscious aims and purposes of those involved in the development of the paradigm. I consider them to be side-effects, flowing from the axiomatics of the very subjectivity of the consultant.

'The Unconscious at Work'

As we have seen, whether working directly from Schein's process consulting paradigm, or following the systems thinking paradigm through Maturana's radical constructivism, both trajectories arrive at the problem of power—as addressed in Foucault's analysis of discursive practices. The limiting horizon of this trajectory, however, is the extent of the subject's reflexivity—the subject's capacity to know the truth about himself.

In order to examine this question of how the unconscious can take its place in a paradigm which also includes the themes of sentience, system, symbolisation and subjectivity—which we have seen in the other approaches we have explored—a recent collection of work edited by Obholzer and Roberts seems useful.[22]

The title of this collection is *The Unconscious at Work: Individual and Organisational Stress in the Human Services*. This in itself raises some interesting issues. What is examined here is human service organisations—organisations which, if they are to put the *good* of the client/patient first, must, by definition, be formed *in relation to* the needs of their clients. The ambiguity of the phrase 'The Unconscious at Work' can be taken—on the one hand—as referring to the unconscious processes *in operation*, in relation to those that are working. On the other hand, it can be taken as referring to *the effects of working*, in relation to clients/patients who *have* unconscious processes that affect what happens in the workplace.

The conceptual framework employed in the book does not address the issues of power which are reflected in the internal market reforms it professes to criticise. Neither is there a discussion of what occasioned these reforms, nor of the inevitable 'ethical' dilemma which underlies the formulation of strategies for providing for the 'good' of the public.

Obholzer's 'Afterword' to the book concludes with the notion of consultancy as 'licensed stupidity', which is teasingly close to the notion of a form of consultancy based on an ethic of 'not-knowing'. However, my criticism of this is the same as that of Schein's process consultancy: that there is no critical examination of the discursive formation within which such 'licensed stupidity' might take its place.

Case studies: (1) 'Shady Glen'

Shady Glen was:

> a specialised hospital for severely impaired elderly people who, without being particularly ill, required intensive, long-term nursing care. It had two wings: the smaller North Wing had three rehabilitation wards for those patients who were thought likely to be able to leave the hospital eventually; South Wing had four 'continuing-care' wards for those who were not expected ever to be able to live outside the hospital again. (Roberts 1994: 75)

Two external consultants were brought in to report to senior managers on the way the continuing-care wards dealt with the stresses of the work itself. The behaviour within the organisation seemed closely linked to the definition of its primary task; indeed, this was deeply enshrined in the way Shady Glen was run:

> ...each discipline or department had had its own discrete task, and was therefore managed as a separate system... (Roberts 1994: 78)

However, the consultants recommended:

> the new definition of a shared task... [requiring] a new boundary around all those involved in patient care. Furthermore, the separation of rehabilitation from continuing-care wards no longer had any rationale, since their previously different aims were now subsumed under a single task definition... (Roberts 1994: 78-79)

This re-definition was a logical development of the current primary task definition that was deeply embedded in the Shady Glen had been organised. Alongside it, the consultants recommended the development of three new means of support for staff:

- Face-to-face contact with hospital management, to review staff needs and the development of new practices.

- Time and a place for staff to reflect together on their work, to be carried out in small groups with continuity of membership.

- Mechanisms for inviting, considering and implementing ideas for change, from everyone in the system, whatever their status (including patients and their relatives).

The change in primary task definition was intended to shift the organisation away from defining itself on the basis of *functional* descriptions of tasks, reflecting the *different* professional groups within the hospital, towards concentrating on the way in which the organisation responded to *the needs of its residents*. It is not clear to what extent open systems modelling played a role in this re-thinking of the overall logic of the organisation, but the approach seems intuitively justifiable from the perspective of the good of the patients but to what extent were the explanations authoritative for the client? Subsequent events suggested they were not.

The smaller staff groups and regular review meetings appear to make a lot of sense as a means of airing the relationship between the experience of what was happening in the organisation, and the ways in which people spoke about their experience. But were these measures truly a mechanism for change and an adequate response to the problem? Indeed, what *was* the problem in terms of the larger context in which the staff were operating? In the presentation of the case of Shady Glen there is no analysis of issues concerning *power*, which might reasonably be expected to arise in the attempt to implement such changes.

A multi-disciplinary team was assigned the project of working through the implications of the change in primary task definition. This is how the story of Shady Glen continues:

> Where task-systems have overlapping boundaries, and their members are part of two management systems, the question of who is managing what—where authority is located—can become critical... The proposed new ward-team boundary, which included staff from other disciplines, needed to be managed by someone with sufficient authority to make decisions about patient care... In the end, the necessary authority was not delegated to the ward sister, and as a result, fundamental change to the continuing-care system as a whole did not take place... The failure to implement the report came as a devastating disappointment to the therapists. The nurses' response was more along the lines of, 'Well, what do you expect?'—the beginning of a move back to the old splits along fault-lines between the different disciplines. (Roberts 1994: 194)

So the system reverted back to a functional form. A 'good idea' was rejected due to the historically dominant ways in which power was exercised. But where was the analysis of this larger context in the first place? If the larger context had been included in the client system, would such a redefinition of primary task ever have been made? Is the larger context itself part of the system of defences against anxiety, or part of the cause of that anxiety? This case presentation is conspicuously silent on the very issues of power which appear most relevant to the outcome. Where were the processes that could bring about an alignment of power and authority in relation to the leadership challenge?

Case studies: (2) 'Thorne House'

In contrast, this second case study concentrates more upon institutional processes between the staff members.

Thorne House was regarded as 'a particularly progressive therapeutic community for the treatment of disturbed adolescents'

(Obholzer & Roberts 1994: 132). Every week, however, the same heated argument would recur during staff meetings, between two individuals advocating different approaches to the work. The role of the external consultants was to address this argument and its underlying concerns. We gain some insight into how this was carried out from the following:

> Thus, what needed to be recognised at Thorne House was the two sides of an unexpressed institutional debate on permissiveness versus control, so that the fight could become the public, ongoing debate within the staff group as a whole that it needed to become. Indeed, this debate taps into the very essence of the adolescent process, with its unconscious struggle between authoritarian and anti-authoritarian parts of the maturing self. (Obholzer & Roberts 1994: 133)

and:

> The child who was hurt by Terence represented all of the staff: 'Look what is happening to us as a result of your decision.' Terence's behaviour expressed not only his own rage, but also the rage all the staff were feeling at parental figures who abuse and fail those whom they should protect. At the same time, first Tony and then Terence were used to voice the group's unacknowledged anxieties about the quality of the service they were offering, anxieties which were split off, projected and finally got rid of by the removal of the 'whistle-blowers'. (Obholzer & Roberts 1994: 130-131)

What was irrupting was a fundamental dilemma concerning authoritarian vs. anti-authoritarian approaches to the organisation of Thorne House. The approach taken by the consultants was to recognise that the unconscious processes of the individuals involved produced in them a tendency towards becoming caught up in the organisational issues associated with particular institutional dilemmas. The key to successful intervention was, therefore, to use group processes as a means of accessing the institutional dilemmas facing the organisation, but in a way that separated these from the individuals' own unconscious processes.

So, it would appear that—besides possession of personal insight— it is useful for managers and other professionals to undergo thorough training in group and institutional processes. This would facilitate an understanding by them of the ways in which their personal anxieties manifest themselves and are defended against—at both the group and institutional level. But is this an entirely adequate prescription for what is required in order to 'maintain a position at the boundary between inside and outside'?

The way in which dilemmas are dealt with by an organisation can be viewed as the specific *strategy* of that organisation.[23] So what are the strategies adopted in Obholzer and Roberts's book, *within* the Tavistock paradigm? The book suggests that:

> Institutional dilemmas (e.g. permissiveness versus control), like personal ones, are anxiety-provoking, and regularly give rise to the kinds of defensive projective processes described above. (Obholzer & Roberts 1994: 133)

Granted, it is important to understand how institutions use individual members to express fundamentally institutional dilemmas. But to what extent does this provide an adequate basis for working through the implications of those dilemmas in *institutional* terms? Is it adequate to trace back everything according to an essence of our own personal dilemmas? And who is to make these interpretations?

Strategies

The first step towards a solution is indeed to understand the anxiety-containing function of institutions. However, this entails not only accepting the problem of Foucault's first 'top-down-vs.-bottom-up' dilemma, but also the implications of the second 'espoused-vs.-in-use' dilemma—the 'cogito' vs. the unthought. In other words, it must be recognised that the anxiety-containing function of the organisation goes beyond the purpose for which the organisation is said to exist.

By re-formulating the primary task in terms of primary process, Armstrong addresses this sense in which the work of the consultant goes beyond the reason that can be *stated* for the existence of the organisation.[24] In this way, then, we might say that he does indeed elaborate the Tavistock paradigm in relation to the second dilemma but the consultants' interpretation of both this notion of primary process, and the interpretation of institutional dilemmas, is itself affected by the third affiliation -vs.-alliance dilemma. However, on the question of the origin of *author-ity* (around which this third dilemma turns) the proponents of the Tavistock paradigm are totally silent. Instead, they suggest a number of courses of action which seem authoritarian rather than authoritative (Obholzer & Roberts (1994: 207-8). These include:

- There *must* be clarity and ongoing discussion about the primary task of the organisation, taking into account changes in the environment.

- Authority structures *need* to be clear.

- It is *essential* that clear and open communication between all sectors involved must be maintained.

- There is a *need* to have work-related staff support systems to contain the anxieties arising from the work itself, as well as out of the process of change.

- Personal support systems *should* be available.

- Managers also *need* support.

With the exception of the first two items, these are all enabling activities, supporting the process of change within the organisation. However, apart from defining the characteristics of the Tavistock consultant's *work*, its says little about the consultant's *role*.

It is, perhaps, the second item in this list which says most about the nature of the Tavistock consultant. He or she is expected to ensure that authority structures possess 'load-bearing' characteristics:

> Consultants to institutions can be regarded as having an analogous role to the architect's, predicting which are the load-bearing structures, and helping to identify what sort of emotional loads these structures are carrying. (Obholzer & Roberts 1994: 209)

This sounds more like a job for a structural engineer than a management consultant. Once more, it is oriented towards the anxiety-carrying role of the organisation, rather than its ongoing development or its continuing viability. In addition, the position of the consultant remains unexamined.

I agree that an understanding of the architecture of organisations can provide crucial insights into the symbolic logic(s) through which they are constituted. However, the metaphor of 'structural architect' is being used here to underpin the consultant's professionalism, rather than to raise questions concerning the nature of that professionalism.

How is it, then, that these questions, concerning the very subjectivity of the consultant, which were first raised as a consequence of the Tavistock paradigm, are now ignored? What kind of strategy might the Tavistock paradigm itself be pursuing *unconsciously*?

It would appear that the answer lies in the way the ontological status of the primary task itself has remained unquestioned. The Tavistock paradigm remains silent concerning the problems associated with the first item in the list above. Although it is suggested that the primary task must be clear and be discussed regularly, apparently the 'licensed stupidity' of the consultant does not extend as far as questioning the axiomatics of the primary task itself! No mention is made of possible problems with the primary task, and its roots—inevitably—in the nature of the discursive and non-discursive formations through which the organisation is constituted.

Therefore it is the unquestioned status of the 'reality' brought into being by the 'private metaphor' of open systems thinking in general, and the primary task in particular, which lies at the root of the shortcomings of the Tavistock paradigm. As in soft systems methodology, this private metaphor installs a language which conceals both the effects of the observer, and—behind these—the effects of power.

Metaphor and metonymy

The notion of the effects of power is informed, perhaps, by another metaphor, installed through that part of the Tavistock paradigm which is concerned with 'winning the peace', supporting the *good* of the Human Service Organisation through the mediating effects of 'healthy' hierarchies. Consequently, in neither Shady Glen nor Thorne House were the institutional dilemmas addressed. So if this selective blindness is not part of the conscious aims and purposes of those involved in the development of the Tavistock paradigm, then perhaps it can be considered a side-effect, flowing from the view taken of the subjectivity of the consultant.

The primary status awarded to unconscious phantasy, and the biological metaphors underlying the formation of object relations, installs yet another metaphor into a privileged position within the paradigm. Working interpretively with the 'counter-transference', under the influence of these metaphors, gives rise to a particular form of subjectivity which itself is no less an effect of power than is the 'reality' of primary task.

In the diagram below,[25] the metonymic characteristics of *speaking* are portrayed as running along chains of association. These escape from *listening*, which depends upon a retroactive effect. Listening, then, always takes place under the retroactive influence of metaphor.

listening

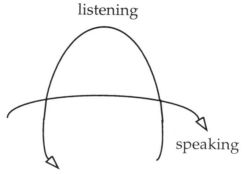

speaking

Privileging the drive over phantasy is to privilege the metonymic effects of the drive over the axiomatising tendency of the metaphorics of phantasy. The Tavistock paradigm, however, cedes primacy to phantasy and thus privileges metaphor over metonymy. We see the effects of this in the way in which the Tavistock paradigm regards the consultant's 'take' on 'reality', and the interpretation of unconscious defences.

Obholzer's notion of 'licensed stupidity' comes *close* to formulating the paradoxical nature of a strategy of intervention based on privileging metonymy, just as his metaphor of the architect points towards an understanding of an organisation in terms of the axiomatics of power which an architecture supports. However, to privilege metaphor over metonymy—even the founding metaphor of the Tavistock paradigm—is to privilege affiliation to that origin, over and above alliance in relation to the challenge of the case. This, then, was how the two realms of power and the unconscious became separated. The separation, inherent in the circumstances surrounding the origins of the paradigm, was installed within the paradigm itself. To seek to escape from this separation would necessarily involve calling the power of the paradigm into question and, with that, the practice of the consultant under its influence. However it is precisely from taking up this challenge—the challenge of the third dilemma—that revolution comes about.

Notes

[1] See Hamel 1996.

[2] The Tavistock Institute of Human Relations was founded in 1946 to pursue inter-disciplinary research and to relate the needs of society to psychological and social services. Its founders had been members of the Tavistock Institute of Medical Psychology ('the Clinic'), which was founded in 1920 as an outpatient unit. Both the Clinic and the Institute continue to be active in the field of consulting to organisations. (See the chapter on the foundation and development of the Tavistock Institute, in Trist & Murray 1990.) The Clinic's approach developed from its 'Consulting to Institutions' workshop, which began in 1980 and is described in Obholzer & Roberts 1994.

[3] A more detailed evaluation of this notion of a 'Tavistock paradigm' can be found in Palmer 1997.

[4] Although the views expressed in this chapter are my own, my particular thanks go to the Working Group on Groups and Organisations for their support in developing these ideas. In particular I would like to thank Barry Palmer for his comments on this text. WGGO was founded in 1994, under the auspices of the Centre for Freudian Analysis and Research. Its aim is to develop understanding of groups and organisations, drawing on members' experience of the organisational intervention and the challenges this presents. This is achieved through reading psychoanalytic and other texts, which throw light upon this experience. At the core of this work is a questioning of the basis of authority (author-ity) of whoever intervenes in the group or organisation: the psychoanalyst in relation to the group, or the consultant in relation to the organisation. Working papers are to be found at www.brl.com, where WGGO has its home page.

[5] See Foucault 1970, 1972; Gordon 1980.

[6] These dilemmas are running themes throughout Foucault's work on the problematics of power/knowledge. See Dreyfus & Rabinow 1982.

[7] This organisational form of the dilemmas is developed more fully in Boxer 1994b.

[8] See Foucault 1986.

[9] Jacques-Alain Miller develops this critique of Foucault in Armstrong 1992.

[10] I am equating 'being' with the self-conscious *ego*, and 'it' with the Freudian *unconscious*: 'Where id was, there ego shall be' (Freud 1933b: 80). In the English translation, the emphasis is upon enlarging 'the organisation of the ego so that it can appropriate fresh portions of the id'. The Lacanian reading (Lacan 1988a: 194), via the original German ('*Wo Es war, soll Ich werden*') places the emphasis on the *there*—that is, upon the id, implying that it is the nature of the id to be always elsewhere and never fully 'drained' by the ego. Accepting the radical Otherness of the unconscious is thus a determining characteristic of any attempt to work in relation to it.

[11] Burchell, Gordon & Miller 1991.

[12] Training Laboratories played a similar role in the USA to that of the Tavistock Institute in the UK by pioneering a new form of practice, with all the attendant challenges of articulating its own processes.

[13] This critique of Schein is elaborated in Boxer 1994a.

[14] See Checkland 1981.

[15] See Checkland & Tsouvalis 1996.

[16] See Maturana & Varela 1987. Lacan had pointed out the fundamental difficulties with this direction in 1955, during his second seminar (Lacan 1988b). The implications of Lacan's view are developed in Appendix I of Fink 1995.

[17] See Von Foerster 1960, Bateson 1972.

[18] See Palazzoli 1986.

[19] See Boxer & Kenny 1992, for a more detailed critique of the use of Maturana's work as the basis for consultational intervention.

[20] David Armstrong takes up this question in a comparison of the approaches of Group Relations Conferences, The Grubb Institute's Organisational Role Analysis, and Gordon Lawrence's Social Dreaming Matrix. See Armstrong 1991.

[21] This is not to suggest that the Tavistock Institute was not itself innovative in relation to its own architecture. Many of its members undertook personal psychoanalysis, as part of the process of constructing its architecture. It adopted a matrix organisation in the early 1960s, which fed upon a growing international network of institutions. See Trist & Murray 1990: 17-27.

[22] For a view of the Tavistock paradigm as a discursive practice, see Palmer 1996.

[23] A good introduction to this approach towards strategy is Hampden-Turner 1990.

[24] See Armstrong 1995.

[25] This is based on an early Lacanian formulation of the relationship between metaphor and metonymy. For an elaboration see Boxer & Palmer 1994.

GROUP SUBVERSION AS SUBJECTIVE NECESSITY— TOWARDS A LACANIAN ORIENTATION TO PSYCHOANALYSIS IN GROUP SETTINGS

Alan Rowan and Eric Harper

Everything which takes effect in the field of analytic action precedes the constitution of knowledge, which doesn't change the fact that in operating in this field we have constituted a knowledge, and one which has proved itself to be exceptionally efficacious...This is also why the more we know the greater the risks. All you are taught in a more or less pre-digested form in the so-called institutes of psychoanalysis—sadistic, anal stages etc.—all this is of course very useful, especially for people who aren't analysts. It would be stupid for a psychoanalyst systematically to neglect them, but he must be aware of the fact that that isn't the dimension in which he operates. (Lacan 1988b: 19)[1]

...shouldn't the true termination of an analysis—and by that I mean the kind that prepares you to become an analyst—in the end confront the one who undergoes it with the reality of the human condition. (Lacan 1992: 303)

Introduction

It is clear that our modern world, and its often celebrated culture of 'modernity', is built upon the legacy of the enlightenment, of which it could be said that 'I' is the state of things ('*L'État c'est moi*', being famously attributed to Louis XIV).

This fundamentally ideological sentiment is also nicely incorporated in the infamous words of Long, a US senator before the US civil rights movement, whose battle-cry for social reform was: 'Everyman a King'. Indeed, the term 'modernity' has come to serve as a broad synonym for capitalism or industrialisation, and the institutional and ideological features that are held to mark off the modern West from other, more traditional societies. The term collects together a set of beliefs into a 'grand narrative'—or 'big story', to use Lyotard's term—which emphasises humanity's progress and its ability to construct the good society, guided by reason, with the goal of undistorted communication between citizens in the cause of human emancipation.

There is thus, within modernity, the construction of a belief in the absolute sovereignty of rationality—in other words, that it is possible to know what is best for everybody. This leads, in turn, to forms of therapy which privilege a transcendent vantage point, a capacity to perceive objectively. It is a view which can be contrasted with that of Lacan who, like Freud, was keen to demonstrate how the unconscious subverts belief in an ideal construction, or end-point. Lacan saw modern man, in particular, as caught up in what he termed 'a service of the goods'. For Lacan, the modern world struggles with and is saturated by the effects of mass consumerism and a co-extensive dedication to social ideals which act as a barrier to desire[2], as he puts it:

> The movement that the world we live in is caught up in, of wanting to establish the universal spread of the service of goods as far as conceivably possible, implies an amputation, sacrifices, indeed a kind of Puritanism in the relationship to desire... (Lacan 1992: 303)

This difference in emphasis—between acquiring knowledge and finding ways to bear our incompleteness—foreshadows, in our opinion, one potential dissimilarity between a Lacanian orientation to group therapy and that of some other schools—a dissimilarity based on the primacy of the subject which, we hope, will become evident as this text progresses.

The word 'modernity', however, also serves to highlight the fact that group psychotherapy is a modern phenomenon. Its origins lie in the psycho-educational groups run by Pratt in the early 1900s for Tuberculosis sufferers which, alongside the work of other pioneering therapists during the first decades of this century, culminated in the group therapy movement proper of the 1940s. This latter development which took place around the same time in both the USA[3] and the UK,[4] is usually viewed as occurring due to the influence of pressures on resources, arising particularly during the Second World War—that is, the need to treat large numbers of people suffering psychological distress in a relatively inexpensive manner.

Such developments, however, did not occur in an intellectual vacuum but were very much influenced by developments in the emerging discipline of sociology. This encompassed the inaugural ideas of

Comte, who was the first to conceive of society as an organism which was not simply reducible to the individuals who made it up, and included such figures as Durkheim, Weber and Marx who each in their own way emphasised the importance of understanding the community, or social totality, as formative in the life of the individual. This drive to understand the social bond was fuelled on the one hand by the revolutionary aspirations of social critics such as Marx and Engels, while on the other hand, there were those (such as Durkheim) who were more focused on and troubled by what they saw as the break-up of traditional roles and social obligations, including a weakening of family ties, as a result of modernisation and industrialisation. Bray neatly illustrates this all too familiar concern as follows:

> Perhaps the most remarkable effect of the urban environment is to be sought in the disappearance of the habit of self-control...The crowd of a town in a moment flashes into a delirious mob... The invention of the new term 'Mafficking' is alone sufficient to indicate the extent of the transformation. Nerves are ever on strain...exploding like a pistol at the mere touch of the hair-trigger...such possibilities of unpremeditated violence constitute a standing menace to the general welfare. (Bray 1907: 145-146)

Freud's position within this arena is – arguably—open to a variety of interpretations. Whilst Freud, Marx and Nietzche are sometimes spoken of as 'masters of suspicion', the question remains whether Freud and his work are in fact subversive, radical, and enable the subject to find a voice, or—alternatively—result merely in some form of moral policing. Zaretsky argues, for example, that Freud's texts destabilised fixed meanings, subverted the ideal of self-control and self-mastery and offered:

> a profound critique of many assumptions underpinning our culture but his criticisms also proved highly adaptable... ultimately, psychoanalysis was reshaped by the culture it influenced so that its critical possibilities were not only largely unrealised, but in fact were turned into modes of oppression. (Zaretsky 1997: 72-3)

Freud's own positioning of himself in relation to culture was, however, somewhat more humble. He states:

I will moderate my zeal and admit the possibility that I, too, am chasing an illusion... I know how difficult it is to avoid illusions; perhaps the hopes I have confessed to are of an illusory nature, too. (Freud 1927: 232...237)

Whilst Freud acknowledges that psychoanalysis may be an attempt to replace one illusion with another, there is a distinction in the type of illusion. Freud advocates, a *Wissenschaft* (a research programme) which should proceed carefully and slowly. This style of research entails the adoption of a state of mind akin to 'free-floating attention'. It might be likened to the stance of the sculptor who tirelessly ponders, waits, and then chips away until some kind of resemblance begins to form. This style of research entails that the properly subjective horizon is occupied by what comes next, by the moment of enunciation as against the already enunciated.

In our opinion the question worth posing here is whether some analytic approaches may have neglected this stance and responded more to the call for individual adaptation to the general welfare, rather than focusing more on a questioning of the subject. We will, however, leave the reader to judge this issue in the light of our argument, while turning now to consider Freud's position on group psychology.

Group psychology and the analysis of identification

Freud wrote about three types of group: the pre-group (primal horde), the established mass or crowd, and civilization at large. Freud did not, therefore, talk directly about the small face-to-face groups most commonly associated with psychotherapy. Psychotherapy groups are characterised by a given number of people (usually 8 to 10) who interact and are aware of one another, who perceive themselves as a group, and who share a common agenda or purpose. Thus mere 'aggregates of people' do not fit this definition, because they do not interact and do not perceive themselves to be a group, even if they are aware of each other—as might be the case, for instance, with a crowd of football fans watching a match. What Freud did clearly display in his work, however, was his continuing interest in human culture and in those aspects of thought, speech and symbolisation shared within the public arena. Indeed, it is clear that, for Freud, psychoanalysis was not characterisable in terms of a supposed focus on the isolated and hermetically sealed individual (as it is caricatured, at times, by some of its less informed critics) but rather he urged us to recognise that:

In the individual's mental life someone else is invariably involved, as a model, as an object, as a helper, as an opponent; and so from the very first individual psychology, in this extended but entirely justifiable sense of the words, is at the same time a social psychology as well. (Freud 1921: 69)

To be a human is thus to be subject to group effects. The effect of the group is a humanisation of the subject through the establishment of social bonds. The institution of the bond brings about a coercion and renunciation of sexual libido and aggressivity. Freud—as early as 1905—implies that to be a member of a group involves a build-up of mental forces, in the form of disgust and shame—due to the imposition of moral ideals—which results in an inhibition of the drive. At this stage in Freud's teaching, civilization (group membership) has an educational function. In his *Introductory Lectures on Psychoanalysis* (1915/16) he expands on this idea and argues that civilization has been created at the cost of drive satisfaction.

In 1921 Freud outlined two forms of social tie: identification and object cathexis. Identification is the earliest and original form of emotional tie with another human. Within a group context there are two forms of identification: with the leader, and with fellow group members. Identification with the leader is an act of tenderness, although is not without murderous implications, for identification involves a wanting to be in the place of the one with whom the subject identifies. The leader incarnates an ego ideal, and this is put in the place of the subject's ego ideal. There is a love by the subject of:

what he once was and no longer is, or else what possesses the excellence which he never had at all... what possesses the excellence which the ego lacks for making it an ideal, is loved. (Freud 1914a: 101)

Love of group members, on the other hand, is an ego-to-ego identification. What is collective in the group is a set of common identifications. Freud did not believe in some form of 'group mind', or 'social mentality' existing independently of the subject, as others had argued (McDougall 1968)[5]. Instead he demonstrated the socially situated and fundamentally subjective bonds of identification and idealisation which bind the members of a large group together. Moreover, he illustrated in works such as *Totem and Taboo* (1913b) and *The Future of an*

Illusion (1927), how belonging to any group whatsoever is built upon one's first relationships (to an object or, in Lacan's terminology, to a (m)other).

In *The Future of an Illusion* Freud points out how an infantile proto-type, a state of helplessness and longing for the father's protection, is transferred to group interactions. There is a searching for a 'benevolent providence', a figure who will protect the subject from those forces that mock all human control and make the individual once again aware of the full extent of their helplessness and insignificance in the face of the universe:

> With these forces nature rises up against us, majestic, cruel and inexorable; she brings to our mind once more our weakness and helplessness, which we thought to escape through the work of civilization. (Freud 1927: 195)

Freud identifies these cruel forces as being the feebleness of our own bodies, and the dangers of nature and human society. Forlorn and without dwelling the adult is in the same position as a 'child who has left the paternal house where he was so warm and comfortable' (Freud 1927: 233). This intolerable experience is tamed through a personifica-tion and humanisation of nature. Through this process there is an attempt to establish a personal relation with the dreaded, perplexing and uncanny experience of human existence (what Lacan refers to as the Real), which is a fundamental dimension at work in the emergence of religious belief.

> When the growing individual finds that he is destined to remain a child for ever, that he can never do without protection against strange superior powers, he lends those powers the features belonging to the figure of the father. (Freud 1927: 204)

In this process the subject hopes to find a *Weltanschauung* which will offer a secure means to live by. This longing for a protective father/ system of thought which can pacify the subject in the face of the unknown—a safety net—becomes a template according to which the subject negotiates his or her interactions within the group.

In the large group, Freud emphasised particularly the function of the leader as central, though this leader may not necessarily be visible (such as the figure of Christ in Christian religions) or in any way incar-nated:

> We should consider whether... an abstraction may not take the
> place of the leader... and whether a common tendency, a wish in
> which a number of people can have a share, may not in the same
> way serve as a substitute. (Freud 1927: 100)

What was necessary, according to Freud, for a large group to come into
existence was some limitation on individual narcissism and the consequent feelings of hostility towards others. This was possible, he maintained, only on the basis of a libidinal or love tie between the individual members of the group. The mechanism he proposed was one
whereby members of a crowd 'have put one and the same object in the
place of their ego ideal and have consequently identified themselves
with one another in their ego' (Freud 1927: 116). The loved object or
leader thus captivates the individual's ego ideal and—based on this
perception of a shared desire with others, who are not objects of the
sexual drive—a further identification (namely, Freud's third form of
identification[6]) takes place, and the group as a whole comes into being.
(It is worth noting in passing that for Freud certain quantitative relationships exist between these terms: thus, the more powerful the ideal,
the more regressed or primitive ego-functioning will be; the more an
object is idealised the less it will function as an object, etc.). Freud
writes:

> The ego ideal opens up an important avenue for the under-
> standing of group psychology. In addition to its individual side
> this ideal has a social side; it is also the common ideal of a fami-
> ly, a class or nation. It binds not only a person's narcissistic
> libido, but also a considerable amount of his homosexual libido,
> which is in this way turned back onto the ego. The want of sat-
> isfaction which arises from the non-fulfilment of this ideal liber-
> ates homosexual libido, and this is transformed into a sense of
> guilt (social anxiety). (Freud 1914a: 96-97)

What is central to the process of identification, be it with the leader or
fellow group members, is an inhibition of the drive. For Freud, the setting of limits to the drive (aggressivity and lust) takes place through
the incitement of people to identifications and aim-inhibited relationships of love. In both *Civilization and its Discontents* and *Group
Psychology and the Analysis of the Ego* Freud argues that it is the inhibit-
ed drive (sensual current) that enables the establishment of bonds of

mutual affection, a 'de-sexualised, sublimated homosexual love for other men, which springs from work in common... love alone acts as the civilizing factor in the sense that it brings a change from egoism to altruism' (Freud 1921: 132). Freud also argues that the subject needs to love if s/he is not to fall ill. Without object cathexes there is no way to discharge a build up of excessive libido, and—instead—the psychic system will be flooded and burdened with unpleasurable stimulus and tension.

Freud believes that this attempt at unification under the sign of an ideal enables the group to attack that which falls outside the group. It gives rise to 'a narcissism of minor differences' in which the group feels the 'right to despise the people outside' and which compensates 'them for the wrongs they suffer within their own unit' (Freud 1927: 193). Group membership involves idealisation of the loved object and projection of hate outwards. This process can only take place at a cost, however. Freud repeatedly highlights the impairment of intellectual functioning in a group—a point that both Bion and Lacan echo in their writings. This intellectual impairment can be read as a hatred of difference.[7]

The group within psychoanalysis—some contexts and dilemmas

Lacan did not focus his thought at any stage in his career on the theory or method of psychoanalysis as applied in psychotherapy groups. Based on this fact one might argue, simply, that this was not his area of clinical interest. On the other hand, as we hope to demonstrate, Lacan's understanding of the 'speaking being' and of the efficacy of psychoanalysis does not preclude working analytically within a group, although it does entail a view of psychoanalysis that privileges the subject. Thus, for the Lacanian psychoanalyst, whereas psychoanalysis *within* a group is at least conceivable, psychoanalysis *of* the group is not. Lacan, however, did devote considerable attention to the distorting effects of 'the group'—for example, with respect to psychoanalysis itself (particularly as manifested around the problems of transmission in psychoanalysis). These observations can be taken as a guide to a clinical conceptualisation of the psychoanalytic group. Our primary aim is, therefore, to extract from Lacan's work a number of key principles, and to illuminate how his 'return to Freud'—as he termed it— throws light on issues such as how one might understand the psychotherapeutic group, and how psychoanalytically one might act in such a setting.

Lacan, in an early paper (Lacan 1947), describes a five-week visit to Northfield Hospital in England, which took place during the Second World War in 1945. He displays no small degree of enthusiasm for the pioneering work that took place there. During this visit he briefly met with both Rickman and Bion and, moreover, described their group studies as reminiscent of the 'miracle of Freud's first steps'. He was also deeply impressed by the way issues of authority were dealt with in these groups, and noted how the group formed around a *task* rather than an authority figure. Lacan speculated that Britain's success in the war was at least in part a consequence of introducing similar ideas to the military.

Throughout Lacan's life and work one can find shadows of this encounter which, it could be argued, was nothing less than profound. For Lacan, however, the question of the group was to be posed not clinically but in relation to the psychoanalytic institution, charged with the transmission of psychoanalysis. The problem centred for Lacan on the necessity of opposing the imaginary ('ego-to-ego') effects of constituted groups, whatever their purpose—whether educational, political, or therapeutic[8]. In Lacan's view, the group-cum-institution offered a fertile ground for narcissistic delusions of the ideal, and idealisations in general, alongside the possibility of pathogenic transferential identifications, or—as Lussier provocatively puts it—the possibility of 'a deadly filiation through the transmission of untouchable magic power' (cited in Wallerstein 1993: 176). Lacan's response to the problem was complex and multifaceted. It ranged from insisting on the fact that psychoanalysis is untransmissable and, therefore that each psychoanalyst must recreate psychoanalysis for him or herself as a subjective act—and, moreover, create it anew each time he or she practices[9]—to insisting that it is ultimately the analyst who must authorise him or herself as an analyst. This analytic position or function is thus not conferrable through an external (that is, institutional) process. Indeed the whole way in which Lacan set up his school sought to deal with these problems of transmission.[10]

In the context of this paper we can allude only briefly to these additional measures—for example, the emphasis on 'Cartels' within a Lacanian approach to analytic training. Cartels are temporary, small work-groups made up of analysts in training and others (that is, literally anybody committed to working on the theme of the Cartel) which are non-hierarchical, but include one member who acts as a 'plus one'[11] and demands work of the group before, over time, the members of the group will be invited to shift to other groups. The aims of a Cartel are twofold: firstly, to produce work (such as a text or texts); and secondly, to work in a context in which the 'family/institutional' pyramid is deconstructed, in order to extend the analytic effect (that is, a subject who speaks for her/himself) into the institution itself.[12] In terms of our present discussion, we can see that Lacan is concerned to enable a group to come into being in a way which is not based on the presence of a master (that is, 'one who knows') or mother, or father, or double, but—instead—on the basis of evoking the subject's desire disengaged from identifications. As we shall see later, this has significant implications for the way a Lacanian approaches psychoanalysis in groups. Before examining this, however—and by way of a counterpoint to Lacan's own position—it is useful to highlight briefly some central features of group psychotherapy as practised today. In doing so we must, of necessity, be selective, and we shall focus on group analysis as pioneered by Foulkes[13].

Foulkes saw the neurotic position as:

> ...in its very nature highly individualistic. It is group disruptive in essence for it is genetically the result of an incompatibility between the individual and his original group. It is at the same time an expression of destructive and aggressive tendencies. (Foulkes 1964: 89)

The process of cure, for Foulkes, involved transforming the patient's neurotic and autistic-like individuality, through free-floating discussion, into open and ever more articulate forms of communication within the group. Foulkes placed great emphasis both on communication— 'working towards an ever more articulate form of communication is identical to the therapeutic process itself' (Foulkes 1948: 69)—and on the power of community. He saw the group as an ideal forum for enabling the growth of healthy individuality and simultaneously curtailing neurotic symptoms based on an implied (in our view highly questionable) ideal: 'the group has an inherent pull towards the socially and biologically established norm' (Foulkes 1964: 90). As Foulkes puts it elsewhere:

> The deepest reason why patients can reinforce each other's normal reactions and wear down and correct each other's neurotic reactions is that collectively they constitute the very norm from which individually they deviate. (Foulkes 1948: 29)

For Foulkes, therapy involved analysis *by* the group *of* the group—including its conductor, whose task it is to focus on the total interactional field rather than on analysis of the individual group member. In elaborating this trend in his thought he coined the term 'group matrix'. This denotes on the one hand the common ground of our social and cultural inheritances, and thus forms the basis on which the group is founded, while on the other hand it refers to how each particular group matrix has a dynamic character in so far as the group takes on various specific traits and characteristics over time. Within this matrix the individual is seen as a 'nodal point' and it is with this (in our opinion) underdeveloped notion that Foulkes perhaps comes closest to Lacan's thinking—the notion that the subject is some sort of more or less fluid or loosely gathered interactional field, with its resemblance to the notion of the subject as subjected to the signifier. However, Foulkes had no such concept as Lacan's 'symbolic'the network of signifiers[14] and fell back, we believe, towards a privileging of the ego and 'concrete experiences' in his overall approach. This is well illustrated by the following passage:

> The most powerful factor in bringing about change and the possibility for further and future progress after the group has ended is based on *ego training in action* and not so much on the insight and interpretation based on words as such, as upon *the ongoing corrective interaction with others*. This is the mainspring of the mutative experience in group analytic psychotherapy. (Foulkes 1990: 295, our emphasis)

For Lacan, however, psychoanalysis does not promise either mastery (corrected interactions) or some form of 'adaptation to reality'- a sort of rational liberation—through, for example, 'ego-training' but is, rather, concerned with the 'discontent in civilization'. Ultimately this means establishing an ethics that proves equal to what one might term the tragedy of the subject, of the one who is ever prey to a gap, a potential calamity, emanating from what is at the very centre of his or her being—namely, the endless and metonymic play (displacement) of desire.

It is our contention that Foulkes, like many other analysts, demonstrates a tendency towards reducing psychoanalytic practice to a broadly psycho-educational orientation, whereby the patient 'learns' to speak with greater sophistication and subtlety under the guidance of 'one who knows'.[15] As Foulkes puts it:

The group has to go downwards and to deepen its understanding of the lower levels of the mind by broadening and deepening
its vocabulary until every group member also understands these
levels. Ideally the whole group should learn eventually to move
over the full range of the scale. (Foulkes & Anthony 1984: 263)

There emerges, therefore, a kind of triumph of the ego over the id.
Foulkes expresses this in his description of how the contents of the
unconscious are:

...cast in primitive symbolic language. This is understood unconsciously and its transmission, or communication, takes place
without consciousness. The group, through processes of progressive communication works its way from this primary, symbolic level of expression into conscious articulate language. This
work in communication is the operational of all therapy in the
group. (Foulkes 1990: 156)

Whatever the therapeutic benefits of this form of praxis—and Lacan
would not deny that suffering may be alleviated in this way—this
approach has for Lacan only a limited relation to psychoanalysis proper, because it removes from centre stage what Lacan sees as Freud's
radical de-centring (or splitting) of the subject[16]. For Lacan the problem
with this approach is that it produces new identifications, the strengthening in each subject of an ideal modelled primarily on that of the
(mature/healthy) analyst, rather than going beyond such identifications and towards the point which Lacan characterises as a point of
'subjective destitution'. This is the point at which the subject discerns
the effects of his or her own desire or 'fundamental fantasy'; it is the
point of assuming one's own cause as subject, without any guarantee
from the desire of another, and it demands from the subject that he or
she gives form, each in his or her own way, to lack of being.[17] At this
point, however, it is necessary to introduce formally some Lacanian
theory, before returning to the issue of psychoanalytic practice within
the group.

Lacan and the subject of psychoanalysis

Some key conceptual areas which—in part, at least—underpin Lacan's
elaboration of classical psychoanalysis are outlined below. These deal,
in turn, with the ego, language, the subject of fading, and 'object a'.[18]

The subject of misrecognition

It is around the question of the subject—a pivotal point in Lacan's teaching—that Lacanian practice unfolds. Throughout the work of Lacan there is a preoccupation with the question as to what the subject is. As Lacan's reading of the subject changed, so did his clinical practice. Lacan first outlined what the subject is primarily through a process of negation, and only later as that which emerges in the act of speaking. The subject is, therefore, not the ego and is to be contrasted to the ego. The ego is that psychic apparatus captured by the specular image and trapped in the mirroring gaze of the other.

The ego, for Lacan, is a fundamentally narcissistic identification or construction which emerges during the Mirror Stage (approximately between 6 and 18 months).[19] This occurs when the infant identifies with the whole form or *gestalt* of the human body—paradigmatically, with a mirror-image of itself as a unified whole, in a position of self-mastery. The infant exists within this imaginary plane as an adaptive ego, striving to reach an unattainable unity with its specular image. This narcissistic structure, made up of identifications supported by ideals, enables the ego to take itself as its own ideal image. The ego, as an imaginary identification, is seen here to include the body.

More pointedly, Lacan argues that this moment—during which 'I is another'—is a fundamentally alienating moment. In other words, this initial sense of identity is not a 'primordial form' but literally belongs to another, and is the cover for a fundamental lack of identity. As Lacan states:

> It is in this erotic relation, in which the human individual fixes upon himself an image that alienates him from himself, that are to be found the energy and the form on which this organisation of the passions that he will call his ego is based. This form will crystallise in the subjects internal conflictual tension which determines the awakening of his desire for the object of the other's desire. (Lacan 1977: 19)

The ego, born in this way, is oriented in a fictional direction (that is, towards the ideal ego manifested in the mirror-image) which remains discordant with the subject's own reality. In other words, the ego is neither autonomous nor the subject of objective knowledge, but is rather a libidinal object of narcissism. For Lacan, the ego is thus 'the seat of illusions' (Lacan 1988a: 2) rather than the psychic agency responsible for adjusting the subject's relations with reality. Moreover, for Lacan, the ego, as reflected image, is responsible for producing a constraining and distorting influence on the subject, who inevitably seeks to reinforce his or her coherence and mastery through imaginary couplings with the other, or in an idealised and utopian image which results in an elision or concealment of the want-to-be or lack of being at the core of subjectivity. The ego thus functions as 'an armour of an alienating identity, which will mark with its rigid structure the subject's whole mental development' (Lacan 1977: 4). It is this ego, ever lured towards imaginary identifications, that Lacan sees as responsible for the false ideology of so-called 'ego-psychology'.

As Muller writes, commenting on the affective tie binding ego-to-ego relationships, and quoting Lacan (his translation):

> ...such a view of psychoanalytic practice as reduced to a dyadic relation, is a practice in which the symbolic register is suppressed in favour of 'a utopian rectification of the imaginary couple', which can arouse in 'everyone of good faith' only the 'sentiment of abjection'. (Muller 1996: 131)

A psychoanalytic therapy which aims at strengthening the ego and/or its defences is therefore, for Lacan, by its very nature alienating. In his terms, it alienates the subject from his or her desire (we will elaborate on this point below). Where Foulkes sees in the group the possibility of sophisticated and deep communication, Lacan sees only the workings of an imaginary ideal of totality—namely the idea that one can have, in or through the group, the perfect body, that there can be the subject without lack, without rupture, integrated and whole.

The subject of language

Language and its constituent parts—'signifiers'—clearly occupy a central place in Lacan's theorising. He begins, simply enough, by pointing out that psychoanalysis works on the symptom only by means of speech. He argues that it is language which brings the human subject into being—though he is careful to be precise about how this occurs.

Prior to the acquisition of language, as described above, the 'I' exists only in 'primordial form' based on a process of imaginary identifications. This attests to the way in which the human infant—like other animals—is capable of functioning in a particular and organised way without language. For example, the pre-linguistic infant (or, better, 'proto-linguistic') is capable of a sense of agency, intention, physical cohesion, continuity in time—and so on—which it shares with any dog or cat. However, this does not imply that dogs and cats have entered the symbolic, can think and reason, or possess a Freudian unconscious. One should not, merely on these grounds, postulate the existence of a subject. Rather there is just 'the-baby-acting-in-this-way', on the basis of particular internal or external stimuli. To a considerable extent, the baby can be seen as functioning pre-symbolically on the model of an analogic machine rather than as a symbolic subject, and as such requires only a continual reading of its immediate environment and bodily states (for instance, its level of hunger) to impel it to alter—or not—the state it is in. This does not require inner symbolic representations, but merely sensory capacities.[20] With the arrival of language all this changes, and the world of signals or natural signs (which clearly exist also for animals, who communicate but do not use language) is replaced by the world of signifiers. Benveniste, a French linguist whose work Lacan refers to in his Seminar III, describes this as follows:

> Consciousness of self is only possible if it is experienced by contrasts. I use 'I' only when I am speaking to someone who will be a 'you' in my address. It is this condition of dialogue that is constitutive of person, for it implies that reciprocally 'I' becomes 'you' in the address of the one who in his turn designates himself as 'I'. (cited in Muller 1996: 67)

Lacan, for his part, is equally sensitive to the importance of indexicals (that is, pronouns such as 'I', 'you', 'he', 'she', and designators such as 'here', 'there', 'now') as constitutive both of the 'speaking being' and the world the subject inhabits as a consequence. He writes:

> What I seek in speech is the response of the Other. What constitutes me is my question. In order to be recognised by the Other, I utter what was, only in view of what will be. In order to find him I call him by a name that he must assume or refuse in order to reply to me. I identify myself in language, but only by losing myself in it like an object. What is realised in my history is not the past definite of what was, since it is no more, or even the present perfect of what has been in what I am, but the future anteri-

or of what I shall have been for what I am in the process of becoming. (Lacan 1977: 86)

Elsewhere Lacan writes of how from sounds 'modulated in presence and absence there is born the world of meaning of a particular language in which the world of things will come to be arranged' (Lacan 1977: 5). For Lacan, therefore, language gives birth, in a simultaneous moment, to the subject as 'I' and to the world of things, and it does so not bit by bit, but rather from the first moment the symbolic takes on a universal character—'as soon as the symbol arrives there is a universe of symbols' (Lacan 1988b: 29). This underlines the point that linguistic elements are constituted by their relationship with other elements of language and not by the use a particular speaker gives to a particular word.[21]

What should be emphasised here is that Lacan has a developed theory of language that is not only sophisticated and complex but radical in its implications. Highlighting the function of metonymy (as displacement), Lacan seeks to demonstrate how the associative linkings of signifier to signifier are constitutive of the de-centred subject of Freud, in which language marks a radical otherness at the core of the subject. Ordinarily, for example, we think we control and produce thought by virtue of our conscious effort. This is true, to an extent. Lacan, on the other hand, emphasises that '*it* thinks'—that language, or what one could perhaps loosely term 'the language machine' thinks the subject. (The term Lacan uses is 'the Other', which carries a number of meanings.[22]) It thinks the subject in tandem with, and despite our consciously directed thought. By this Lacan highlights the fact that thought 'just comes'. Miller (1995) illustrates this as follows:

How do we grasp the phenomenon of talking in analysis? Lacan privileges the gaps. He chooses to define the unconscious—and it is only one definition among many—as 'impediment failure, split... in a spoken or written sentence something stumbles'. Freud is attracted by these phenomena and it is there that he seeks the unconscious. There something other demands to be realised—which appears as intentional, of course, but of a strange temporality. What occurs, what is produced in the gap, is presented as *the discovery*. (Miller 1995: 9-10)

Freud illustrates this fact with parapraxes—one only finds out what the thought is after it comes out—thus thought is both always working in us, and always running along on its own in such a way that we do not necessarily know what is happening any more than one knows why one's eyes blink when subjected to an air blast—it is just a brute fact. Out of this 'it', or 'subject of language', there is constructed—through symbolic identifications—a more delimited 'I', an I identified with particular signifiers as master signifiers.[23] These signifiers should be regarded as nonsensical, as non-rational elements of the unconscious, for they are in a sense 'simply there', simply 'in' a person. For instance, words like 'shy', 'kind', 'cruel', 'tough', 'democrat', 'nationalist', and so on, are all signifiers which can organise a person's life, and it is through such networks of signifiers that my desire is invariably elaborated in a manner particular to me.[24] Yet at this very moment there is, for Lacan, an elision, because by knowing these master signifiers one does not thereby 'know' what one is. Rather, what one is remains unknown, remains a process whereby 'it'—the unconscious—constantly reveals itself through language and in thought at the moment of enunciation.

When we identify a self, as the philosopher Hume pointed out, we actually identify a body of thoughts going on in our consciousness. It is, in part, this image that leads to the illusion that there is a substantive 'I' who creates and directs thought. As Freud put it in his famous aphorism *'Wo Es war, soll Ich werden'*—which Lacan translates as 'Where it was there must I become'[25]—the truth of the subject is tied to a want-to-be, or coming into being, in which we must never lose sight of the subject's radical eccentricity to itself. For Lacan, these philosophical reflections on language take us to the very heart of Freud's discovery—namely, to the fact that the unconscious is essentially linguistic in nature. As Lacan puts it, the unconscious is 'that part of the concrete discourse insofar as it is trans-individual, that is, not at the disposal of the subject in re-establishing the continuity of his conscious discourse' (Lacan 1977: 49). In his analysis Lacan has done away with the notion of so-called 'deep structure' with the implication that, in psychoanalysis, we can have access to some extra-linguistic conceptual reality. Rather, language functions 'according to the laws of a closed order' (Lacan 1977: 152). There is the signifier and the signified, but the signified does not refer—as it does for Saussure—to an underlying concept, but rather to *another* signifier, for 'no signification can be maintained other than by reference to another signification' (Lacan 1977: 150).

While this return to the role of language in psychoanalysis constitutes one of Lacan's most important revisions of Freudian theory[26] it would be a mistake to assume that he is simply elaborating a version of post-structuralist doctrine, which characterises the subject as purely an effect—or entity—'of discourse'.[27] Many commentators on Lacan have made this mistake. As a working psychoanalyst, Lacan was only too well aware of subjects who resist, deny, and displace the linguistic effects at which the psychoanalyst aims whilst he or she 'directs the treatment' (a phrase Lacan uses to emphasise that it is the treatment rather than the patient that one 'directs'). Thus, while Lacan's subject necessarily exists in a state of self-division, it is also necessary to recognise each subject's particular identity, which is characterisable as a certain stability within the self-structure, which in turn motivates resistance. Indeed it is this singularity of the case that must be recognised in psychoanalysis if it is to produce effects. For Lacan the singularity of the subject represents the particular way conflicting discourses—the web of symbolic relations—organise the subject and in turn produce that subject's uniqueness. Language is not simply internalised, or swallowed whole (as it were), but is uniquely organised in each individual as a result of the unconscious functions of repression and desire. The destiny of the subject situated amidst a multitude of discourses is the production of original effects, a particular organised constellation of signifiers. These represent the permeable boundaries of the subject— the word 'subject' designating here not the Cartesian subject of self-knowledge, but that which 'goes well beyond what is experienced "subjectively" by the individual, exactly as far as the truth he is able to attain' (Lacan 1977: 55).

To be subject to fading

Lacan, especially in his later work, attempted to create a science of the real, a psychoanalysis of 'object a'.

'Object a' is that which is not symbolised, and—as such—lies outside of the signifying chain. It is *real*, not symbolic. It is that which remains behind (as it were) after the subject is constituted through language. 'Object a' represents something outside of that with which one can identify.

This 'outside something'—which Lacan classifies as a 'remainder' or 'remnant'—escapes symbolisation and defines the subject as a sexual and desiring being—or, to use Lacan's term, as a 'want-of-being'. Lack and desire are understood by Lacan as co-extensive terms. This 'left over' from primary repression thus denotes an object which can never be attained, but which sets desire itself in motion. 'Object a' is not *the* breast, penis, oral, anal or scopic object, but that which is inscribed or evoked in relation to all of these partial objects as it exists (and insists) both within the subject and within the Other. It is thus opaque to the subject who is—nonetheless—subjected to its pull. In a sense, it is also the opposite to the object of narcissism (the ego), by being 'that thing' the subject seeks beyond him or herself and 'in' the Other. What becomes crucial in analysis is precisely that which cease-lessly escapes symbolic inscription and refuses to be put into words. Laurent describes this as follows:

> Psychoanalysis, as a practice of dis-identification, as rupture by the unchaining of the subject of the unconscious, and of the establishment of identifications, produces an emptiness and in this operation leaves a remainder. This operation permits the analysand-subject new possibilities. (Laurent 1995b: 9)

The direction of the treatment comes about through allowing that which escapes representation ('object a') to drive the analysis to an end. A movement from an endless over-production of meaning ends when one could say the subject can come to trust his or her want-of-being. For this to take place, there must be a crossing of the plane of identification. This entails a breaking away from the belief in a subjec-tive capture by an ideal, the objectifying gaze of the Other, which Lacan describes as 'somewhere in the Other, from which the Other sees me, in the form I like to be seen' (Lacan 1979: 268). This comes about through separation, an encounter with the lack in the Other, a realisa-tion that the Other is barred and does not contain the truth. Not all of the subject can be represented (in the Other); that which remains non-represented is 'object a', around which the drives circulate.

At the moment of separation, therefore, there is a *fading of the sub-ject*, such that the subject is unable to constitute him or herself into exis-tence through identifications. There is a gap in meaning which lies at the navel of analysis, and is marked by anxiety. The subject is anguished when denied the possibility of taking up an imaginary point in the Other and, at the same time, he/she is confronted with questions concerning his or her own being: 'Why did I marry this kind of man? Why do I sleep with so-and-so when they are not my kind of man? Why have I not seen my mother for 5 years?', and so on. Such questions represent a state of ignorance, of not-knowing. Here the subject is divided between 'truth' and knowledge. The truth of the subject's being lies elsewhere, and the story the subject told him or herself about their own life no longer acts as an alibi. The subject is faced with some new possibility, a new way of being, which involves changing his/her relationship to the world. This renunciation of dear and cherished assumptions represented in fantasy about who and what I am is to stumble upon the incomprehensible, the incomplete, and to fall pray to non-sense (the unimportant, arbitrary, paradoxical). At this moment of fading the subject will try to reconstitute him or herself in an existence through identification. However, the 'object a'—which is unrepresentable and lies between signifiers—breaks the signifying chain. Consequently, the subject is unable to link together signifiers, and there is a loss of identification with unpleasant and indeterminable effects. An encounter with 'object a' thus involves a loss of reality, a going beyond the pleasure principle. Fading is a structural manifestation of the phenomenon of depersonalisation. It denotes a place where the subject might not exist, a place of non-existence open only to a potential existence or a 'want-to-be'.

This 'fading of the subject' is used by Lacan to highlight the fact that, in the act of speaking, the subject's speech can never fully express the subject. This is due to the structural division of the subject brought about by primary repression. In the present moment there is a manifestation of the subject, due to the function of the signifier (which is always in relation to another signifier). However, the signifier reduces 'the subject in question to being no more than a signifier, to petrify the subject in the same movement in which it calls the subject to function, to speak, as subject' (Lacan 1979: 207). This entails a disappearance of being, that primordial loss and refusal of *jouissance* which occurs when a drive is taken up and inscribed within the symbolic universe.

For Lacan, clinical practice takes place within the order of the non-realised. The unconscious is constituted by that which is essentially non-realised, refused, what Lacan refers to as 'the structuring function of a lack' (Lacan 1979: 29). Clinical practice aims to bring the subject to a place where he/she can trust his/her want-of-being, this want-of-being denoting the order of the non-realised.

Laurent puts this as follows:

You have to address the true meaning of what the analysand says within the signifying chain, and the true meaning analytic interpretation has to address is not the effect of signification but rather the product or remainder of the first encounter between the subject and the Other—the remainder of that experience, *das Erlebnis* in Freudian terms, the remainder of jouissance... [Lacan writes:] 'Interpretation is not open to any and all meanings. The effect of interpretation is to isolate in the subject a kernel, a *Kern* to use Freud's own term, of non-sense, that does not mean interpretation is in itself nonsense...' Lacan adopted this term and described the *Kern* of the subject as a signifier isolated in its deeper meaning—separated from meaning, the binary signifier standing for anything that makes sense, thus separating out in the chain of signifiers what remains at the level of nonsense, the master signifier, S1. (Laurent 1995a: 31)

Practising psychoanalysis in the group context

Firstly, as should be evident from Lacan's positioning of the ego in the mirror stage, there is, in the Lacanian approach, no privileging of 'ego-functioning' or reinforcement of so-called 'healthy identifications' which the subject may hold. Such identifications, however culturally valid within a particular milieu, are—for Lacan—always subjectively alienating. Whether one sees oneself as a freedom fighter or a terrorist is not the point for psychoanalysis, though clearly the way in which master signifiers define and guide the life of a particular subject will be explored. This is a process Lacan describes as 'rectification'. It involves confrontation with and mapping of the various synchronic and diachronic associative linkings to master signifiers. The purpose of this, however, is merely to pave the way to *interpreting* the fantasy that supports such identifications, for it is only through the fantasy and the subject's relation to 'object a'—and ultimately to his or her void of being—that one may approach unconscious desire.

This should not be taken to mean that group identifications do not occur, but only that 'group-as-a-whole' phenomena are based on the presupposition of a fictional entity, or ideal, which holds out to each the promise of narcissistic completion. What the analyst must do in these situations is to put 'group-as-a-whole' phenomena into question by addressing, within the group, what form of life they lead to, and what attempts are made within the group to sustain them. To the question 'can one truly speak for all?', Lacan answers 'no'.

The second point to be made is that, for Lacan, there is no end-point or ideal synthesis to be aimed at in the work. To follow this path is to silence or close-up the unconscious. Synthesis and integration imply adaptation, but adaptation to what? To society? To life's routines? To psychoanalytic ideals in the form of an ideology of the psychological-ly mature or strong man/woman? All these pathways merely take one down the road of suggestion and its many derivatives, captivating the subject within what Lacan termed the 'lure of the already there'.

This 'lure of the already there' is beautifully illustrated by Blay-Neto in a clinical example of how a group might attempt to avoid the unknown:

> I found that my serenity was the result of my leading the group to function within an area that was familiar to me, by imposing my fantasies on them: the group developed them for me as though they were their own. Thus a comfortable situation was reached... But this comfortable situation could only be main-tained by sacrificing the therapeutic process; so, dressing up the unknown with familiar clothes, the unknown would never have the conditions in which to become known. (Blay-Neto 1985: 252)

A third line of criticism can be directed towards those approaches with-in the field of group psychotherapy which base themselves on a read-ing of some form of pre-established code in relation to the group. In this approach the analyst places him or herself in the position of 'one who knows', whose knowledge and 'privileged language' serves the function of deciphering presupposed individual and/or group phe-nomena. For Lacan, such 'translations' are always suspect and invari-ably result in the most dulling and stereotypical of interpretative styles. In Lacan's terms what is produced here is a master discourse which seeks to dominate the subject, leading often enough to that depressing phenomena—frequently seen, for example, in analytic institutions—namely, *identification with the analyst*. Alternatively, this approach opens the pathway to outright rejection, as was evident in Dora's negative reaction to and ultimate dismissal of Freud in the face of his insistent misreading of her desire. In place of this seeking out of presupposed correspondences to the words one hears, the analyst should, Lacan argues, attend instead to the subject's associative path-ways—which is a form of *de-translation* or *emptying out* of meaning—and by so doing remain in the position he or she designated as that of the analyst.[28]

To illustrate the above, we can turn to Plato's *Symposium*. In the *Symposium*, the intellectual elite find themselves gathered together debating the nature of Eros. Each of the speakers offers his thoughts on love. When Socrates speaks he does not attempt to replace one discourse of mastery with another, but puts into question all the preceding discourse. Socrates is provocative and brings about a rupture, 'a breaking down of a beautiful discourse that knows nothing of what is said, characterised by its *Nichtigkeit*, emptiness' (Lacan 1960-61: 11/1/61]). Socrates thus employs an interpretative style in which he shows his interlocutors that absurd consequences follow from holding certain opinions about the world. As Lacan puts it, 'it is to bring the effect of his questioning to bear on the consistency of the signifier' (Lacan 1960-61: 14/12/60). Socrates shows them that nothing holds their arguments together. For Socrates, one might say group subversion was already a subjective necessity.

Lacan, relies on what he designated a cornerstone of analytic practice—namely, the 'desire-of-the-analyst'. He raises, squarely, the issue of analytic intentionality. This is often enough elided, but remains crucial, in both individual and group settings. Lacan states: 'it is ultimately the analyst's desire which operates in psychoanalysis' (Lacan 1996). What might this mean? On one level it refers simply to that desire the analyst displays in listening to the unconscious. On another level it refers to the nature of the analyst's desire, which Lacan described as a desire for 'absolute difference'—the defining elements of one's always particular subjectivity. To achieve this the analyst must not respond to the subject's demands—for love, relief of suffering, and so on—but must produce in the subject and through the analytic work a truth, a subjective knowledge of suffering (unconscious signifiers) or, more loosely put, a new discourse. This emerging discourse will of necessity have its master signifiers, but with the crucial difference that these will not represent the ideals (the ego ideal) already imposed upon the subject. Instead the new master signifiers will be those produced by the subject, to the extent that the analyst sustains the subject's desire for bringing forth within the analysis 'object a' as the cause of desire. The subject thus becomes detached from his or her ideal(s), which simultaneously deprives the subject of the imaginary satisfaction of becoming or embodying the loved ideal. At this point there occurs what Lacan called a moment of 'subjective destitution', a loss of fundamental references, which leaves the subject no longer questioning the other's desire (embodied by questions such as: 'What does the other want of me?' 'Am I worthy?', and so on) but instead facing the truth of his or her own desire. This raises an ethical point—the experience of the lack of any guarantee. Lacan puts it this way:

> In order to reach the point beyond the reduction of the individ-
> ual's ideals, it is as 'object a' of desire, as what he has been for the
> Other in his erection as a living being, as wanted or unwanted
> when he came into the world, that the subject is called upon to
> be reborn in order to know if he wants what he desires... Such is
> the sort of truth that Freud brought to light with the invention of
> psychoanalysis. (quoted in Julien 1994: 101)

Lacan puts the related ethical point as follows: 'the only thing of which one can be guilty, at least in the analytic perspective, is to have given up on one's desire' (Lacan 1992: 368). What the psychoanalyst is aiming at, therefore, is nothing less that a re-subjectivisation of the subject. This entails a re-appraisal of the subject's fundamental fantasy and—consequently—a distancing from it. The Lacanian analyst, at this point, is clearly far way from the perspective of (for example) Foulkes, who suggests that 'individual psychotherapy is thus a form of group psychotherapy without being aware of it' (Foulkes 1990: 155). This practice emphasises the reverse of the Lacanian approach, which is focused upon the subject, and on how this subject constitutes his or her world in the act of desire. The world, and the group, are not pre-givens, and to objectify them is to create a fiction and a refuge which, instead of evoking desire, will merely confer a sense of identity, a being-for-another.

Foulkes states that:

> Group psychotherapy simply brings back the problems to where
> they belong. The community is represented in the treatment
> room. Validations and norms are restated and modified by com-
> parison, contrast and analysis. Communication leading to a
> shared experience and understanding is the terms of the group.
> (Foulkes 1990: 155)

This, for Lacan, can only be an *alienating* moment, best captured in the notion of 'strengthening the ego'. For Lacan, desire is repressed by a strong ego, not a weak ego. In complete contrast to Foulkes, Lacan argues that analysis:

...must aim at the passage of the speech, joining the subject to another subject, on the other side of the wall of language. That is the final relation of the subject to a genuine Other, to the Other who gives the answer one doesn't expect, which defines the terminal point of analysis. (Lacan 1988b: 246)

Thus what is essential is to encounter unconscious desire, an 'inmixing of otherness' at the core of one's being, brought about by the emergence of repressed signifiers and—with this—the question which is not at all containing, but which provokes anguish: 'what do you (it) want of me?'

At this point it might be useful to introduce an example from our own experience. A group for HIV positive people had been running for about one and a half years. During one session a man with AIDS, who was soon to die, said: 'What would happen if someone in this group died?' Silence followed. After some time, someone said 'can we look the beast in the eye?' A long silence followed. After this very long silence the man continued: 'I cannot play the game of social niceties anymore. A friend of mine who I was to have dinner with won a big business contract. I could not get excited. It just does not work anymore. I didn't know what to say to him. Tell them about my constant diarrhoea and vomiting?' More silence, and then another group member said: 'People say, oh we are all going to die, yes, but when you are HIV positive, death is in your face, the veil is removed'. To this another person responded: 'Only to be re-veiled until you get sick'. Analyst: 'OK let's end on that'.[29]

This example illustrates how the analyst punctuates the discourse at a point where there is a lack, a point of non-existence open to existence, a loss of familiar identifications and thus a point of anguish and of ignorance. The subject puts him or herself in question, and—there—questions desire. There is evoked a sense of being with something that determines me. At the very moment when this is unfrozen and in movement, there is thus an opening of the unconscious, in the place of repetition, which is what the analyst is after. Additionally there is within this example the signifier 'death' which, for Lacan, is fundamentally linked to desire as the limit of one's being, and as something that has a particular place in analysis. Death and the anxiety of death are to be *lived against*, rather than avoided or otherwise elided. It must be situated in order to be lived with, which is, in part, what this analytic 'punctuation' achieves.

Let us now, however, turn our attention to a second cornerstone of clinical practice, to *love* which, in psychoanalysis, is called 'transference'. There is no analysis without transference, and it is through transference that the subject's 'conditions of love' emerge. Indeed, one can go as far as saying that it is in the *analysis* of transference—rather than its manipulation (that is, a cure by 'suggestion')—through which psychoanalysis manifests its unique function whereby the analysand is called upon to investigate his or her own unconscious. As Freud states, one finds in transference:

> ...what might be described as a stereotype plate (or several such) which is constantly repeated—constantly repeated afresh—in the course of the person's life, so far as external circumstances and the nature of the love-objects accessible to him permit, and which is certainly not entirely insusceptible to change in the face of recent experience. (Freud 1912: 99-100)

For Freud, the analyst is thus taken up into one of the series of archaic imagoes, belonging to the patient's unconscious, which represent a 'compulsion to repeat, and in the end we understand that this is his way of remembering' (Freud 1914b: 150). For Lacan one of the key questions concerning transference was *what* is repeated? His first response was to argue that what was repeated is essentially an imaginary relationship (to the analyst) which leads to a stagnation of the analytic work. It is, in effect, that moment in which: 'the analyst goes astray and equally takes his or her bearings' (Lacan 1952: 103). Later he was to argue that the transference was a *repetition*, but a repetition of a demand emerging in speech and—as such—a message calling for the analyst's response in an inverted form. In simple terms, the wish for—say—a kiss from or some closeness to the analyst has to be 'found again', elaborated and informed by the analysand's fantasy, as a movement of desire, which marks the subject with a wish to kiss, to be close to, and so on.[30] In a third development of his thinking in his seminar devoted to transference (1960-1961), Lacan refined this position also and argued that the idea of a re-inscription of a demand in the act of speaking was too general a notion of transference. In its place Lacan formulated the concept of 'the desire of the analyst', which implies the analyst should occupy the 'empty place' of the Other's desire, acting as an (enigmatic) cause of unconscious desire. This produces transference, and allows the analysand's own unique truth to emerge based on a desire proper to the analyst—namely, a desire for 'absolute difference'. For Lacan there is, therefore, a desire that is specific to analysis and to the analyst/analytic function. At the same time this evokes transference and tends in the opposite direction to identification.[31] In the group setting this implies a form of functioning specific to the analyst and necessarily divorced from the other relationships in the group, which are of a different character. It is fascinating to see that in many ways Foulkes argues precisely this point. For example, in one of the few places in which he mentions transference between group members he describes such phenomena in terms of aberration and as 'a psychotic type of transference' (Foulkes 1990: 245). Moreover, he is at pains to argue in another paper that the term transference should be reserved for Freud's 'classical notion' of transference, and that one should avoid calling other aspects of the so-called psychotherapeutic relationship by this name. In the same article he is critical of the notion of counter-transference, stating that: 'The Trojan horse of counter-transference threatens the walls that have guarded the splendid isolation of the psychoanalyst's situation' (Foulkes 1990: 141-143). The Lacanian analyst would agree. Lacan himself, discussing Freud's treatment of the Dora case, situates its failure squarely upon Freud's active counter-transference, which Lacan labels as the sum total of 'his prejudices passions and difficulties'.[32] For Lacan, there are invariably counter-transference effects: the analyst feels or experiences this or that when with a patient. However, these effects belong to the analyst and must be kept silent, for there is no telepathy, and no unconscious to unconscious communication that evades the signifier. It is the subject's signifiers that count, which puts the focus on handling the transference in such a way as to ensure it does not disrupt the analysand's speech.

Let us return to the case of the *Symposium* to illustrate the above. Following a discourse which Socrates concludes with a description of Eros as a desire of what one lacks, Alcibiades bursts onto the scene. Wounded, he presents a complaint (symptom) and demands that Socrates take away his ills. Alcibiades does not want to produce his own knowledge, but would love Socrates to give him knowledge. Alcibiades is operating under the assumption that there is something to know and this creates transference effects. Alcibiades' love of Socrates is both an obstacle and agent in the case, a means by which he seeks a knowledge of what is most intimate to himself. Put another way, Socrates incarnates an object ('object a') and—as such—is turned into the beloved object which will fill up the lack in Alcibiades' life.

Socrates and Alcibiades are engaged in a seduction. This seduction of Socrates produces—for Alcibiades—a form of pleasure which leads to *nothing*. Socrates remains silent and takes his bearings on his own want-of-being (that is, he resolves to be empty, and not to signify his presence). Socrates' silence demonstrates a certainty in not knowing, a desire that remains non-metonymised and open to being surprised by what is said. When Socrates does speak it is a speech act which aims to decipher the convergence and overlap of signifiers. He offers what amounts to an interpretation:

> You seem to me quite sober, Alcibiades. Otherwise you wouldn't try to conceal your real object with such an apparatus of artful circumlocution, and then slip it in at the end by way of after-thought... (Plato 1951: 112)

Plato does not specify the 'interpretation' which Alcibiades makes in response to Socrates' intervention; for Lacan it is always the case that while the analyst *offers* an interpretation, it is the analysand who *makes* the interpretation.

As for transference, it is important to note that—if it is too strong—there will be love and no work; if it is too weak there will be lack of desire, and—in most cases—a repetitive call for help. Too much hatred, meanwhile, will bring the treatment to an end. Moreover, to directly interpret the transference leads, Lacan claims, onto the plane of an 'I-you', ego-to-ego, or imaginary dialectic which only tends to fixate or trap the analysand at this level, while the analyst—in turn—becomes an omniscient other. What then is the Lacanian aiming at in interpretation? What is the effect one is attempting to produce here? Lacan is clear on this point. Insight as knowledge will not do, for knowledge is subject to commodification and—as such—can be assimilated by the neurotic without any change in his or her neurotic structure. Indeed, it is for this reason that Freud's early interpretations, now culturally appropriated and commodified, no longer work in analytic practice.

The analyst thus aims not at telling the truth, but at *enabling the truth*[33] *to appear*. As Lacan suggests:

> Interpretation must introduce into the synchrony of the signi-fiers that compose it something that suddenly makes translation possible—precisely what is made possible by the function of the Other in the concealment of the code, it being in relation to the Other that the missing element appears. (Lacan 1977: 233)

In this quotation Lacan is condensing a number of issues. Firstly, he indicates that the aim of interpretation is to *evoke*, to make something *possible* for the subject—which is clearly different from the analyst offering a descriptive narrative to the analysand. No matter how accurate or sense-making one presumes this description to be, it necessarily alienates and objectifies the subject. Secondly, he indicates that what is aimed at is the appearance of a missing element in relation to the subject's unconscious which can be recognised by the subject, thus enabling the analysand to experience—bit by bit—what is subjectively avoided ('the repressed') and—ultimately—that which sustains his or her desire (the subject's 'fundamental fantasy'). When it comes to the issue of how one (in practice) interprets, Lacan is purposively reticent, eschewing all formulas such as the injunction to be 'simple, clear, concrete and direct' which some classical authors have frequently put forward as the *sine qua non* of a good interpretation. Instead, Lacan favours a style that privileges equivocation and the homophonic possibilities available through language, which allow the analyst the best possibility of introducing the subject to that which falls—in a sense—*between* signifiers, in that space of absence made evident when we simply place two signifiers together in an endless attempt to articulate our being. For Lacan, a style which privileges allusion is both a duty and a necessity for the psychoanalyst.

Illustrating this clinically is not easy. As the psychoanalytic reader or psychotherapist will know, the most profound interpretative acts can easily appear mundane without recourse to a good deal of the text of the particular patient or analysand's speech. Nevertheless a brief example may help.

In a group run by one of the authors, a group member began to talk about the very public difficulties in relationships and loss of status being experienced by the British Royal Family. The patient's speech was resonant with other themes—such as the vicissitudes of love, one's place in and outside of the family, relationships with parental figures, and the relationship to and between the group's therapists (in this case a male/female pair working as co-therapists). He might have commented further on any of these.[34] However, this particular group member focused his concerns on the loss of status the Royal Family was suffering. The analyst's interpretation was directed at this anxiety, as a point of potential subjectification for this group member, whose comments represented other people as—in the end, and hopelessly—all too similar. Simply by picking up on an often repeated signifier in the

words of the patient—'distinguish'/'distinguished'—the interpretation, such as it was, sought recognition of the patient's speech, and to
evoke its resonances, ambivalences, and points of equivocation. The
analyst said: 'your concerns seem to centre on the absence of a distinguished presence'. In doing so, the analysand's current struggle and
abject failure to distinguish himself in a high profile profession, to fulfil the role of the distinguished mother's son (who, during his childhood, and in place of the 'undistinguished' and failed oedipal father,
truly was the apple of her eye), to be fully present in the group, to enter
any form of love relationship, to distinguish himself from others without denigration or idealisation, along with his tendency to take flight
in daydreams of narcissistic grandiosity, were put in question and a
response awaited. Awaited, that is, because it is the analysand's unconscious that—in the end—interprets, by means of producing unconscious signifiers.

As stated earlier, there is no aspiration here to present a paradigm
interpretation, but merely to try and show how the Lacanian analyst
focuses more on the *play* (and resonances) of signifiers, and where this
may lead, in contrast to an interpretative style that seeks to emphasise
transference interpretations, or to supply potentially definitive and
alternative meanings for the analysand's speech. One could say—cari-
caturing somewhat—that rather than make the unconscious conscious,
the Lacanian is more interested in giving unconscious processes free
rein; in place of a serious interpretation, the Lacanian emphasises the
unconscious series.

A psychoanalysis oriented in this way is thus not focused on what
the subject may or may not *learn* as a consequence of his or her exposure to the group or indeed to psychoanalysis itself. Rather, what is
aimed at is a transformation in the nature of the individual's subjectivity, which brings along with it an end to neurotic suffering, though
not—as Freud pointed out—an end to 'common human unhappiness'.
Beyond this, it is not a transformation which promises all that much.
Lacan suggests that what is on offer is the possibility of taking up in
relation to another the position of analyst—defined as 'the supposed
subject of knowledge' and, as such, embodying a function that can
work against repression and for 'absolute difference'. On the other
hand, perhaps one may also hope to be more humorous or ironic in the
face of the insistence of unconscious functioning—one's own and others' alike. For our part, what we hope is clear at this point is how Lacan
stresses again and again the 'subject' of psychoanalysis as its sole sup-

port and guide. For the Lacanian psychoanalyst this remains the case in the group setting, whatever benefit (which at times may be considerable) the social aspect of this situation might bring to a patient in terms of developing—for example—greater social and cultural sophistication and/or resilience. To that extent, the direction of the treatment remains fundamentally the same in the group setting as in the individual case,[35] for one cannot alter this focus without losing what is at the heart of psychoanalysis—namely, the speaking subject, which is where, we would argue, psychoanalysis itself necessarily both begins and ends.

Notes

[1] In quoting Lacan we have, as far as possible, restricted ourselves to published translations in English, at times depending on other authors' translations of passages from Lacan's works not yet available in English in their original form. This is in the belief that it allows the English reader better access to relevant secondary material.

[2] 'Desire', for Lacan, designates *unconscious* desire. Moreover, for Lacan, during the moment at which one recognises one's desire by naming it, one recognises something new, something not already present in one's world. It is in this that the efficacious action of analysis—its performative dimension—is realised.

[3] For example, Schilder 1936; Wender 1940; Wolf 1949.

[4] For example, Foulkes 1948; Bion 1961.

[5] Our position here is not that these group processes do not exist. Rather, we maintain that 'the group', as indicating a natural order, is both an entification and a totalisation. Writing from a slightly different perspective, Schwartz makes a similar point about organisations, attributing their destructive narcissistic processes to 'an obscuring on the part of the organisation, of the source of the resources it employs'. He continues: 'The point to be noted here is that, in the most fundamental sense with regard to the exchange relationships of work, the organisation is not a party in the transaction. The organisation, strictly speaking, is simply a patterning of this very complex relationship. This is at least one meaning that can be given to Karl Weick's... observation that the organisation does not exist, only the process of organising does. Thus bringing the organisation in as the main party in the transaction is already an act of obscuration' (Schwartz 1990: 42).

[6] Freud summarises the three forms of identification as follows: 'First, identification is the original form of emotional tie with an object, secondly, in a regressive way it becomes a substitute for a libidinal object-tie, as it were by means of introjection of the object into the ego; and thirdly, it may arise with any new perception of a common quality shared with some other person who is not an object of the sexual instinct. The more important this common quality is, the more successful may

this partial identification become, and it may thus represent the beginning of a new tie' (Freud 1921: 107-108). In terms of group psychology, it is the first and third forms of identification which Freud emphasised.

7 Whilst such group processes exist in large groups, the point is that psychoanalytic practice simply does not extend as far as the crowd or mass, though psychoanalytically informed action can exert and influence—that is, when this action is in the guise of an ethics of truth (or liberation) based on freedom from illusion. Of course, this is not to say that misuses do not occur. One might simply point to the oppressed forms of sexuality produced by some psychoanalytic discourses (for instance, Socarides 1978) which are in sharp contrast to Freud's own ethical position. See Lewes 1995 for a wider discussion of this issue. In the setting of the small interactive group, the less remote leader—*qua* analyst—must forge a bond that is fundamentally different from that which is available through identification.

8It is perhaps interesting to note that various aspects of this problem have recently been addressed by a number of IPA analysts. Kernberg has written a highly critical article on the way institutional trainings in psychoanalysis tend to inhibit the creativity of psychoanalytic candidates—for example, by displaying monolithic tendencies regarding theoretical approaches; by accentuating hierarchical relations among psychoanalytic faculty members; by discouraging original contributions; and by neglecting controversies regarding psychoanalytic technique, and so on. Wallerstein in his report on the Fifth IPA Conference of Training Analysts (July 1991) points out the difficulty of transmission in psychoanalysis by highlighting the twin dangers of 'petrification'—namely the stultification of analytic creativity produced by tribe-like, trade school or semi-religious approaches to training—and 'chaos'—namely the risk of embodying ever more maverick and delinquent approaches to psychoanalysis within an ethos of 'anything goes'. Lacan, for his part, actively addressed this problem from the 1960s onwards. See Kernberg 1996; Wallerstein 1993, Lacan 1990.

9 In Lacan's terms, the psychoanalytic act creates the psychoanalyst, and not *vice versa*.

10 Despite Lacan's innovations many of his critics have argued that his efforts to overcome such problems ultimately failed, leading to identifications within Lacan's school that are as problematic as other schools and institutions. (See, for example, Roustang 1976.) On the other hand, the present authors would—given space—wish to argue that, certain aberrations aside, a Lacanian orientation, whereby each subject is systematically confronted with the question of 'the desire of the analyst', both during his or her formation as an analyst and in relation to how the institution itself functions not as a guarantor but as a support to this, is ultimately *helpful* in supporting analysis against 'filiation' to or within the psychoanalytic community.

11 Lacan states of this function that: 'the task of directing will not constitute a form of leadership whose services rendered might be capitalised on into access to a higher rank and no one will be inclined to regard himself demoted for entering at a rank of base level work... This in no way implies an inverted hierarchy, but a circular organisation where—easy to program—functioning will take on consistency with experience' (Lacan 1990: 97).

[12] Other measures instituted by Lacan in this vein include: membership of the school was not restricted to analysts/trainees; all members had equal voting rights; the instigation of 'the pass' as a means to examine the question of 'the end of analysis'. See Lacan 1995, 1996, or—for a more critical review of these measures—Roudinesco 1990.

[13] We have chosen to focus here on the work of Foulkes as he is clearly a founding-father in this field. As he stated, whilst speaking to a British audience about this form of psychotherapy, 'I may claim a right in its definition, as I was the first to practice it in this country (and as later turned out anywhere in this form) and the first to use the name since Trigant Burrow, whose work lay back 30 years and who had abandoned this name in favour of phyloanalysis' (Foulkes 1990: 147). We do not, however, wish to set up Foulkes as a straw-man for Lacan. At the same time we do wish to offer a critical reading of a stance and emphasis clearly present in Foulkes. In doing, so we rely heavily on quoting from Foulkes' own writings, but must leave the reader to engage more fully with Foulkes' work as a whole. For a different approach from ours—one which emphasises potential points of integration between Foulkes and Lacan—the reader is referred to Laxenaire 1983. Our own view, however, is that this author ultimately fails to engage with what is most radical in Lacan.

[14] Lacan writes: 'the passion of the signifier now becomes a new dimension of the human condition in that it is not only man who speaks but that in man and through man *it* speaks (*ça parole*) that his nature as woven by effects in which is to be found the structure of language of which he becomes the material and that therefore here resounds in him, beyond what could be conceived of by a psychology of ideas, the relation to speech' (Lacan 1977: 284). It is interesting to speculate on whether Foulkes drew (as did Lowenstein and Hartmann) on Buchler's once popular linguistic theories which divided language between cognitive and expressive functions, with interpretation moving from the former to the latter and resulting in insight or knowledge of the self. Lacan's concept of the signifier, however, renders this distinction obsolete as linguistic elements have no intrinsic expressive or cognitive powers, but take on value only in relation to other signifiers. See Leader 1996 for a more extended discussion.

[15] See, for example, Alexander & French 1946.

[16] This issue, of course, highlights the fact that, to quote Wallerstein, 'psychoanalysis world-wide today... consists of multiple and divergent theories of mental functioning, of development, of pathogenesis, of treatment, and of cure' (Wallerstein 1988: 5) which is, perhaps, a somewhat more benign framing of this point.

[17] In describing this process Lacan writes: '...the fundamental mainspring of the analytic operation is the maintenance of the distance between the I—identification—and the (a)' (Lacan 1979: 273]). A few lines earlier he writes: 'any analysis that one teaches as having to be terminated by identification with the analyst reveals, by the some token, that its true motive force is elided. There is a beyond to the identification, and this beyond is defined by the relation and the distance of the object a (*objet petit a*) to the idealising capital I of identification' (Lacan 1979: 271-2).

[18] Unfortunately, a certain amount of glossing in relation to Lacan's work is inevitable here, particularly as Lacan constantly elaborated and reworked his ideas on psychoanalytic theory and practice throughout his life. The interested reader is referred to Fink 1995, Lee 1990, and to Lacan's own published work, including the extremely useful commentaries on Seminars I and II and on Seminar XI—Fink, Feldstein & Jaanus 1995. At this point it may be worth stating that Lacan (in some ways like Bion) had a preference for using symbols where possible, which—unlike words—resist concretisation and have fewer pre-formed images attached to them.

[19] There is considerable support for Lacan's view of infant development from within developmental psychology, which is carefully reviewed in Muller 1996. See especially chapters 1 to 4.

[20] A mercury thermometer is a good example of a rudimentary analogic machine; the height of the mercury measures the temperature, although it does not symbolise it.

[21] Wittgenstein makes a similar point when he argues that there can be no such thing as a private language. See Wittgenstein 1958.

[22] Lacan characterises the Other as follows: 'the Other is, therefore, the locus in which is constituted the I who speaks to him who hears, that which is said by the one being already the reply... But this locus also extends as far into the subject as the laws of speech, that is to say well beyond the discourse that takes its orders from the ego' (Lacan 1977: 141).

[23] 'Master signifiers' are valorised signifiers. They confer identity, are embodied in the ego ideal, and we maintain our sense of self-worth by attempting to live up to them.

[24] Lacan is uncompromising on the point, he writes: 'if what Freud discovered and re-discovers with a perpetually increasing sense of shock has a meaning, it is that the displacement of the signifier determines the subjects in their acts, in their destiny, in their blindness, in their end and in their fate, (their innate gifts and social acquisitions notwithstanding), without regard for character or sex, and that, willing or not, everything that might be considered the stuff of psychology, kit and caboodle *will follow the path of the signifier*' (quoted in Felman 1987: 43).

[25] Lacan sees the *Standard Edition* translation as deeply unfortunate and misleading. In translating this phrase as 'Where the id was, there the ego should be' a misconception in analysis has grown up around the idea that the ego should take precedence over the id. Moreover, for Lacan it risks misapprehending the very nature of the unconscious: 'The status of the unconscious, which, as I have shown, is so fragile on the ontic plane, is ethical. In his thirst for truth, Freud says, whatever it is I must go there because somewhere this unconscious reveals itself' (Lacan 1979: 33).

[26] In his paper 'The Function and Field of Speech and Language in Psychoanalysis' (1953) Lacan states: 'As far as I am concerned, I would assert that the technique cannot be understood, nor therefore correctly applied, if the concepts on which it is based are ignored. It is our task to demonstrate that these concepts take on their full meaning only when oriented in a field of language, only when ordered in relation to the function of speech' (Lacan 1977: 39).

[27] As Alcorn 1994 quite rightly illustrates.

[28] This method does not preclude so-called 'constructions' in analysis, but these are never seen as an end in themselves but part of a journey. Moreover they should arise spontaneously and be based on the actual speech of the analysand.

[29] This example invariably brings in Lacan's use of the variable session, which cannot be discussed in detail here. Simply put—however—Lacan sought to establish a way to end the session that was psychoanalytic rather than conventional (that is, based on clock time). Arguments as to the so-called 'containing' function of the non-variable session do not impress the present authors, nor is there apparent empirical support for this. Moreover, the heat generated by this Lacanian innovation leaves us somewhat bewildered given that many of the so-called brief and/or family-systems therapies have—since their inception—implicitly used variable sessions without undermining their therapeutic effect!

[30] Freud illustrates this approach in his discussion of the way he deals with just such a wish in *Studies on Hysteria*. See Freud & Breuer 1895: 302-3. See also the discussion in Forrester 1990: chapter 7.

[31] It is also worth quoting Freud at this point: 'If the patient puts the analyst in the position of his father (or mother) he is also giving him the power which his superego exercises over his ego... But at this point a warning must be given against misusing this new influence. However much the analyst may be tempted to become a teacher, model and ideal for other people, and to create men in his own image, he should not forget that it is not his task in the analytic relationship, and indeed that he will be disloyal to his task if he allows himself to be led on by his inclinations. If he does he will only be repeating a mistake of the parents who crushed their child's independence by their influence, and he will only be replacing the patient's earlier dependence by a new one' (Freud 1940: 38).

[32] Simply put, Freud was unable to perceive the importance of Dora's homosexual attachment to Frau K.

[33] Truth for Lacan, is not an absolute. Rather, it emerges in discourse, though always as half-truth: 'All I can do is tell the truth. No that isn't so. I have missed it. There is no truth that in passing through awareness does not lie, but one runs after it all the same' (Lacan 1979: 7).

[34] One can perhaps imagine the possibility of interpretations concentrating on the attack on the disappointing therapists/parental figures, or in relation to the patient's impoverished and impoverishing inner objects, and so on.

[35] To the reader who asks 'why run a group if this in the case?' our response is fairly pragmatic and without, therefore, a strong theoretical rationale. In our experience, the main factors relate to issues such as reducing costs or seeing more patients—which is one force at work within public health services. Running groups is one possible means of maximising scarce resources. There is also, however, the more positive side of our experience which suggests that some people—especially those who present problems of isolation and/or significant difficulties in relationships—can benefit from the social and psycho-educational aspects of simply being in a group. Moreover, there are some patients—again, based on our experience—who demonstrate a willingness or preference to engage in group-

based psychoanalytic work, and who are less willing (for whatever reason) to commit themselves to individual psychoanalysis. This is frequently related to the fact of being able in a group to engage more at one's own pace, rather than from the first being faced with the fundamental rule, the imperative 'free associate'.

LEVINAS AND THE QUESTION OF THE GROUP

Steven Gans

Emmanuel Levinas is responsible for at least two inaugural transformations of contemporary philosophical culture. Firstly, from 1930 onwards, he introduced Husserlian phenomenology and—at the same time—Heideggarian thought to the French philosophical scene. This had such an enormous impact that—it is fair to say—every significant French philosopher, psychoanalyst and thinker has, since then, been formed and informed by Levinas's work.

Secondly, Levinas transformed phenomenology through the introduction of *otherness*—'the traumatism of the other'.

Levinas died aged 89 at the end of 1995. To quote from Derrida's obituary for Levinas, this second innovation:

> ...produced a discreet but irreversible mutation, one of those very powerful, very singular, very rare provocations that in history, after more than 2000 years, will have indelibly stamped the space and body of dialogue between Jewish thought and its others, the philosophies of Greek origin and of other Abramic monotheisms. That mutation has happened, it has happened through him. Through Emmanuel Levinas, who had for this immense responsibility, I believe, a conscience at once clear, confident, calm and modest, like that of a prophet. (Derrida 1995a: 4)

Levinasian ethics advocates the 'one *for* the other', rather than, 'the one *against* the other'. It calls for the rescue of *saying* from the ossification of the *said*; for attunement to the living rhythms of dynamic time rather than to the frozen time of totalising theory; and for a *between* of responsible relatedness.

To be sure, an argument can be made for a Levinasian reading of Freud. After all, the psychoanalytic context engenders proximity through the attentiveness of one to the other. However, its project is cast in terms of a quest for self-understanding, no matter how much consciousness is obstructed by the hide-and-seek game of the unconscious and the turbulence generated by repressed desire. It is a *taxonomy* of pathology—a *meta-psychology*—which informs the gestures of analytic intervention, intended to release the analysand from pro-grammed constriction, and to free him/her for fuller participation in life-play—for work and love.

Freud's therapeutic ambition announces a return to an Aristotelian notion of functional good, a wellness that amounts to becoming better at playing life's games. Levinas, on the other hand, invokes the Platonic 'Good beyond Being'. The face of the other in singular and infinite difference, Levinas suggests, obliges me to respond with a 'here I am'; I am responsible even for the other's responsibility, for bringing out the Good in the other. Thus, the other obliges me to take him/her by the hand to relieve his/her suffering. This requires noth-ing less than the rupture of my own interiority, the disruption of my reflexive narcissism. This means a shift from being good at 'me first' games, towards *responsible relatedness*, towards 'putting the other first'.

I propose that a way beyond what appears an impasse—or even a polarisation—between Levinas and Freud, is to develop a practice which retrieves the ethical dimension of Freud's sensibility. In section one of this chapter I comment on *Jokes and Their Relation to the Unconscious*. I show that Freud was always already finely attuned to the other, in a Levinasian sense. I then go on to discuss *Group Psychology and the Analysis of the Ego* as a prescient deconstruction of the psychoanalytic movement's tendency toward orthodoxy and insti-tutionalisation—of celebrating the *said* at the expense of *saying*. Section two is a critical account of R.D. Laing's attempt to superimpose exis-tential phenomenology and communication theory on psychoanalytic group practice. Section three lays out the tenets of Levinasian ethics as a basis for re-inscribing ethics in the heart of psychoanalytic practice, a practice which seems to have lost touch with the issues of responsibil-ity, suffering, the community and justice. In section four I present some critical reflections on Levinas as posed by Jacques Derrida in *The Gift of Death*, as a challenge to those who might attempt to develop an ethi-cally oriented psychoanalytic practice.

1. Freud's ethical sensibility

An early indication that Freud was exquisitely sensitive to the Levinasian distinction between the saying and the said, between per-formance and representation, ethics and epistemology, comes out in his discussion of a well-known Jewish joke which he classified as 'scep-tical', and indexed as 'truth a lie (Jewish)':

Two Jews set out in a railway carriage at a station in Galicia. 'Where are you going?' asked the one. 'To Cracow' was the answer. 'What a liar you are!' broke out the other. 'If you say you're going to Cracow, you want me to believe you're going to Lemberg. But I know that in fact you're going to Cracow—so why are you lying to me?' (Freud 1905: 115)

The humour of this joke turns on an exaggerated—even absurd— problematising of propositional truth. The interlocutor knows/assumes that he could never expect a straight answer from a member of the same 'clan'. There is an almost Talmudic resonance to the outrage at the offence of having told the truth—that is, as Freud puts it, the 'Jesuitical truth'. The second speaker assumes that the first expects him to lie so, by merely stating the propositional truth, he has indeed committed a duplicity.

As Freud remarks: '[I]s it the truth if we describe things as they are without troubling to consider how our hearer will understand what we say?' (Freud 1905: 115). Putting the hearer or other *first* is the heart of the Levinasian injunction 'for the other', which can only take place in *saying*, in the intimacy of *relatedness*, rather than in the domain of the abstract and impersonal *said*. It is the difference between passing messages and speaking; between replaying pre-recorded tapes—repeating stereotypical 'numbers', as many analysands do in their compulsive manner of non-relating—and genuinely *relating in* the conversation.

I would argue that Freud's life and practice was far more informed by the distinction between the saying and said, by the 'one for the other' instead of 'one against the other', than his formal theoretical work suggests. His contribution to 'Jesuitical truth', like the answer of the travelling Jew in the railway carriage, must be deconstructed or '*unsaid*' in order to arrive at a sense of the destination of his *saying*, embedded in the official said of his published work.

Group Psychology and the Analysis of the Ego provides an opportunity for separating the public exoteric/epistemological dimension of his work from the esoteric/ethical dimension of his practice. Freud's reflections on group phenomena were never meant to be solely academic. My reading is that his so-called 'social psychology' was actually intended as a myth of the founding of the psychoanalytic movement. Freud's apologetic intention is to render intelligible the explosive defections of some of his closest colleagues, as well as to justify his sometimes vitriolic denunciations of them. Whatever else the stakes in play might be, the work is a polemic against the disloyal sons by the 'father', Freud. At an esoteric level, then, Freud is taking responsibility for the responsibility of the 'sons', by revealing the origin of their irresponsibility.

Historically, Freud's psychoanalysis was a hybrid discipline which set out to subvert the modern contract. The modern contract constructed a Chinese wall between things and humans. The discourse of the scientific community was granted privilege with regard to *things* (natural law), and the discourse of the political community was granted status and power over *human* legislation (political law). Entitlement to speak within one or the other of these bifurcated modern fields required an adherence to the special language, assumptions and technologies of each—experimental method for the one, real politic for the other. It also meant adherence to the modern contract and the suppression of hybrid phenomena and disciplines. When Freud's research and publications criss-crossed the boundaries between the neurophysiological and the social-psychological, he was shunned and ostracised from the 'proper' scientific community. He stood accused of making up scientific fairy tales.

Freud established the psychoanalytic movement: its theory, practice, and institution, within the excluded middle of modernity. It was 'a science of persons'. The therapeutic application of this hybrid discipline generated an economy for its member practitioners. Freud was the progenitor of the original—hence, according to him, *only*—psychoanalytic group, composed of those who had been psychoanalysed by him or someone he had analysed. Only by direct transmission, then, by experiencing one's own unconscious repressions in the presence of an anointed psychoanalyst, does one become fit to conduct the psychoanalytic ritual and participate in psychoanalytic discourse. Only an alchemical transformation within the psychoanalytic crucible authorises one to practice and speak as a psychoanalyst.

Having established the post-modern psychoanalytic organisation and institution as an alternative to the modern hegemony, Freud found himself the fantasy-focus of the psychoanalytic group. His response to this was to analyse and address the group itself. He wrote:

> Although group psychology is only in its infancy, it embraces an immense number of separate issues... Anyone who compares the narrow dimensions of this little book with the wide extent of group psychology will at once be able to guess that only a few

parts chosen from the whole material are to be dealt with here.
And they will in fact only be a few questions with which the
depth-psychology of psychoanalysis is specially concerned.
(Freud 1921: 70-71)

The question Freud poses regarding the group and—by implication—
the psychoanalytical group, is the Levinasian question of *responsibility*.
How is it possible to be responsible in a group, since the first victim of
collective or group thinking is responsibility? And is it not *responsible
relatedness* which is the precondition of psychoanalytic attentiveness?
Freud cites Le Bon, who wrote:

...the individual forming part of a group acquires, solely from
numerical considerations, a sentiment of invincible power which
allows him to yield to instincts which had he been alone, he
would perforce have kept under restraint. He will be the less dis-
posed to check himself, from the consideration that, a group
being anonymous and in consequence irresponsible, the sentiment of responsibility which always controls individuals disappears entirely. (Freud 1921: 74)

So, having constituted the psychoanalytic group, Freud analysed the
forces he had unleashed. He posed to the group the conundrum that
the very libidinal ties which hold it together diminish—if not altogether eradicate—individual responsibility, the precondition of analytic
practice. Grouping is a regressive process, which returns its members
to the condition of the primal horde. It is through subjection to and
identification with the primal father, the strong independent leader,
that the members of the group are bound.

'Even today,' commented Freud, 'the members of a group stand in
need of the illusion that they are equally and justly loved by their
leader' (Freud 1921: 123). Consequently, 'The individual gives up his
ego ideal and substitutes for it the group ideal as embodied in the
leader' (Freud 1921: 129).

The primal father enforced abstinence as a means of establishing the
emotional tie between himself and the group. In a similar fashion,
Freud prevented his sons from 'saying', since speaking in the name of
psychoanalysis means adherence to the official version of what has
been *said* by Freud himself. In this case, how is it possible for a group
of sorcerer's apprentices who are in hypnotic rapport or transference

with Freud—a group of Freudian clones—to convene individually the analytic session, which is predicated on the principle of responsibility performed as attentiveness to the other, as the 'one *for* the other'?

The problem of the conflict and incompatibility between the *exoteric* repetition of the analytic catechism—which is supposed to inform psychoanalytic practice—and the *esoteric* therapeutic potency of responsible relatedness, is indeed exacerbated by the development of group psychoanalysis. It is as if groups were convened to re-enact, confirm and replicate the psychoanalytic myth of the primal horde. Group members incorporate as their ego ideal the leader/analyst who is feared and loved. The group in turn bands together to perform the ritual murder of the father/leader. The father/analyst is 'hopeless, useless, knows nothing'.

After the 'murder', the brothers/sisters form the leaderless community which operates according to group norms. All members have equal rights and must observe equal prohibitions. This memorialises the murdered father/analyst who becomes eulogised in his absent presence as the hero/deity who was—after all—showing the way to the promised land of free-relatedness.

But the question remains: how is there even a remote possibility of responsible relatedness, of the 'one for the other', in the context of this imitation of Freud, this Freudian passion-play? How can the individual analyst ever reconcile the contradiction inherent in the ego idealisation of psychoanalytic group leadership—namely, Freud's injunction to be a psychoanalyst, *like* him, yet *not* to be like him? How can one be one's *own* independent, strong, leader/founder, yet remain faithful to the leader/founder?

In practice this paradox confronting the followers of Freud has led to the numerous splits, schisms and proliferation of new psychoanalytic schools and cults that are legion within the psychoanalytic movement. The would-be leader identifies him/herself with Freud on the one hand, yet introduces new theory, practices and orthodoxy on the other—for example, Klein and Lacan among others. While claiming these innovations amplify, deepen or elaborate what was already implicit in Freud (that they are 'returning' to Freud), these new schools often dismantle and resurrect psychoanalysis in forms that would be unrecognisable to the founding father.

A relatively recent and well-known attempt to reincarnate Freud, and to break out of the impasse of the self-replication of psychoanalytic dogma, was made by R.D. Laing. Laing's approach to groups

involved replacing Freud's libidinal interpretation of group identification with a theory of group *totalisation* as the basis for its cohesion.

2. Laing's self psychoanalysis.

Drawing on Sartre's *Critique of Dialectical Reason*, Laing, like Freud,
founds his analysis of the group on a mythological, primal state of
nature. In a 'state of nature' every other is one too many, since man
exists in an environment characterised by scarcity. Laing takes the 'one
against the other', the serial grouping of individuals, such as—for
example—a bus queue, as the starting-point and basis of his analysis
and ethic. 'As long as scarcity remains our destiny, evil is irremediable
and this must be the basic of our ethic' (Laing and Cooper 1971: 114).
Each other *totalises* or *objectifies* others, as in Hegel's master-slave
dialectic, in order to impose and enforce a recognition of their identity.
'Whether I kill, torture, enslave or simply mystify', Laing writes, 'my
aim is to suppress the other's freedom' (Laing and Cooper 1971: 114).
In other words, I am the author, director and central character of my
life scenario and others are merely the supporting cast... Yet if each
runs the risk of subordination, appropriation and objectification by the
others, how do humans overcome this inherent contradiction and
relate to one another in the first place?

Laing answers that it is in response to *external threat* that a group is
formed. As a survival strategy against external menace, each person in
the group about to be formed totalises the group, and realises that he
or she is integrated within it. Thus each is included in the totalisation
of the others. 'The being in the group of each is thus an interiority or
bond of interiority' (Laing and Cooper 1971: 114). In Laing, *group identification* displaces the role of the Freudian father as ego ideal.

It is a small dialectical jump for Laing (after Sartre) to show how the
survival group develops into a pledged group, and then moves
towards organisation and institution. The group is based on the group
identification of the group members due to terror and violence, in
order to prevent the threat of serial dissolution.

However, this entails that my obligation to others in the group is
regulated by a reign of terror:

> The fundamental structure of the pledged group is violence—
> terror—since I have freely consented to the possible liquidation
> of my person. My pledge to the group invites violence and death

if I default... The group institutionalises its identity through the construction of agreement, of a 'we' and an us/them dichotomy. In agreement, the multiplicities of identities disappear... all are realised in each. (Laing and Cooper 1971: 150)

Consequently, the identification of the individual with the group becomes the basis of an existentially inauthentic false-self system, which dominates self-presentation in everyday life.

An individual's persona, mask, self, identity and relations to others are constituted through totalisations and interiorisations of group norms. As Laing puts it: 'Each person... internalises their relation to the group as a quasi-objective totality (Laing and Cooper 1971: 158). Being in the group, in its interiority, is 'manifested by a double failure to which each has given his consent: powerlessness to leave, and powerlessness to be integrated' (Laing and Cooper 1971: 158).

Only through the mediation of meta-perspectives—that is, my view of the other's view of me—do I regulate my sense of inclusion or exclusion from the group. The attempt to manipulate and control the other's perception of me—and hence, my identity within the group—is the operation Laing calls 'collusion'. The job of the existential analyst is to reveal and frustrate collusion, the reciprocal validation of false self-identifications within the group. This serves to unbind false ties and the violence which regulates them, returning the individual to a more authentic or true way of relating. As Laing remarks—collusion is always clinched when self finds in other someone who will 'confirm' the false-self that self is trying to make real, and *vice versa* (Laing 1969: 93). The inability to establish complementary relationships is expressed by Sartre in the often-quoted line from *No Exit*—'hell is other people'.

My question is this: can a form of analysis, set up to generate, read and then dismantle collusive relationships, ever be *responsible*? Can self-psychoanalysis, oriented towards interpreting internalised meta-perspectives, foster *responsible relatedness*? Given his starting point of internalised reflexivity, and a totalising dialectic based on natural scarcity, it is hard to see how Laing's revisionist psychoanalytic project can lead to authentic, let alone responsible, relatedness. Even if it is possible to overcome collusion, does this not simply return the group to its original seriality, the war of each *against* all? This problem is vividly illustrated in Laing's account of his approach to existential group psychoanalysis.

Laing provides a sample of his 'Bionesque' group work which concentrates on analysis and frustration of 'the self's' search for a collusive complement or 'false identity'. This, Laing argues, is the 'most cogent meaning' of Freud's dictum that analysis should be conducted under conditions of maximal frustration.

According to Laing, the role of the existential group analyst is to provide conditions for group members' *self*-disclosure. This means the therapist must not allow him/herself to collude with patients' attempts to assimilate the therapist into their phantasy or false-self system, usually expressed in the form of 'the therapist knows the answer to my problems... if I can only get the answer out of him/her.' The art of the therapist is to dispel the illusion of 'an answer' to suffering, and show how seeking 'the answer' from 'one supposed to know' perpetuates the state of need and demand that is the source of the suffering in the first place.

Laing describes three group members, Jack, Bill and Richard, in their attempts with one another and him (as analyst) to find and sustain a collusive identity.

Bill wanted to see himself as superior, but felt inferior to others. He was like his parents—'empty, dull and uninteresting.' He saw the analyst as having what he lacked. The analyst was strong, educated, understanding and appreciative. But the analyst didn't give these things to him. He complained that the analyst, the 'ideal other', was frustrating and unsatisfying. His 'technique' was unexciting, dull, empty and uninteresting.

Jack also felt deprived, but aspired to be a good husband and parent. He wanted to *give* but found he resented those to whom he felt impelled to be generous. Bill and Jack formed a collusive relationship in the group, based on each confirming the other in their false identity. Jack confirmed Bill's pseudo superiority in exchange for being confirmed by Bill as a 'giver'.

Laing reports that:

> ...the collusive confirmation of each counterfeited genuine friendship. One thing was clear in listening to them. When they talked together Jack was never more 'Jack' as Jack saw himself. Bill was never more 'Bill' as he saw himself. Each confirmed the other in his illusory identity. (Laing 1969: 103)

When Bill began to express sexual feelings toward Jack the collusion collapsed.

Richard, in contrast, could not enter into collusive pairing. Laing characterises him as an extremely schizoid individual: 'he could only *be* by himself'. Relationship threatened loss of identity—being engulfed, fused, merged, losing separate distinctiveness. He could only be a *voyeur*. He couldn't play the same game with anyone for fear of being destroyed by the other. For Laing, Richard represented a story of ultimate collusion—that is, apparent non-collusion.

The problem with Laing's analytic approach is that it operates within the enclosure of reflexive interiority, so that it precludes in advance a relation of 'one *for* the other'. Laing's early group work was the springboard for his now famous critique of psychiatry. His inter-personal communications version of existential psychoanalysis led him to a paradigm shift away from the collusive interaction between psychiatrist and patient, as engendered by the medical model. Laing no longer saw suffering in terms of the symptoms of a disease but, instead, attempted to illuminate the social interpersonal intelligibility of suffering within the context of family and group miscommunication and collusive meta-perception.

Nevertheless existential praxis, because of its interiorisation and totalisation of the other, and because of its centripetal dialectical thinking, closes off the potential for ethical relatedness. Laing eventually broke away from the formalism of the psychoanalytic group's rules and procedures, in an attempt to establish a more convivial 'conversation' within the group. But, as far as we know, he never abandoned his quest for a dialectical ontology of human relatedness, as the basis for re-visioning Freudian psychoanalysis. This amounts to a subordination of ethics to knowledge and power, rather than privileging ethical responsibility.

3. *Levinas and the responsibility of relatedness*

Levinas would argue that the problem with psychoanalytic theorising is the same as that with all metaphysical and philosophical thought—namely, that reason is awarded primacy and hence ethics, or 'the other', is subordinated to a totalising system.

Psychoanalysis reduces and assimilates the infinite otherness of the other to the *same*—to a mere example within the generality of a metapsychological or ontological phenomenological system. Yet the heart of Freud's actual practice is a response to the singular suffering of each and every other; hence his careful attention to an in-depth analysis of the other's personal history.

Why not restore to Freudian practice its ethical sensibility? This would mean the analyst turning away from conceptual constructions and artificial groupings, and returning to the *between* of relatedness, in order to attend to the suffering of the other.

In a short essay entitled 'Useless Suffering', Levinas compresses his teaching into a saying that is quite beyond and different from traditional theory. He argues that suffering cannot be integrated by consciousness or theory. It cannot be systematised by reflexive totalising thought, whether analytic, dialectic or existential. Suffering cannot be grasped, because it revolts us. It cannot be assimilated, appropriated, integrated, made 'my own'. Unbearable, unanswerable, suffering ruptures the self-enclosure of interiority. It is traumatic. Suffering leads thought to move into reverse gear; it is a revulsion, a reversal, a move from the ordinary centripetal appropriation to a centrifugal flight. It is a move outside itself toward otherness. The alterity of suffering amounts to a denial and refusal of meaning or sense. It is an absurdity, an obscenity, pure evil. Suffering opens us to our vulnerability, more passive than any receptive sensibility. Unremitting suffering, as such, is *useless*; it is gratuitous pain *for nothing*, reaching beyond the early-warning signal of a symptom calling for attention. Pain in its undiluted form swallows up the entirety of consciousness. It exhausts me and leaves me bereft, withdrawn to the limit of my dissolution. But, Levinas argues, suffering exposes us to the fundamental dimension of ethics, to the face of the other and the basic ethical dilemma: *how do we respond to the other's pain and suffering?*

As Levinas puts it:

> Is not the evil of suffering—extreme passivity, impotence, abandonment and solitude—also the unassimilable and thus the possibility of a half opening, and more precisely, the possibility that wherever a moan, a cry, a groan or a sigh has passed there is the original call for aid, for curative help, for help from the other ego whose alterity, whose exteriority promises solution? (Levinas 1988: 158)

Levinas proposes that the meaning of suffering—which initially is enclosed upon itself and is without recourse, exit or relief—is to enable me to suffer *for* the useless suffering of the other person:

The just suffering in me for the unjustifiable suffering of the other opens upon suffering the ethical perspective of the inter-human. (Levinas 1988: 158)

It is through suffering, then, through suffering for the suffering of someone else, that the human bond is established and forms the supreme basis for ethical responsibility.

The practice of this ethical relatedness is epitomised by Levinas in a footnote, in which he cites a brief excerpt from a Talmudic dialogue that—he suggests—'reflects the conception of the radical hurt of suffering, its intrinsic and uncompensated despair, its confinement and its recourse to the other person, to medication *exterior* to the imminent structure of hurt' (Levinas 1988: 158).

Rav Hiya bar Abba falls ill and Rav Yohanan comes to visit him. He asks him 'are your sufferings fitted to you?'. 'Neither them nor the compensations they promise.' 'Give me your hand' the visitor of the ill man then says. And the visitor lifts the ill man from his couch. But then Rav Yohanan himself falls ill and is visited by Rav Hanina. Same question: 'are your sufferings fitted to you?' Same response: 'Neither them nor the compensations they promise.' 'Give me your hand' says Rav Hanina, and he lifts Rav Yohanan from his couch. Question: Could not Rav Yohanan lift himself by himself? Answer: the prisoner could not break free from his confinement by himself. (Levinas 1988: 166)

Levinas' *'give me your hand'* is the gesture of attentiveness to the other that is perhaps the very heart and soul of psychoanalytic therapy. Compassion for the suffering of the other transforms the useless suffering into suffering that has meaning for me, for it is my non-indifference, my responsibility for the other, the 'one for the other', that constitutes the *between* of human relatedness. Only through my responsibility for the other person do I enter into intimacy and meaningful relatedness with an other. The opposite—reason detached from the intimacy of responsible relatedness—is the road to hell. This is the road of twentieth century consciousness, which has uncoupled itself from ethics and instituted the modern contract: the alliance of knowledge, power and discourse in the service of science and politics. 'It is no accident that the century has produced two world wars, totalitarianism of right and left, Hitlerism and Stalinism, the Gulag and the genocide of

Auschwitz and Cambodia' (Levinas 1988: 62). Levinas cites the Holocaust of the Jewish people as paradigmatic of gratuitous human suffering, when 'evil appears in its diabolical horror' (Levinas 1988: 162). For Levinas, any attempt to explain or justify the neighbour's pain is odious and the source of immorality. This includes psychologistic explanations which pathologise suffering.

What are the consequences for psychoanalytic practice, the psychoanalytic group and institution as well as group psychoanalysis, if we take Levinas' ethical exhortation and obligation to heart? Does Freud already practice psychoanalysis ethically (in a Levinasian) sense by responding to the singularity of the other with a 'here I am, give me your hand, speak to me of your suffering', despite Freud's formal metapsychological exposition and the staging of himself as hero and prophet in his writing? Can the analytic frame bracket the question of good (the 'one *for* the other') versus evil (the 'one *against* the other')? Must not responsible and therapeutic relatedness come from *saying*, from singular responses to the infinite otherness of the vulnerable and the suffering other, rather than from a conceptualised recycling of the *said*, which categorises and reduces the other to the same through totalising, synchronic and systematised theory?

But without its theory, what is the justification for the psychoanalytic ritual—for example, the analyst's technique or skilful means of interpreting and resolving the so-called 'transference'? What, other than theory, would authorise the convening of psychoanalytically oriented therapy or therapy groups? If the analyst owns up to a practice informed by ethical teaching then the question arises: why set up the artificial boundaries of the analytic session, why privilege what happens *in* as opposed to *outside* the analytic framework? Why charge for being what one is obliged to be as an ethical human being, however short one might fall from the mark of ethical responsibility?

Levinasian ethics clarifies how and why psychoanalysis works in all its various transformations and proliferations. Taking the other by the hand, metaphorically or literally, converts useless suffering into meaningful inter-human intimacy, and brings out the good between people in the 'one for the other', through responsible relatedness. Giving the other my hand, in the Levinasian or Talmudic sense, is perhaps what heals, is that which is *therapeutic* in the psychoanalytic encounter—namely, converting the other's meaningless or useless suffering into a surrender to the inter-human bond. Yet this ethical practice subverts the very principles on which the psychoanalytic movement is founded: its ritual, institutions, theory, knowledge, power and language.

Does ethics render analytic practice redundant or superfluous? Would the daily obligation to the other, to convert useless suffering into meaningful and responsible relatedness, displace the formal ritual of the analytic session? And yet, perhaps the analytic session offers the framework within which the Levinasian ethics of responsible relatedness can occur in its most provocative form. Once theory is bracketed or sidelined the opportunity for intimacy and proximity, for having time for another, is perhaps most likely to occur in the encounter of the therapeutic relation. The guidelines of the analytic ritual, of offering space and time to and for the other, calls upon the analyst to put the other (the client or patient) *first*. As long as the analyst refrains from totalising or conceptualising the infinite otherness of the other, which emerges through the symptoms, stories, dreams and wishes that the patient brings, the patient is heard, a hand is given and their suffering is made meaningful. The therapeutic relation illustrates the significance of what Levinas means when he claims that *we are hostage to the other through substitution.*

Substitution does not mean taking the other's place—rather, the reverse. It is taking responsibility for the other's responsibility. As long as the other avoids the experience of trauma, the blow to their interiority that every genuine relation to an other brings about, he/she remains locked in the prison of isolation that is egoic consciousness. The saying or gesture of the analytic encounter has the potency to give the other the courage to enter the between of intimate relatedness. The 'here I am' and substitution is the response of the ethical analyst to the call of the suffering of the patient. The sound of my voice, the gesture of my welcome and receptivity, my sensitivity to the nearness and distance that the other may or may not be able to tolerate, amounts to giving the other my hand. In time, the hand comes to lift them out of the suffering of their self-enclosed belief systems, and the terror of the unknown and unknowable otherness of the other and others from which they have withdrawn.

It is my non-indifference to the point of substitution that may inspire the other to unsay their repetitive self-destructive and destructive 'self-system', and come to speak with me, to say and be heard, as if for the first time in their lives.

If ethics and the intimacy of responsible relatedness is what is at work in analysis (what makes it therapeutic) how can Freud's directive which insists on analytic neutrality be maintained? Yet does not this recommendation protect the analyst from incorporating the other's suffering? The boundaries of the analytic situation, the development of a meta-relationship (a relationship about the others' relationships), is constituted to prevent the 'transference' of the other's suffering on to the analyst. Is not the ethical analyst who gives the other their hand in substitution, exposing their own vulnerability to being captured and overwhelmed by their patient's suffering? Is this not illustrated in the above Talmudic footnote when Rav Yohanan falls ill after healing Rav Hiya bar Abba?

The ethical welcome must be unconditional; it cannot be responsible if it is artificial and contrived, a mere imitation or simulation. This means *the analyst is exposed to the other's suffering to the degree he/she is ethical*. Yet the conversion of the other's useless suffering to meaningful relatedness is carried out through *my just suffering*, my *substitution* for the other which takes on the responsibility for the other's responsibility. Just suffering means that the ethical analyst can never have a good conscience, be complacent or naive. As one develops a sense of responsibility he/she assumes ever greater responsibility. I always have one responsibility more than my patient or client—responsibility for the others' responsibility. Nevertheless, this just suffering of the analyst is not useless and therefore need not bring on illness.

Given the infinite otherness of every other, can we practice ethical relatedness in a group, or—in other words—is *ethical* group analysis possible? This raises a difficult issue for the Levinasian inspired psychoanalytic practitioner. How do we meet our just obligations to all the *other others*, if our responsibility to any one is already infinite? Put in another way, how do we move from ethics—the 'one for the other'—to politics, the relation with more than one? How do we move from dynamic interpersonal responsiveness to the totalising perspective of the group, without violence, and without lapsing into the 'one against the other', underpinned by the social construction of the 'us and them'?

4. Derrida and the question of responsibility in the group

For Levinas, what binds the group is a living bond or pact where each pledges responsibility for each other. As he puts it: 'one is not only responsible for everyone else, but responsible also for the responsibility of everyone else' (Levinas 1989: 225).

Derrida, in *The Gift of Death*, raises a number of issues with regard to responsibility and the other, which problematise the possibility of a Levinasian 'pact' and—consequently—the project of an ethically oriented group psychoanalytic practice.

Derrida traces the history of European responsibility and finds that it contains a hidden secret. At its core it incorporates *demonic rapture*. What we call responsibility originates in the mystery rites of sexual enthusiasm, fervour and fusion that are later incorporated and 'overcome' in Platonic rationalism, and then repressed in the Christian ideal of love. Derrida resurrects a Freudian thesis and argues that this secret sexual undercurrent is the glue of the group mind. Sexuality releases demonic madness and excess. Platonic rationalism is the antidote, which amounts to a reassemblage of the soul in flight from the body, sex and death. For Socrates, philosophy is the practice of *dying*, the overcoming of mysteries through reason.

Responsibility is lost when it is subordinated to knowledge—as in Platonic philosophy—and relegated to conscious decisions based on 'the technical deployment of a cognitive apparatus'. One must know the good to do good, but knowing—which is the vigilance of the self over death—amounts to a withdrawal into reflexive interiority. As a result of this detachment of the soul, the self-thematising assemblage I take to be me cannot relate to the other as transcendent. For responsible action to take place, that action must occur *before* or *beyond* theoretical and thematic determination.

Christianity transforms Platonism by exposing the soul to the *mysterum tremendum* of Christ. According to Derrida, this plunged Europe into a new abyss of responsibility, based on a new secret and a new relation to death. The condition of Christian responsibility is that infinite love should renounce itself in order to become finite and incarnated. The other is loved as a finite and singular other. To assume responsibility, then, is to accede as a singular mortal individual to the gift of infinite love. However, I can never live up to the task, hence the transformation of responsibility into guilt and original sin. If guilt is inherent in Christian responsibility, then responsibility becomes contradictory. I must respond as a singular individual, and answer for my actions, but I am always guilty because of my very finite limitations and inability to respond in tune with absolute goodness and love. Placed in its historical context, the notion of responsibility appears highly paradoxical. It becomes even more problematic when Derrida considers the question of responsibility to the 'other *others*', through an analysis of the parable of Abraham and Isaac.

The story of Abraham's decision to sacrifice Isaac is a transgression of the so-called 'ethical' order. Abraham puts his duty to the Absolute Other (God) before his bond to his fellow man, family and community. He refuses accountability for his action in the name of an infinite obligation to the absolute. However, because he offers his unconditional love through the death of his son, God prevents the sacrifice and acknowledges Abraham's total responsibility to the Absolute. Yet the terrifying ordeal of responsibility facing Abraham is, Derrida argues, 'the most common and everyday experience of responsibility' (Derrida 1995b: 68). How is this so?

I cannot respond to any other without sacrificing an *other* other, *other* others. My absolute sacrifice to the singular other who calls me, and to whom I respond with 'here I am', means that I must fail in my responsibility to all the other others—in short, to the rest of my fellows at that very moment of response. Perhaps this means that my response to one rather than another is ultimately arbitrary and unjustifiable. As Derrida puts it *'tout autre est tout autre'*. Every other (one) is every (bit) other (Derrida 1995b: 68). For example, by fulfilling my obligation to a colleague by writing this piece, am I not sacrificing and betraying—in the process—my other obligations, my responsibility to the other others, to those suffering and starving, and those closest and dearest?

To the extent that each and every other is infinitely other for Levinas, then every other is akin to the Divinity and—as absolute—obliges me to make absolute sacrifice in the manner of Abraham. For this reason, Derrida accuses Levinas of being unable to distinguish in his thinking between the order of ethics and religion, between the alterity of every other human being and God (Derrida 1995b:84).

To the extent that this is so I cannot but fail in or betray my responsibility to and for the other others at the moment I am engaged in my responsibility to any *one* other. The hyper-responsibility of Levinasian ethics, even if such an ethical responsibility were possible, seems to rule out an ethically founded politics, or ethical practice in a group situation. As soon as the third person comes into proximity, my unconditional welcome and attention to the other becomes compromised—much as a third person coming into the bedroom would interrupt a couple making love. The entry of the third, for Levinas, transforms the ethical event back to a social one, which becomes re-inscribed in the language and operations of the *said*: institutions, law, consciousness and the privileging of being and knowledge. Yet Levinas holds out the promise of the advent of justice in the group. It might arise that, from the *between* of responsible relatedness and proximity, a third might be welcomed by each of the members of a former duo. The trio might then move toward a just interrelationship.

If an ethically inspired group analysis were possible, such a group would focus its attention on the question of justice and the just opportunity of responsible relating, wherein each member of the group would attend to all the others. Such an experiment in ethical group practice would be timely, if it could indeed contribute to the relief of suffering within groups—such as the family, the work group, the community, and even the psychoanalytic group and organisations.

BIBLIOGRAPHY

Alcorn, M. (1994) 'The subject of discourse: reading Lacan through (and beyond) post-structuralist contexts', in *Lacanian Theory of Discourse Subject Structure and Society*, ed. Bracher et al., New York: New York University Press.

Alexander, F. & French, T. M. (1946) *Psychoanalytic Therapy*, New York: Ronald Press.

Althusser, L. (1976) *Positions*, Paris: Editions Sociales.

Anthony (1983), 'The Group-Analytic Circle and Its Ambient Network', in Pines 1983.

Anzieu, D. (1971) 'L'illusion groupale', *Nouvelle Revue de Psychanalyse* 4:73-93.

Armstrong, D. (1991) 'Thoughts bound and thoughts free: reflections on mental process in groups', paper read to an open meeting of the Department of Psychotherapy, Cambridge University, 16th March 1991.

Armstrong, D. (1995) 'The analytic object in organisational work', paper presented to the ISPSO Annual Symposium, London, July 1995.

Austen, J. (1995) *Sense and Sensibility*, London: Penguin Books.

Baron, C. (1987) *Asylum to Anarchy*, London: Free Association Books.

Bateson, G. (1972) *Steps to an Ecology of Mind*, New York: Ballantine.

Bellow, S. (1970) *Mr. Sammler's Planet*, London: Weidenfeld & Nicholson.

Bendix, R. (1966) 'A memoir of my father', *The Canadian Revue of Sociology and Anthropology* 2, 1.

Bettleheim, B. (1969) *Children of the Dream*, London: Thames & Hudson.

Bion, W. (1952), 'Group dynamics: a review', *International Journal of Psycho-Analysis* 23, 2.

Bion, W. (1961) *Experiences in Groups*, London: Tavistock.

Bion, W. (1967) *Second Thoughts*, London: Heinemann.

Bion, W. (1982) *The Long Weekend, Part of a Life*, Abingdon: Fleetwood Press.

Bion, W. (1985) *The Other Side of Genius: Family Letters*, Abingdon: Fleetwood Press.

Bion, W. (1991a) *Learning from Experience*, London: Karnac.

Bion, W. (1991b) *Elements of Psychoanalysis*, London: Karnac.

Blay-Neto, B. (1985) 'The Influence of Bion's Ideas on my Work', in *Bion and Group Psychotherapy*, ed. M. Pines, London & New York: Tavistock/Routledge.

Blegler, J. (1966) 'Psychoanalysis of the psychoanalytic frame', *International Journal of Psycho-Analysis* 48: 511-519.

Bollas, C. (1987) *The Shadow of the Object*, London: Free Association Books.

Borch-Jacobsen, M. (1988), *The Freudian Subject*, Stanford: Stanford University Press.

Boxer, P. (1994a) 'Schein: Process Consultation', working paper, Working Group on Groups and Organisations, Centre for Freudian Analysis and Research, London.

Boxer, P. (1994b) 'The future of identity', in *Managing the Unknown by Creating New Futures*, ed. R. Boot, J. Lawrence & J. Morris, London: McGraw-Hill.

Boxer, P., & Kenny, V. (1992) 'Lacan and Maturana: constructivist origins for a 3∞ cybernetics', *Communication and Cognition* 25, 1: 73-100.

Boxer, P., & Palmer, B. (1994) 'Meeting the Challenge of the Case', in *What Makes Consultancy Work—Understanding the Dynamics*, ed. Casemore et al., London: South Bank University Press.

Bray, R. (1907) *The Town Child*, London: Fisher Unwin.

Britton, R. (1985) 'The Oedipus complex and the depressive position', *Sigmund Freud House Bulletin* 9: 7-12.

Britton, R. (1994) 'The blindness of the seeing eye: inverse symmetry as a defence against reality', *Psychoanalytical Inquiry* 14, 3: 365-378.

Britton, R., Feldman, M. & O'Shaughnessy, E. (1989) *The Oedipus Complex Today: Clinical Implications*, ed. J. Steiner, London: Karnac.

Brown, D. & Zinkin, L., eds. (1994) *The Psyche and the Social World: Developments in Group Analytic Theory*, London: Routledge.

Brown, D. (1985) 'Bion and Foulkes: Basic Assumptions and Beyond', in Pines 1985.

Brown, D. (1994) 'Self Development Through Subjective Interaction: A Fresh Look at "Ego" Training in Action', in Brown & Zinkin 1994.

Brown, J. (1961) *Freud and the Post-Freudians*, Harmondsworth: Penguin.

Budd, S., & Hopper, E. (1992) 'The reception of psychoanalysis in Great Britain: a sociological approach', unpublished paper, International Association for the History of Psychoanalysis, Conference on a Comparative History of the Early Stages of Psychoanalysis in Europe, Brussels.

Burchell, G., Gordon, C., & Miller, P. (1991) *The Foucault Effect: Studies in Governmentality*, London: Harvester Wheatsheaf.

Burman, R., & Roel, G. (1986) personal communications.

Burrow, T. (1927) *The Social Basis of Consciousness*, New York: Harcourt, Brace & World.

Canetti, E. (1960) *Crowds and Power*, New York: Seabury Press.

Chasseguet-Smirgel, J. (1984) *The Ego Ideal*, New York: Norton.

Checkland, P. (1981) *Systems Thinking, Systems Practice*, Chichester: John Wiley & Sons.

Checkland, P., & Tsouvalis, C. (1996) 'Reflecting on SSM: the dividing line between "real world" and "systems thinking world"', working paper in Systems and Information Sciences, University of Humberside.

De Mare, P. (1972) *Perspectives in Group Psychotherapy*, London: Allen & Unwin.

De Mare, P. (1991) *Koinonia*, London: Karnac Books.

Derrida, J. (1995a) 'Emmanuel Levinas, Adieu', *Liberation* 28th December, 4.

Derrida, J. (1995b) *The Gift of Death*, Chicago & London: University of Chicago Press.

Dor, J. (1997) *Introduction to the Reading of Lacan. The Unconscious Structured Like a Language*, London: Jason Aronson.

Dreyfus, H. & Rabinow, P. (1982) *Michel Foucault: Beyond Structuralism and Hermeneutics*, New York: Harvester.

Erikson, E. (1959) *Identity and the Life Cycle*, New York: International Universities Press.

Ezriel, H. (1950) 'A psychoanalytic approach to group treatment', *British Journal of Medical Psychology* 23: 58-74.

Fairbairn, W. R. D. (1994) 'The Moral Defence', in *Psychoanalytic Studies of the Personality*, London: Routledge & Kegan Paul.

Felman, S. (1987) *Jacques Lacan and the Adventure of Insight: Psychoanalysis in Contemporary Culture*, Cambridge: Harvard University Press.

Ferenczi, S. (1955) *Final Contributions to the Problems and Methodology of Psychoanalysis*, ed. M. Balint, trans. E. Mosbacher et al., London: Maresfield Reprints.

Fink, B. (1995) *The Lacanian Subject. Between Language and Jouissance*, Princeton: Princeton University Press.

Fink, B., Feldstein, R., & Jaanus, M., eds. (1995) *Reading Seminar XI: Lacan's Four Fundamental Concepts of Psychoanalysis*, Albany: Suny Press.

Fink, B., Feldstein, R., & Jaanus, M., eds. (1996) *Reading Seminars I & II: Lacan's Return to Freud*, Albany: Suny Press.

Fonagy, P. (1989) 'On tolerating mental states', *Bulletin of The Anna Freud Centre* 12: 91-115.

Forrester, J. (1990) *The Seductions of Psychoanalysis: Freud Lacan and Derrida*, Cambridge, Cambridge University Press.

Foucault, M. (1970) *The Order of Things*, London: Tavistock Publications.

Foucault, M. (1972) *The Archaeology of Knowledge*, London: Tavistock Publications.

Foucault, M. (1978) *History of Sexuality: An Introduction*, New York: Pantheon.

Foucault, M. (1986) *The Care of the Self—Volume 3: The History of Sexuality*, London: Allen Lane.

Foulkes, S. (1948) *Introduction to Group-Analytic Psychotherapy*, London: Heinemann.

Foulkes, S. (1964) *Therapeutic Group Analysis*, London: George Allen & Unwin.

Foulkes, S. (1975) 'A Short Outcome of the Therapeutic Processes in Group-Analytic Psychotherapy', in *Spheres of Group Analysis*, ed. T. Lear, London: Group Analytic Society.

Foulkes, S. (1983) *Introduction to Group-Analytic Psychotherapy*, London: Maresfield Reprints.

Foulkes, S. (1984) *Therapeutic Group Analysis*, London: Karnac Books.

Foulkes, S. (1986) *Group Analytic Psychotherapy*, London: Maresfield Library.

Foulkes, S. (1990) *Selected Papers on Psychoanalysis and Group Analysis*, London: Karnac Books.

Foulkes, S., & Anthony, E. (1984) *Group Psychotherapy: The Psychoanalytic Approach*, London: Karnac.

Freud, S. (1900) *The Interpretation of Dreams*, S.E. IV-V, London:Hogarth.

Freud, S. (1905) *Jokes and Their Relation to the Unconscious*, S.E. VIII, London:Hogarth.

Freud, S. (1912) 'The Dynamics of Transference', S.E. XII: 99-108, London:Hogarth.

Freud, S. (1913a) 'On Beginning the Treatment', S.E. XII: 121-144, London:Hogarth.

Freud, S. (1913b) *Totem and Taboo*, S.E. XIII: 1-161, London:Hogarth.

Freud, S. (1914a) 'On Narcissism: an Introduction', S.E. XIV: 67-102, London:Hogarth.

Freud, S. (1914b) 'Remembering, Repeating and Working-Through', S.E. XII: 147-156, London:Hogarth.

Freud, S. (1915) 'Observations on Transference-Love', S.E. XII: 159-171, London:Hogarth.

Freud, S. (1916-17) *Introductory Lectures on Psychoanalysis*, S.E. XIV: 275-284, London:Hogarth.

Freud, S. (1920) *Beyond the Pleasure Principle*, S.E. XVIII: 1-64, London:Hogarth.

Freud, S. (1921) *Group Psychology and the Analysis of the Ego*, S.E. XVIII: 65-143, London:Hogarth.

Freud, S. (1923) *The Ego and the Id*, S.E. XIX: 1-66, London:Hogarth.

Freud, S. (1924) 'The Dissolution of the Oedipus Complex', S.E. XIX: 171-179, London:Hogarth.

Freud, S. (1925) *An Autobiographical Study*, S.E. XX: 1-74, London:Hogarth.

Freud, S. (1927) *The Future of an Illusion*, S.E. XXI: 1-56, London:Hogarth.

Freud, S. (1930) *Civilization and its Discontents*, S.E. XXI: 57-145, London:Hogarth.

Freud, S. (1933a) 'Why War?', S.E. XXII: 195-215, London:Hogarth.

Freud, S. (1933b) *New Introductory Lectures on Psycho-Analysis*, S.E. XXII: 1-182, London:Hogarth.

Freud, S. (1939) *Moses and Monotheism*, S.E. XXIII: 1-137, London:Hogarth.

Freud, S. (1940) *An Outline of Psychoanalysis*, S.E. XXII: 139-207, London:Hogarth.

Freud, S., & Breuer, J. (1895) *Studies on Hysteria*, S.E. II, London:Hogarth.

Fromm, E. (1963) 'The Revolutionary Character', in *The Dogma of Christ*, New York: Holt, Rinehart & Winston.

Fromm, E. (1984) *The Working Class in Weimar Germany: A Psychological & Sociological Study*, trans. Barbara Weinberger, Cambridge, Mass: Harvard University Press.

Gaddini, E. (1992) *A Psychoanalytic Theory of Infantile Experience*, ed. A. Limentani, London: Routledge.

Garland, C. (1980) *The Proceedings of the Survivor Syndrome Workshop*, London: Institute of Group Analysis.

Gordon, C., ed. (1980) *Power/Knowledge. Selected Interviews and Other Writings by Michel Foucault 1972-1977*, New York: Harvester Press.

Grinberg, L., et al. (1975) *Introduction to the Work of Bion*, Perth: Clunie Press.

Grinberg, L., et al. (1985) 'Bion's Contribution to the Understanding of the Group', in Pines 1985.

Halton, W. (1994) 'Some Unconscious Aspects of Organisational Life: Contributions from Psychoanalysis', in Obholzer & Roberts 1994.

Hamel, G. (1996) 'Strategy as revolution', *Harvard Business Review* July-August.

Hampden-Turner, C. (1990) *Charting the Corporate Mind: From Dilemma to Strategy*, Oxford: Blackwell.

Heidegger, M. (1967) *Being and Time*, trans. J. Macquarrie & E. Robinson, Oxford: Blackwell.

Hoggett, P. (1997) 'A review of Obholzer & Roberts, *The Unconscious at Work: Individual and Organisational Stress in the Human Services*', Vol. 7, Pt. 1, No. 41: 131-8 Free Associations.

Hopper, E. (1965) 'Some effects of supervisory style: a sociological analysis', *British Journal of Sociology* 16, 3: 189-205.

Hopper, E. (1980) 'Report', in Garland 1980.

Hopper, E. (1981) *Social Mobility: A Study of Social Control and Insatiability*, Oxford: Blackwell.

Hopper, E. (1985) 'The Problem of Context In Group Analysis', in *Bion and Group Analysis*, ed. M. Pines, London: Routledge & Kegan Paul.

Hopper, E. (1987) 'Discussion of Segal, H., "The clinical usefulness of the 'death instinct'"', *The Bulletin of the British Psychoanalytical Society* 7: 39-45.

Hopper, E. (1989a) 'Psychotic anxieties and society: fission (fragmentation)/fusion and aggregation/massification', unpublished paper, Annual Conference of the Royal College of Psychiatry, Cambridge.

Hopper, E. (1989b) 'Aggregation/massification and fission (fragmentation)/fusion: A fourth basic assumption?', unpublished paper, VIIIth International Conference of the International Association of Group Psychotherapy, Amsterdam.

Hopper, E. (1991a) 'Borderline and narcissistic conditions: psycho-analytical and group analytical modes of treatment', panel discussion at the Annual Conference of the American Group Psychotherapy Association, San Antonio: InfoMedix Cassettes.

Hopper, E. (1991b) 'Encapsulation as a defence against the fear of annihilation', *International Journal of Psycho-Analysis* 72, 4: 607-624.

Hopper, E. (1993) 'Hope and dread in a group of child survivors of the Shoah. Panel on Trauma', panel discussion on trauma presented at the Annual Conference of the American Group Psychotherapy Association, San Diego: InfoMedix Cassettes.

Hopper, E. (1994) 'Il tempo del cambiamento', in *Nel Nome Del Gruppo*, ed. F. di Maria & G. Lavanco, Palermo: F. Angeli.

Hopper, E. (1995) 'Das soziale unbewußte in der klinischen Arbeit: Reflexionen uber die "komplette interpretation" und die "Quadratur des therapeutischen Dreiecks"', *Psa-Info* 44.

Hopper, E. (1996a) 'The social unconscious in clinical work', *Group* 20, 1: 7-42.

Hopper, E. (1996b) 'Das gesellschaftliche Unbewußte in der klinischen Arbeit: Reflexionen uber die "vollstandige Deutung" und die "Quadratur des therapeutischen Dreiecks"', *Gruppenanalyse* 6, 1: 67-113.

Hopper, E. (1997) 'Traumatic experience in the unconscious life of groups: A Fourth Basic Assumption', *Group Analysis* 30, 4: 439-470.

Horney, K. (1937) *The Neurotic Personality of our Time*, New York: Norton.

Jacobson, E. (1964) *The Self and the Object World*, New York: IUP.

Jacobson, E. (1971) *Depression*, New York: IUP.

Jaques, E. (1989) *Requisite Organisation: The CEO's Guide to Creative Structure and Leadership*, Aldershot: Gower.

Jaques, E. (1995) 'Why the psychoanalytical approach to understanding organisations is dysfunctional', *Human Relations* 48, 4: 343-365.

Joffe, W. (1969) 'A critical review of the envy concept', *International Journal of Psycho-Analysis* 50: 533-545.

Joseph, B. (1989) *Psychic Equilibrium and Psychic Change: Selected Papers of Betty Joseph*, London: Routledge.

Joseph, E. (1982) 'Normal in psychoanalysis', *International Journal of Psycho-Analysis* 62, 3: 3-13.

Julien, P. (1994) *Jacques Lacan's Return to Freud. The Real, the Symbolic and the Imaginary*, trans. D.B. Simiu, London: New York University Press.

Jung, C. (1951) *On Synchronicity*, Collected Works, vol. 8: §§ 965-97; 816-868.

Kaes, R. (1979) 'Introduction a l'analyse transitionelle', in *Crise, Rupture et Depassement*, ed. R. Kaes et al., Paris: Dunod.

Kernberg, O. (1980) *Internal World and External Reality: Object Relations Theory Applied*, New York: Aronson.

Kernberg, O. (1984) 'The couch at sea: the psychoanalysis of organisations', *International Journal of Group Psychotherapy* 34, 1: 5-23.

Kernberg, O. (1986) 'Institutional problems of psychoanalytic education', *Journal of the American Psychoanalytic Association* 34: 799-834.

Kernberg, O. (1989a) 'The temptations of conventionality', *International Review of Psychoanalysis* 16: 191-205.

Kernberg, O. (1989b) 'Paranoiagenesis in Organisations', in *Comprehensive Textbook of Group Psychotherapy*, 3rd edition, ed. H. Kaplan & B. J. Sadcock, Baltimore, MD: Williams & Wilkins.

Kernberg, O. (1989c) 'The narcissistic personality disorder and the differential diagnosis of antisocial behaviour', in *Psychiatric Clinics of North America: Narcissistic Personality Disorder* 12, 3: 723-729.

Kernberg, O. (1991) 'The Moral Dimensions of Leadership', in *Psychoanalytic Group Theory and Therapy: Essays in Honour of Saul Scheidlinger*, ed. S. Tuttman. Madison, CT: IUP.

Kernberg, O. (1993) 'The couple's constructive and destructive superego functions', *Journal of the American Psychoanalytic Association* 41: 653-677.

Kernberg, O. (1996) 'Thirty methods to destroy the creativity of psychoanalytic candidates', *International Journal of Psycho-Analysis* 77: 1031-1040.

Khaleelee, O., & Miller, E. (1985) 'Beyond the Small Group', in *Bion and Group Psychotherapy*, ed. M. Pines, London: Routledge & Kegan Paul.

King, P. & Steiner, R., eds. (1991) *The Freud-Klein Controversies 1941-1945*, London: Tavistock.

Kinston, W., & Cohen, J. (1986) 'Primal repression', *International Journal of Psycho-Analysis* 67: 337-56.

Klein, E. (1993) personal communication.

Klein, M. (1997a[1928]) 'Early Stages of the Oedipus Conflict', in *Love, Guilt and Reparation and other works 1921-1945*, London: Vintage.

Klein, M. (1997a[1945]) 'The Oedipus Conflict in the Light of Early Anxieties', in *Love, Guilt and Reparation and other works 1921-1945*, London: Vintage.

Klein, M. (1997b[1952a]) 'The Mutual Influences in the Development of Ego and Id', in *Envy and Gratitude and other works 1946-1963*, London: Vintage.

Klein, M. (1997b[1952b]) 'Some Theoretical Conclusions Regarding the Emotional Life of the Infant', in *Envy and Gratitude and other works 1946-1963*, London: Vintage.

Kohon, G. (1988) *The British School of Psychoanalysis*, London: Free Association Books.

Kohut, H., & Wolf, E. (1978) 'The disorders of the self and their treatment', *International Journal of Psycho-Analysis* 59: 414-425.

Koller, P. (1993) 'Contribution to panel on Trauma', paper presented to Annual Conference of American Group Psychotherapy Association, San Diego: InfoMedix Cassettes.

Koller, P., et al. (1992) 'Psychodynamic group treatment of post-traumatic stress disorder in Vietnam Veterans', *International Journal of Group Psychotherapy* 42, 2: 225-245.

Kroll, L. (1992) personal communication.

Lacan, J. (1947) 'La psychiatrique anglaise et la guerre', *Evolution Psychiatrique* 1: 293-318.

Lacan, J. (1960-61) 'Seminar VIII: Transference and Its Subjective Reality', unpublished translation by Cormac Gallagher.

Lacan, J. (1977) *Écrits*, trans. A. Sheridan, London: Tavistock.

Lacan, J. (1979) *The Four Fundamental Concepts of Psycho-Analysis*, ed. J.-A. Miller, trans. A. Sheridan, London: Penguin.

Lacan, J. (1988a) *The Seminar of Jacques Lacan—Book I: Freud's Papers on Technique 1953-1954*, ed. J.-A. Miller, trans. John Forrester, Cambridge: Cambridge University Press.

Lacan, J. (1988b) *The Seminar of Jacques Lacan—Book II: The Ego in Freud's Theory and in the Technique of Psychoanalysis, 1954-1955*, ed. J.-A. Miller, trans. John Forrester, Cambridge: Cambridge University Press.

Lacan, J. (1990) *Television. A Challenge to the Psychoanalytic Establishment*, London, W.W. Norton.

Lacan, J. (1992) *Seminar VII: The Ethics of Psychoanalysis*, ed. J.-A. Miller, trans. D. Potter, New York: Norton.

Lacan, J. (1995) 'Proposition du 9 Octobre 1967 sur le psychoanalyst de L'École', *Analysis—Journal of the Australian Centre for Psychoanalysis* 6: 1-13.

Lacan, J. (1996) 'On Freud's 'Trieb' and the Psychoanalyst's Desire', in *Reading Seminars I & II: Lacan's Return to Freud*, ed. B. Fink, R. Feldstein, & M. Jaanus, Albany: Suny Press.

Laing, R.D. (1969) *Self and Others*, New York: Pantheon/Random House.

Laing, R.D., & Cooper, D.G. (1971) *Reason and Violence*, New York: Vintage/Random House.

Lasch, C. (1977) *Haven in a Heartless World*, New York: Basic Books.

Lasch, C. (1978) *The Culture of Narcissism*, New York: Basic Books.

Laurent, E. (1995a) 'Alienation and Separation', in B. Fink et al. 1995.

Laurent, E. (1995b) 'Psychoanalysis and science', *Newsletter of the London Circle of the European School of Psychoanalysis* 3: 9.

Lawrence, G. (1991) 'Won from the void and formless infinite: experiences of social dreaming', *Free Associations* 2, 22: 259-294.

Laxenaire, M. (1983) 'Group Analytic Psychotherapy According to Foulkes and Psychoanalysis According to Lacan', in *The Evolution of Group Analysis*, ed. M. Pines, London: Routledge.

Le Bon, G. (1920) *The Crowd: a Study of the Popular Mind*, London.

Le Roy, J. (1994) 'Group Analysis and Culture', in *The Psyche and The Social World*, ed. D. Brown & L. Zinkin, London: Routledge.

Le Vine, R. (1973) *Culture, Behaviour and Personality*, Chicago: Aldine.

Leader, D. (1996) 'Strategies, tactics and standard treatment', *Journal of the Centre of Freudian Analysis and Research* 7: 46-52.

Lee, J. (1990) *Jacques Lacan*, Boston: Twayne Publishers.

Levinas, E. (1988) 'Useless Suffering', in *The Provocation of Levinas*, ed. R.L. Bernasconi & D. Wood, London & New York: Routledge.

Levinas, E. (1989) 'The Pact', in *The Levinas Reader*, ed. S. Hand, Oxford: Basil Blackwell.

Lewes, K. (1995) *Psychoanalysis and Male Homo-sexuality*, London: Jason Aronson.

Mahler, M. S., & Furer, M. (1968) *On Human Symbiosis and the Vicissitudes of Individuation*, New York: IUP.

Malan, D. (1979) *Individual Psychotherapy and the Science of Psychodynamics*, London: Butterworths.

Malinowski, B. (1937) *Sex and Repression in a Savage Society*, London: Routledge & Kegan Paul.

Marcuse, H. (1955) *Eros and Civilization: A Philosophical Inquiry into Freud*, Boston: Beacon Press.

Maslow, A. (1954) 'The instinctoid nature of basic needs', *Journal of Personality* 22: 340-341.

Maturana, H. & Varela, F. (1987) *The Tree of Knowledge: The Biological Roots of Human Understanding*, Boston: New Science Library.

McDougall, W. (1920) *The Group Mind*, London: Cambridge University Press.

McDougall, W. (1968) *Social Psychology*, New York: G.P. Putnam & Sons.

Merleau-Ponty, M. (1962) *The Phenomenology of Perception*, London: Routledge & Kegan Paul.

Merleau-Ponty, M. (1964) 'The Child's Relation with Others', in *The Primacy of Perception*, Northwestern U.P.

Miles, B. (1993) 'Contribution to panel on Trauma', paper presented to Annual Conference of the American Group Psychotherapy Association, San Diego: InfoMedix Cassettes.

Miller, E., & Rice, A. (1967) *Systems of Organisation: The Control of Task and Sentient Boundaries*, London: Tavistock.

Miller, J.-A. (1992) 'Michel Foucault and Psychoanalysis' in T.J. Armstrong, *Michel Foucault: Philosopher*, London: Wheatsheaf Harvester.

Miller, J.-A. (1995) 'Contexts and Concepts', in B. Fink et al. 1995.

Miller, P., & Rose, N. (1988) 'The Tavistock programme: the government of subjectivity and social life', *Sociology* 22, 2:171-192.

Mitchell, S. (1994) *Hope and Dread in Psychoanalysis*, New York: Basic Books.

Mitscherlich, A. (1963) *Auf dem Weg zur vaterlosen Gesellschaft: Ideen zur Sozial-Psychologie* (On the Way to a Fatherless Society: Ideas on Social Psychology) Munchen: R. Piper.

Moreno, J. (1934) *Who Shall Survive?*, Washington, D.C.: Nervous and Mental Disease Publishing Company.

Moreno, J. (1959) 'Interpersonal therapy, group psychotherapy and the function of the unconscious', *Psychodrama* 2.

Moscovici, S. (1981) *L'age des foules* (The Age of the Crowds), Paris: Fayard.

Mosse, J. (1994) 'Introduction: The Institutional Roots of Consulting to Institutions', in Obholzer & Roberts 1994.

Muller, J. P. (1996) *Beyond the Psychoanalytic Dyad: Development Semiotics in Freud, Peirce and Lacan*, London: Routledge.

Nitsun, M. (1996) *The Anti Group*, London: Routledge.

Obholzer, A. & Roberts, V., eds. (1994) *The Unconscious at Work: Individual and Organisational Stress in the Human Services*, London: Routledge.

Ortega y Gasset, J. (1976) *La Rebelion de las Masas* (The Revolt of the Masses), Madrid: Expasa-Calpe.

Palazzoli, M.S., et al. (1986) *The Hidden Games of Organisations*, New York: Pantheon Books.

Palmer, B. (1996) 'In which the Tavistock paradigm is considered as a discursive practice', working paper, Working Group on Groups and Organisations, Centre for Freudian Analysis and Research.

Palmer, B. (forthcoming) 'The Tavistock Paradigm: Inside, Outside and Beyond', in *Institutions, Anxieties and Defence*, ed. R. Hinshelwood & M. Chiesa.

Parsons, A. (1957) *Belief, Magic and Anomie*, New York: The Free Press.

Pedder, J. (1988) 'Termination reconsidered', *International Journal of Psycho-Analysis* 69: 495-505.

Pines, M. (1978) 'Psychoanalysis and group analysis', *Journal of Group Analysis* 11, 1: 8.

Pines, M. (1983) *The Evolution of Group Analysis*, London: Routledge.

Pines, M., ed. (1985) *Bion and Group Psychotherapy*, London: Routledge.

Plato (1951) *The Symposium*, trans. W. Hamilton, London: Penguin Books.

Pollack, G. & Ross, J. (1988) *The Oedipus Papers*, New York: International Universities Press.

Puget, J. (1989) 'Groupe analytique et formation', *Revue de psychotherapie psychoanalitique de groupe* 13: 137-54.

Rajchman, J. (1991) *Truth and Eros: Foucault, Lacan and the Question of Ethics*, London: Routledge.

Rayner, E. (1990) *The Independent Mind in British Psychoanalysis*, London: Free Association Books.

Reich, W. (1962) *The Sexual Revolution: Toward a Self-Governing Character Structure*, New York: Noonday Press.

Rice, A. K. (1965) *Learning for Leadership*, London: Tavistock.

Richards, A. (1948) *Hunger and Work in a Savage Tribe*, Glencoe: The Free Press.

Roberts, V. (1994) 'Till Death Do Us Part: Caring and Uncaring in Work with the Elderly', in Obholzer & Roberts 1994.

Roth, P. (1995) *Portnoy's Complaint*, London: Vintage.

Rouchy, J.-C. (1987) 'Identité culturelle et groupes d'appartenance', *Revue de psychotherapie psychoanalytique de groupe* 9: 31-41.

Roudinesco, E. (1990) *Jacques Lacan & Co.: A History of Psychoanalysis in France, 1925-1985*, trans. Jeffrey Mehlman, Chicago: University of Chicago Press.

Roustang, F. (1982) *Dire Mastery: Discipleship from Freud to Lacan*, trans. N. Lukacher, Washington: American Psychiatric Press.

Rustomjee, S. (1993) 'Traversing the Psychoanalytic Pathway', paper presented at the Third Pacific Rim Regional Congress, Taiwan.

Sandler, J. (1984) 'The past unconscious, the present unconscious and interpretation of the transference', *Psychoanalytic Inquiry* 4.

Schein, E. (1969) *Process Consultation: Its Role in Organisation Development*, London: Addison-Wesley.

Schein, E., & Bennis, W. (1965) *Personal and Organisational Change Through Group Methods: The Laboratory Approach*, New York: Wiley.

Schilder, P. (1935) *The Image and Appearance of the Human Body*, London: Kegan Paul, Trench, Trubner.

Schilder, P. (1936) 'The analysis of ideologies as a psychotherapeutic method, especially in group treatment', *American Journal of Psychiatry* 93: 601.

Schwartz, H. (1990) *Narcissistic Process and Corporate Decay*, London: New York University Press.

Serrano, A. (1990) 'Transferential and Cultural Issues in Group Psychotherapy', in *The Difficult Patient in Group*, ed. B. Roth et al., Madison, Conn.: International Universities Press.

Sheldrake, R. (1987) *New Science of Life: Hypothesis of Formative Causation*, London: Paladin Books.

Simon, B. (1992) 'Incest—see under Oedipus Complex: the history of an error in psychoanalysis', *Journal of the American Psychoanalytic Association* 40: 955-988.

Socarides, C. (1978) *Homosexuality*, New York: Aronson.

Spector-Person, E. (1992) 'Romantic Love: At the Intersection of the Psyche and the Cultural Unconscious', in *Affect: Psychoanalytic Perspective*, ed. T. Shapiro & R. Emde, New York: International Universities Press.

Spillius, E., ed. (1988) *Melanie Klein Today*, London: Routledge.

Steiner, J. (1985) 'Turning a blind eye: the cover-up for Oedipus', *International Review of Psycho-Analysis* 12: 161-172.

Steiner, J. (1990) 'The retreat from truth to omnipotence in Oedipus at Colonus', *International Review of Psycho-Analysis* 17: 227-37.

Steiner, J. (1993) *Psychic Retreats*, London: Routledge.

Stephane, A. (1969) *L'Univers Contestationnaire* (The Antiestablishment Universe), Paris: Petite Bibliotheque Payot.

Stewart, H. (1992) 'Interpretation and other agents for psychic change', *International Journal of Psycho-Analysis* 71: 61-70.

Stokes, J. (1994) 'The Unconscious at Work in Groups and Teams: Contributions from the Work of Wilfred Bion', in Obholzer & Roberts 1994.

Strindberg, J.A. (1992) *Miss Julie*, London: Reed Consumer Books.

Sutherland, J. (1985) 'Bion Revisited: Group Dynamics and Group Psychotherapy', in Pines 1985.

Trist, E. (1985) 'Working with Bion in the 1940s: the Group Decade', in Pines 1985.

Trist, E., & Murray, H. (1990) 'Historical Overview: The Foundation and Development of the Tavistock Institute', in *The Social Engagement of Social Science: A Tavistock Anthology—Volume I*, ed. E. Trist & H. Murray, London: Free Association Books.

Turquet, P. (1975) 'Threats to Identity in the Large Group', in *The Large Group: Dynamics and Therapy*, ed. L. Kreeger, London: Constable.

Tustin, F. (1981) *Autistic States in Children*, London: Routledge & Kegan Paul.

Von Foerster, H. (1960) 'On self-organising systems and their environments' in *International Tracts in Computer Science and Technology and their Application*, vol. 2, ed. M.C. Yovits & G. Cameron, Oxford: Pergamon Press.

Wallerstein, R. (1988) 'One psychoanalysis or many?', *International Journal of Psycho-Analysis* 71: 5-21.

Wallerstein, R. (1993) 'Between chaos and petrification: a summary of the fifth IPA conference of training analysts', *International Journal of Psycho-Analysis* 74: 165-178.

Weber, M. (1947) *The Theory of Social and Economic Organisation*, ed. T. Parsons, New York: Oxford University Press, New York.

Wender, L. (1940) 'Psychotherapy: a study of its application', *Psychiatric Quarterly* 14: 708.

Winnicott, D. (1954) 'Mind and its relation to psyche-soma', *British Journal of Medical Psychology* 27.

Winnicott, D. (1965) *The Maturational Process and the Facilitating Environment*, New York: International Universities Press.

Wittgenstein, L. (1958) *Philosophical Investigations*, second edition, ed. G.E.M. Anscombe & R. Rhees, trans. G. Anscombe, Oxford: Basil Blackwell.

Wolf, A. (1949) 'The psychoanalysis of groups', *American Journal of Psychotherapy* 3: 525-558.

Zaretsky, E. (1997) 'Bisexuality, capitalism and the ambivalent legacy of psychoanalysis', *New Left Review* 223: 69-89.

Zinkin, L. (1979) 'The collective and the personal', *Journal of Analytic Psychology* 24, 3: 227-250.

Index